# Passage to Pesach

*Preparing for Passover
through Text and Tradition*

# PASSAGE TO PESACH

*Preparing for Passover through Text and Tradition*

Frances Weinman Schwartz

UAHC Press  ·  New York, New York

**Library of Congress Cataloging-in-Publication Data**

Schwartz, Frances Weinman.
    Passage to Pesach : preparing for Passover through text and tradition / Frances
Weinman Schwartz.
      p. cm.
    Includes bibliographical references and index.
    ISBN 0-8074-0858-1 (pbk. : alk. paper)
    1. Passover. 2. Seder. 3. Haggadah. I. Title

BM695.P3S3935 2003
296.4'37—dc21                                          2002042981

For Stuart, always

and for my parents, Frank Weinman
and Teri Vidor Weinman (*z"l*)

We Jews are all born of wanderers, with shoes
under our pillows and a memory of blood that is ours
raining down. We honor only those Jews who changed
tonight, those who chose the desert over bondage,

who walked into the strange and became strangers
and gave birth to children who could look down
on them standing on their shoulders for having
been slaves. We honor those who let go of everything but freedom, who ran, who revolted, who fought,
who became other by saving themselves.

Excerpted from "Maggid" by Marge Piercy

# Contents

# Acknowledgments

Credit for *Passage to Pesach* must first go to Rabbi Hara Person, editorial director of the UAHC Press and a classmate from Hebrew Union College–Jewish Institute of Religion, New York campus, where I received a master's degree in Judaic studies. "Francie," Hara began, "we've been talking about publishing a book exploring various Pesach themes, and we agree that you are the person to write it." "Oh, you mean a new Haggadah?" "No, we don't mean a Haggadah," answered Hara. "Oh, are you talking about another 'how to prepare/conduct a seder' book?" I asked. "No, we don't mean that either. What we had in mind is a book based on and explaining Jewish texts for adult study during the weeks prior to Pesach that broadens their understanding of the holiday. I know this is not much to work with, but we feel sure that you could expand the concept." These few words, whose message was supposed to be uplifting, instead left me truly bewildered.

So I contacted my mentor and dear friend Eugene B. Borowitz, Sigmund L. Falk Distinguished Professor of Education and Jewish Religious Thought at Hebrew Union College. Several years before, Gene had asked me to co-author a book with him. That wonderful learning experience and exercise in collaboration became *The Jewish Moral Virtues* (Jewish Publication Society, 1999). His complete confidence in my ability led me to accept Hara's invitation. Thank you, Gene, for your continued friendship and faith in me. I next spoke to Dr.

Phillip Miller, director of the HUC–JIR library in New York and a good friend. Phil's help in finding the many books on HUC's shelves that became my Pesach "Bibles" enabled my research to progress quite smoothly. Bushels of thanks to Phil and to the HUC circulation librarian Lou Massone for locating obscure references eagerly and pleasantly. Much appreciation to Laurel Wolfson, deputy librarian of the HUC-JIR Klau Library in Cincinnati and managing editor of *The First Cincinnati Haggadah, An Interactive Facsimile Edition,* for agreeing without hesitation to our use of several illustrations from this fifteenth-century masterpiece. Danny Levine, president of J. Levine bookstore in Manhattan, lent his bibliophile expertise to my search for the most noteworthy Haggadot currently in print.

A note of gratitude is directed to Rabbi David Wechsler-Azen for consenting to be my *chevruta* partner in the formative stages of *Passage to Pesach* to discuss the wealth of Jewish midrash that surrounds the five special Shabbatot. Thanks also are in order to two HUC classmates: Rabbi Fred Greene suggested many additional Pesach texts to me, and I found Rabbi Ariel Friedlander's HUC rabbinic thesis, which delves into many explanations for traditional seder rituals associated with Elijah's cup, quite enlightening. Passages from *The Open Door,* the new Haggadah published by the Central Conference of American Rabbis, the rabbinical arm of the American Reform Movement, added contemporary verve to my words. Many thanks to my project editor, Christine Sweeney, and copy editor, Debra Hirsch Corman, for their eagle-eyed proficiency. Many thanks to all the others at the UAHC Press who helped to create this book, including Ken Gesser, Stuart Benick, Rick Abrams, and Liane Broido.

Wonderful memories of the seders led by my father, Frank Weinman, shaped my *n'shamah,* my Jewish soul, early on; thank you, Dad, for everything. More recently, the seders led by my *machatenum,* Rabbi Marvin Bash, and overseen by my *machatenister,* Deborah Bash, have allowed me to glory in many hours of song, prayer, and family togetherness. A general thank-you to friends and family members for your unflagging support and forbearance, and for tolerating my many months of distraction with grace and understanding when I was completely consumed in writing.

I've saved my last and highest praise for my husband Stuart, without whom *Passage to Pesach* would never have been completed. Stu read every word of the manuscript and tempered his criticism with con-structive encouragement. A "stealth mensch" if there ever was one, uncomfortable accepting acclamation, no matter how low-keyed, you light my path daily with your wit, your thoughtfulness, your love.

# PART I

## Introduction

# Preparing for Passage

Rabbi Ishmael said: The one who learns in order to teach will be
granted adequate means to learn and to teach; but the one who
learns in order to practice will be granted adequate means to learn
and to teach, to observe and to practice. (*Pirkei Avot* 4:6)

Of all the Jewish holidays our people celebrate today, Pesach ranks as
the most popular. A recent survey confirms it: close to 90 percent of
American Jewry not only know about Pesach, but actually "observe
and practice" its rituals by attending a seder—a truly amazing statistic!
Wherever Jews find themselves on the fourteenth of Nisan, the Hebrew
date that begins Pesach, they are sure to search out a seder. As far away
from home as Katmandu, the sky-high capital of the Himalayan country of Nepal, hundreds of young trekkers flock to a by-now-legendary
seder. Elsewhere people listen to music singing the praises of a "Reggae
Passover," a blend of West African and Caribbean rhythms, and add "I
Go Die-O" to their more traditional "Dayeinu" renditions. For the last
several years, many of our own seder tables have hosted toys depicting
the Ten Plagues alongside the more usual holiday symbols, plates, and
wine cups. And at last count, well over four thousand different editions
of Pesach Haggadot have been published, to guide our passage through
observances in every possible cultural leaning and language.

Pesach is truly a memorable occasion, marking our creation as a
people. Today Pesach is filled with joy and happiness as we annually
commemorate our passage from slavery to freedom. However, at other
times in our history Pesach has taken place in atmospheres of apprehension and fear. It is important to remember these Pesachs as well.
When conditions were perilous, celebrating this holiday of redemption

strengthened our conviction to fight for freedom with our last breath. It is said that at Pesach in 73 C.E., three years after the Temple in Jerusalem was destroyed, the last Jewish holdouts clinging to life on Masada committed suicide rather than submit to their capture, enslavement, and inevitable death by the Romans. Almost two millennia later, Pesach marked another desperate effort by remnants of the Jewish people. In April 1943, in the Warsaw Ghetto, young Jews observed Pesach as best they could and then battled German troops for six weeks of desperate, heroic combat.

In his recent autobiography, noted writer Herman Wouk explains the meaning of absolute freedom in times of personal trauma. On a visit to Israel in 1955, Wouk came to know David Ben-Gurion, the first president of the then-new Jewish state. "When we were leaving, [Ben-Gurion] came out with his straight Zionist line . . . 'You must return here to live,' he said. 'This is the only place for Jews like you. Here you will be free.' 'Free?' I ventured to reply. 'Free? With enemy armies ringing you, with their leaders publicly threatening to wipe [you] out, with your roads impassable after sundown—free?' 'I did not say safe,' the old man retorted. 'I said free.'"

Our first Pesach was anything but safe. Hastily exiting Egypt, facing unknown terrain and hostile peoples, the former slaves didn't know what their new lives would be like. Nevertheless, the Book of Exodus describes the attire and the attitude of the Jewish people leaving Egypt, with "loins girded, sandals on your feet, and your staff in your hand" (12:11). Protracted wanderings between the slavery of Egypt and the freedom of the Promised Land introduced Jews to life as permanent passage. With Egypt portrayed as archetypal enemy and Jerusalem symbolizing ultimate synthesis and wholeness, we seem fated to wander *b'midbar*, "in the wilderness," endlessly. Our time in the desert has assuredly strengthened our survival skills, even to this day enabling us to roll with the punches of uncertainty and marginality, blossoming during periods of calm and well-being.

As we gather in our homes each year to commemorate the beginning of our journey, we look ahead to "next year in Jerusalem," even as we remember "last year in Egypt." We are well aware of our shifting point on a Jewish spiritual continuum, somewhere between, as we read in the Haggadah, "starting in disgrace and ending in praise." Perhaps the holiday of Pesach continues to be celebrated by such large numbers of

Jews precisely because we pay homage to our progress in private, within an extended family unit, where disgrace can be forgiven and praise easily forthcoming, at least for one or two nights a year.

The whole notion of family is broadening in ways we never would have imagined just decades ago, enriching and delighting us. The definitions of family have expanded to include significant others of whatever sexual predilection. The Jewish household includes intermarried couples, Jews-by-choice, and Jewish children whose lives may have begun in Asia or South America, Eastern Europe or native America.

It is to our children that Pesach especially speaks, with its built-in mechanisms to keep them (and us) curious and awake through the lengthy seder. Who can resist the earnest expression on the face of a child struggling to ask the Four Questions for the first time, or a child's smile of satisfaction upon gleefully finding the *afikoman* ahead of older siblings and assorted cousins? Pesach is the quintessential festival of gladness and togetherness. The pain of recalling past humiliations, "We were slaves unto Pharaoh in Egypt," eases when we revel in our present joys and the promise of generations yet to come.

As we watch the scampering of nephews and nieces, children and grandchildren, we also reflect on those whose life passages have ended. Their memories are honored by children who bear their names and who may even share similar physical characteristics. Of course, those no longer with us are ever present in our thoughts during Pesach, especially when we look at the seder table set with wine goblets or seder plates they have bequeathed to us.

Narratives in both the Books of Genesis and Exodus relate that the Patriarch Joseph, though long dead, had a very real, physical presence during the first Pesach. Joseph tells his brothers, "I am about to die. God will surely take notice of you and bring you up from this land to the land God promised on oath to Abraham, to Isaac, and to Jacob." So Joseph made his brothers take an oath. They swore, "When God has taken notice of [us], [we] shall carry up [Joseph's] bones from here" (Gen. 50:24–25). Sure enough, right after "Pharaoh let the people go," and "the Israelites went up armed out of the land of Egypt," we hear that, indeed, "Moses took with him the bones of Joseph" (Exod. 13:17–19).

Jewish liturgist Lawrence Hoffman notes that if we take the bones of our ancestors with us, figuratively as well as literally, we will go through life armed with whatever we need. Playing on the similarity of two Hebrew words, Hoffman transforms mere physicality into the core of individual character. He explains that Israel took out of Egypt not Joseph's bones, *atzamot,* but his essence, *atzmiyut.* Equipped for life's journeys with the essence of our ancestors in the form of family memories and models of behavior, we can succeed even *b'midbar,* in the wilderness passages of our lives.

Pesach's observance is not diminished by its private rather than public venue. Exactly the opposite occurs, as it has for several thousand years. Yes, the Bible describes transcendent Temple sacrifices during which thousands gathered amidst the splendors of ritual objects made of gold and priestly vestments encrusted with gems. But the Bible also depicts how these vast assemblies were immediately followed by picnics on wooded hillsides near the Temple Mount itself, where the sacrifice was eaten in small family groups (Exod. 12:3–8). The first Jewish philosopher, Philo of Alexandria, Egypt, who lived while the Temple still stood, in the middle decades of the first century C.E., relates that the outdoor feasts commemorating the Exodus were already moving indoors, the earliest versions of our contemporary seder celebrations.

Then, as now, during these intimate gatherings, something wonderful occurs. As Philo puts it, "On this day every dwelling is invested with the outward semblance and dignity of a temple." Thus our very homes become vested with a sacred quality previously reserved for central, public spaces. Two centuries after Philo, the Rabbis codified the vast collection of oral law and customary practice into the Mishnah. One of its books, *P'sachim,* explains in great detail the leveling significance of the Pesach seder. "The meal is not just for a special class or an elite group of Jews. Everyone should participate, even the poor."

The Pesach meal simplifies social relationships and sets up what the rabbinic scholar Baruch Bokser describes as an "atmosphere of *communitas,*" an inclusive environment that liberates individuals from the regimented social structures that normally separate. The welcoming atmosphere of a Pesach seder encourages us to mull over Judaism's central values in a place of trust. The embracing atmosphere of the seder permits, indeed requires, each person to join in the observances, whatever our degree of Jewish learning, belief, or ritual participation.

It is to those who want to increase their knowledge of seder and Pesach activities that this book is dedicated. It is to individual learning that we now turn. My aim in writing *Passage to Pesach* has been *torah lishmah,* "learning for its own sake," about this most ubiquitous of Jewish holidays. *Passage to Pesach* hopes to encourage an enriched, text-based understanding of why we do what we do, when we do it. Pesach is more than matzah. Its reach defines us as individuals as well as a people. We discover our own place in this wonderful tradition by reflecting on the countless memories and applications our heritage affords us.

Our study begins some weeks before the onset of the holiday. After a historical survey, *Passage to Pesach* focuses on each of the five special Shabbatot that lead to the seder. The Rabbis assigned each of these Sabbaths an additional Torah and haftarah reading, which serve as our focus here. Shabbat Sh'kalim, the "counting-taxing Sabbath," is celebrated at the New Moon of the month of Adar, at least six weeks before Pesach. At the second special Sabbath, Shabbat Zachor, the Sabbath closest to Purim, we study the wealth of material interpreting memory. The third special Sabbath is called Shabbat Parah, connecting the ancient mysterious cleansing ceremony of the red heifer to a discussion of Jewish purity in general. When Jews sacrificed the paschal lamb at the Temple at Pesach, they were required to be ritually pure. The fourth special Sabbath, Shabbat HaChodesh, is observed as the Jewish month of Nisan begins, when Moses gave the laws of Pesach to the Children of Israel just prior to the Exodus. And finally, Shabbat HaGadol brings us back to individual longings. On this Sabbath closest to Pesach, the extra haftarah reading discusses the prophet Elijah as the herald of the Messiah, a reminder of Elijah's role in the seder, now only a few days away. We are told what awaits us when the Messiah comes: a massive reconciliation of parents and children, truly a miraculous event!

As we arrive at the first night of Pesach, we will once again pause for a brief look at the development of the Haggadah. Then our passage continues with an examination of the seder itself by detailing, not four cups of wine, but the "Six Cups" central to our holiday meal. In the "First Cup" we explore the myriad meanings of matzah in the celebration of Pesach. The items on our seder plate reveal new interpretations in the "Second Cup." The "Third Cup" takes us through the miracles of the Exodus, from the horrors of the Ten Plagues to the ultimate revelation of creation, our children, and their roles in the Pesach festivities. Our point of view then shifts from created to Creator. The "Fourth Cup" guides the study of the many blessings and praises to God found in the Haggadah, from the *Hallel,* the special psalms we sing, to our last songs of the evening, "Echad Mi Yodei-a?" (Who Knows One?) and "Chad Gadya" (An Only Kid). In the "Fifth Cup" we turn to the prophet Elijah and the messianic dreams of the Jews. We end with "Miriam's Cup," a discussion of feminist themes that have recently taken their deserved place in our Pesach celebration.

But we can't leave this discussion of every Jew's favorite holiday without passing from the historic events preceding it to its ultimate destination: the giving of Torah at Mount Sinai, celebrated at Shavuot. *Passage to Pesach* concludes by commenting on the daily counting of the *Omer,* which begins on the second night of Pesach and continues for the next forty-nine days. As we count, we update the ancient practice of sacrificing a measure of grain from the first spring harvest and remember all of the associations surrounding the Exodus we have just celebrated. Thus we finish as we began, way back at Shabbat Sh'kalim, numbering our way through the Jewish tradition.

We attempt several things here. We expand our lead time to Pesach to discern new layers of meaning in the added sacred texts we study. We broaden our understanding of traditional symbols and activities surrounding Pesach practices. And we extend our comprehension of the grand meaning of Pesach, from one week during which we abstain from bread, to seven weeks culminating in our seminal covenant with God, accepting with gratitude the Law God gave us.

During Pesach week, we read from the Song of Songs, the deeply moving, passionately romantic biblical ode. Some sages have described the work as an intense human courtship, commingling lust and love in exploding desire. Others interpret the work more allegorically as the ultimate love song between God and the people of Israel. While in the past I have opted for the more earthy interpretation, I also embrace a literary understanding of Song of Songs that takes into account the full scope of Pesach. In this scenario, God begins to court Israel while the people are still in Egypt, earning their respect and love as they witness each succeeding plague, until finally they are freed. The traditional engagement period, *eirusin,* is cemented by the miracle at the Red Sea;

the *chuppah* takes place on top of Mount Sinai, with Torah as *ketubah*. And we receive our wedding present from the Eternal: the Land of Israel.

May we always glorify our gifts to God with song and blessing, and may these continue to mark our learning passages, lighting the way as we work toward our own final redemption, and that of the world entire.

# Ancient Pesach: How Many Passages?

> Your lamb shall be without blemish, a yearling male. . . . All the
> assembled congregation of the Israelites shall slaughter it at twi-
> light. (Exod. 12:5–6)

Thus Pesach was first celebrated by shepherds, anxious to insure the
continued fertility of their sheep and goats. Every spring they chose an
unblemished young male animal (rather than female, so as not to kill a
pregnant animal and her unborn lamb or kid) and sacrificed it as an
offering to the deity in charge of such things. If female sheep proceeded
to bear healthy offspring that year, the people knew they had pleased
their god. If newborn lambs were born prematurely and stayed
scrawny, or sickened and died shortly after birth, the people knew their
god was displeased with their offering. They would resolve to search
for a more suitable sacrifice next year.

> In the first month, from the fourteenth day of the month at
> evening, you shall eat unleavened bread until the twenty-first day
> of the month. . . . No leaven shall be found in your houses. . . .
> For whoever eats what is leavened shall be cut off. . . . (Exod.
> 12:18–20)

Thus Pesach was first celebrated by farmers, desperate for a successful first harvest of the year. By not allowing their staple food, bread,
to rise before eating it for one week each spring, the people were doing
without to demonstrate their fidelity to the god responsible for such
things. If too much rain washed away the seed, or too little rain produced a diminished harvest, the people knew their god was displeased

with their efforts. They would resolve to be more diligent regarding what they did or did not eat next year.

> Three times a year you shall hold a festival for Me; You shall observe the Feast of Unleavened Bread . . . at the set time . . . and none shall appear before Me empty-handed. (Exod. 23:14–15)

Thus Pesach was first celebrated as a pilgrimage festival, along with the other holy harvest days of Shavuot and Sukkot. Jews gathered at the Temple in Jerusalem, greeting family and friends they hadn't seen since their last trip to the most sacred city. After the men watched a priest sacrifice their animal on the Temple altar, they brought the fresh meat back to their wives, who roasted it and then served it outdoors as a special holiday meal.

> They shall take some of the blood and put it on the two doorposts and the lintel of the houses in which they are to eat it. . . . And the blood on the houses . . . shall be a sign for you . . . when I see the blood I will pass over you, so no plague will destroy you. (Exod. 12:7, 13)

Thus Pesach was first celebrated in the private dwellings of Hebrew slaves living in Egypt. Understanding that their freedom was imminent, they made hasty plans to leave the land in which they had lived for four hundred years. The animal blood they daubed on the outside of their houses protected them from an evil inflicted on the Egyptian firstborn so terrible that Pharaoh finally released the Jews, but only after feeling the power of their God firsthand.

All of the Torah passages above contain elements of our primal holiday's origins. At various times in our long history, we observed Pesach differently, based on where we lived, what we did for a living, and our social or political status. This chapter discusses Pesach's biblical and rabbinic beginnings, dealing with the ancient roots of Pesach. Other related topics, such as medieval and modern observances based on actual manuscripts or printed seder texts, will be reviewed in the chapter exploring the history of the Haggadah.

A few words are in order as to the historic reality of the Exodus. In recent years, some academicians and clergy have suggested that the Exodus may never have happened. Other scholars and rabbis have maintained a more conservative stance, in favor of a historic Exodus. *Passage to Pesach* will not enter this debate. At a certain point, most scientific absolutes must make room for personal faith, pulling the rug out from under the surest intellectual premise. Whether or not it actually occurred, millions of Jews and non-Jews continue to base their fundamental spiritual beliefs on the veracity and commemoration of some form of the Exodus narrative. And so shall we.

Not even Moses himself knew many of the details of the Exodus when he and Aaron first appeared to Pharaoh requesting permission to sacrifice to God as a ruse to free the Israelites. In God's name, Moses asked Egypt's ruler:

> Let My people go that they may celebrate a festival for Me in the wilderness. . . . Let us go a distance of three days. . . . (Exod. 5:1, 3)

Pharaoh retaliated by making life even more difficult for the slaves, forcing them to find their own straw to use in their brick making. Several plagues later, Pharaoh pretended to give in, offering to free only some of the slaves. Moses quickly set him straight:

> We will all go, young and old; we will go with our sons and daughters . . . our own livestock, too, shall go along with us . . . we shall not know with what we are to worship *Adonai* until we arrive there." (Exod. 10:9, 26)

Two chapters later, the Book of Exodus describes how the very first Pesach was celebrated: indoors, eating the entire *pesach* sacrifice, not in some remote wilderness area as first proposed to Pharaoh, but in Egypt, under the noses of the hated taskmasters. The whole family consumed the offering and then waited through the long night, making last-minute plans for the next day's departure (Exod. 12:10–11, 34).

In the historic time of the Bible, the Israelites left Egypt, and forty years passed. At last the people entered the land God had promised them, led by Joshua, the young military commander picked by Moses to succeed him. The time of year they crossed the Jordan River has a definite "Pesach aura" about it. "The people came up from the Jordan on the tenth day of the first month" (Josh. 4:19), precisely forty years to the day that their parents and grandparents selected the lamb they would sacrifice, commemorating the first Pesach on the fourteenth day of the first month, Nisan. "And Joshua set up in Gilgal the twelve stones they had taken from the Jordan. He charged the Israelites: 'In time to come, when your children ask their fathers, "What is the meaning of those stones?" tell your children . . .'" (Josh. 4:20–22). Today, our entire seder evening is devoted to children inquiring and parents patiently responding to carefully scripted questions ascertaining the meanings of all the strange things we do, only on this night. The passage in the Book of Joshua recalls the journey's early commemoration, a preview of thousands of Pesachs yet to come.

Once Joshua led the Israelites across the Jordan River, the first act there involved the entire male population and also suggests *Pesach Mitzrayim*, the first, Egyptian Pesach.

> At that time *Adonai* said to Joshua, "Make flint knives and proceed with a second circumcision of the Israelites." . . . Now, whereas all the people who came out of Egypt had been circumcised, none of the people born after the Exodus had been. . . . The men of military age who had left Egypt had perished . . . it was [their sons] that Joshua circumcised. (Josh. 5:2, 5–7)

In the first Pesach, blood taken from animal offerings protected Hebrew homes; flowing blood dimming the lives of the Egyptian first-borns served as the catalyst that led to the Jews' departure from slavery. In this Pesach, taking place forty years after the first, blood drawn from the Israelite males confirmed the covenant God had made with the patriarch Abraham and all of his descendants, welcoming them as free individuals into the Promised Land. "And *Adonai* said to Joshua, 'Today I have rolled away from you the disgrace of Egypt'" (Josh. 5:9). After the men had recovered from the wounds related to their circumcision, they offered the *pesach* sacrifice.

"On the day after the *pesach* offering . . . when they ate of the produce of the land, the manna [the breadlike food that nourished the people throughout their wilderness wanderings] ceased" (Josh. 5:11–12). From now on, Israel had to work the land in order to eat. Freedom is not an unqualified gift. It entails responsibilities as well as entitlements. The people had to work hard to fashion their own home on the land that God gave them, using the Torah as their moral compass.

Close to six hundred years passed. King David vastly expanded the territory under Israel's flag. His son Solomon solidified God's rule by building the Temple in Jerusalem, where the Ark of the Covenant finally found a permanent home. But political disaffection tore apart David's kingdom, and foreign gods were worshiped throughout Israel and Judah. In the eighth century B.C.E., the Northern Kingdom of Israel fell to the Assyrians, who threatened the very gates of Jerusalem in the Southern Kingdom of Judah before being routed. Succeeding Judean kings worshiped false gods; many idols replaced the One God at altars scattered in high places throughout the land.

Toward the end of the seventh century B.C.E., eight-year-old Josiah was crowned king. In the eighteenth year of his reign, while priests were repairing the Temple, they made a startling discovery. The Bible relates that "the High Priest found a scroll of the Teaching in the House of *Adonai*" (II Kings 22:8). This testament, alleged to be the Book of Deuteronomy, was read to King Josiah, who "rent his clothes" (II Kings 22:11) because the people had been so wicked for so long. Ordering all the priests of Judah to demolish their local altars and come to the Temple in Jerusalem, Josiah's decree also effectively ended the intimate home celebration of Pesach. Using the centralizing national structure of the Temple as mandated in Deuteronomy, Josiah demanded a refashioning of the entire Jewish worship apparatus, beginning with the commemoration of the Exodus.

> The king commanded all the people, "Offer the *pesach* sacrifice to *Adonai* your God as prescribed in this scroll of the covenant." Now the *pesach* sacrifice had not been offered in that manner in the days of the judges . . . or during the days of the kings of Israel and Judah. Only King Josiah . . . offered such a *pesach* sacrifice to *Adonai* in Jerusalem. (II Kings 23:21–23)

Conveniently for Josiah, Deuteronomy is clear about the proper manner of celebrating Pesach.

> You are not permitted to slaughter the *pesach* sacrifice in any of the settlements . . . but at the place where *Adonai* your God will choose to establish God's name, there alone shall you slaughter the *pesach* sacrifice, in the evening, at sundown, the time of day you departed from Egypt. You shall cook and eat it at the place *Adonai* your God will choose; in the morning you may start back on your journey home. (Deut. 16:5–7)

Thus Pesach became the premier pilgrimage festival of the Jews, until the destruction of the Second Temple in 70 C.E. dictated a return to a home celebration.

But things are rarely that simple. In 586 B.C.E., Babylonia conquered Jerusalem and destroyed Solomon's Temple, exiling the priestly families and the higher classes, the more educated Jews. Approximately seventy years later, Cyrus of Persia dethroned the Babylonian monarch and allowed a small band of Jewish pioneers to return to Jerusalem. After several false starts, they were able to rebuild the Temple, an austere, downscale version of the earlier palace of God.

The Book of Ezra describes the first Pesach of the Babylonian returnees. Notice how the emphasis shifts from the people to the priests, with a new prominence given to ritual distinctiveness.

> The returned exiles celebrated the Pesach on the fourteenth day of the first month. For the priests and Levites had purified themselves. . . . They slaughtered the *pesach* offering for all the returned exiles. The Children of Israel who had returned, together with all who joined them in separating themselves from uncleanness of the nations of the lands to worship *Adonai* God of Israel, ate of it. (Ezra 6:19–21)

For the remaining two hundred years of Persian dominance of the land of Judea, as it was then called, we hear little about Jewish holiday celebration, or any other subject concerning the Jews. But there is a curious mention of another Jewish temple built hundreds of miles from Jerusalem to accommodate a colony of Jewish soldiers serving the Persian king at the remote Egyptian outpost of Elephantine on the upper Nile. The military outpost was first established in the early years of the sixth century B.C.E., perhaps by Jews escaping Babylonian exile after the fall of Jerusalem. A papyrus written by the Persian ruler Darius in 419 B.C.E. gives the Jewish garrison permission to eat unleavened bread and bans the general consumption of beer (since it is based on leavening grains) and other leaven for the seven days of Pesach. That the Jewish soldiers received official sanction from the king to celebrate this one particular holiday (and no other) reveals both the tolerance of the Persian monarch and the importance of following the required Pesach observances.

Alexander the Great destroyed the Persian empire in 332 B.C.E., introducing the Greek way of life to most of the then-civilized world. At the same time, the priestly cults surrounding the Temple entrenched their authority over the Jews of Judea and the Diaspora, the growing Jewish population living outside the physical borders of Judea since the Babylonian exile. Written sources from the period concur that the many rituals of Pesach were conducted amidst the splendors of a physically enhanced Temple Mount, with scores of priests performing the rites of Pesach commanded by Torah. In the second century B.C.E., Jews again achieved their independence, as the Jewish Maccabeans conquered the Syrian-Greeks, toppling King Antiochus and his rule of religious repression. Jewish kings and High Priests alike copied mannerisms of highborn Greek aristocracy. The more seriously inclined Jewish intellectuals found aspects of Greek philosophy, with its extensive study of the ideal forms in the natural world, to be worthy of their focus. Once again, the lure of an intimate meal eaten at home, with its opportunities for thoughtful, lively discussion, drew Jews back to private celebrations of Pesach, as it had before the Temple rites made Pesach a public observance. *Chavurot,* table-fellowship groups emphasizing worship around food, gained prominence among many Jews.

No Jew epitomizes the changing rhythms of Jewish observances at that time more typically than Philo, the first Jewish philosopher. He lived not in Palestine, but in the city of Alexandria, Egypt, the most cosmopolitan city of its day, a great beacon of commerce and home to a large wealthy Jewish population. Referring to Pesach as the "Crossing-Feast," Philo wrote, "So joyful were they that in their vast enthusiasm and impatient eagerness, they sacrificed without waiting for their priest. This practice reminded [the Jews] of their duty of thanksgiving." Philo, called the "great spiritualizer" of the Bible by noted scholar Baruch Bokser, was attuned to the individualistic yearnings that existed in tandem with the pageantry of the structured Temple Pesach rite.

This emphasis on far-ranging, intelligent speech surrounded by fine food and wine looks backward to Plato's symposia and forward to the paragon of Haggadah discussion by the five Rabbis of B'nei B'rak during the seder meal. The Haggadah tells us that the Rabbis became so engrossed in intricate points of Pesach observance that they debated through the night. Early the next morning, their astonished students called their attention to the hour; it was time to recite the morning *Sh'ma.*

We also take note of another seminal meal, which occurred around 30 C.E. in Jerusalem. Though named by its twilight time and final utterances, the Last Supper remains paramount in Christian theology because of the words spoken by the charismatic Jewish preacher Joshua, his name better known in Greek as Jesus. The Books of Matthew, Mark, and Luke from the Greek Scriptures (New Testament), written many decades after Jesus' crucifixion, place major importance in identifying the Last Supper as a Pesach seder.

> Now on the first day of Unleavened Bread the disciples came to Jesus, saying, "Where will you have us prepare for you to eat the passover?" He said, "Go into the city to a certain one and say to him, 'The Teacher says . . . I will keep the passover at your house . . . with my disciples.'" And the disciples did as Jesus had directed them, and they prepared the passover. (Matt. 26:17–19, RSV)

This passage is included to make two points. First, at this time, at the height of the glory of the Jerusalem Temple, practicing Jews (as the authors of Matthew, Mark, and Luke almost certainly were) also noted the importance of observing Pesach in a private home with a group of close associates. Second, the need to pick a place ahead of time implies that many preliminary tasks had to be done even before a simple meal could proceed. Unleavened bread, matzah, and ceremonial wine had to be obtained. The environment had to be chosen carefully to befit a place where serious words were spoken and blessings to God were offered.

The Jewish rebellion against Roman rule, begun in 66 C.E., led to the destruction of Jerusalem and the decimation four years later of the Temple. With the loss of the central place to gather together and worship God, Jewish scholars known as rabbis, or teachers, quickly made into formal doctrine what had existed for years as *minhag,* informal though widely practiced custom. Thus in 200 C.E. the redaction of the Mishnah, the codification of Jewish legal statutes, reflected several centuries of religious and cultural activity.

Several Pesach observances we usually associate with the seder existed even while the Temple still stood. Blessings and benedictions on wine and food, eating matzah and bitter herbs, reciting six psalms of praise (113–118) known as *Hallel,* were common ways to celebrate Pesach two thousand years ago, in addition to offering the holiday sacrifice at the Temple in Jerusalem. Sometime in the second century C.E., before the Mishnah's final editing, three sections of the Pesach liturgy became standard. The recital of the Four Questions, what later became the embellishment of the twenty-sixth chapter of Deuteronomy known as the *Magid* seder section, and the *Hallel* all became relatively fixed parts of the festive meal as we know it today.

The text entitled *P'sachim,* one of the books included in the Mishnah, deals in ten chapters with the laws concerning the holiday festival. Chapters 1–4 explain leavened and unleavened bread, chapters 5–9 discuss the sacrificial service, and chapter 10 specifically explains early laws of the seder meal. For several hundred years after these chapters appeared, two parts of *P'sachim* were referred to separately, called respectively *Pesach Rishon* (the First Pesach) and *Pesach Sheini* (the Second Pesach). *Pesach Sheini* (chapters 1–4 and 10), which includes regulations that cover the individual celebration of the home holiday, is actually significantly older than *Pesach Rishon* (chapters 5–9), the description of the more ancient Temple rite. This is one more indication of the importance of the home Pesach ritual, whose emphasis on family speaks to its lasting popularity.

Because Jews were no longer able to observe Pesach as a pilgrimage holiday celebrating national independence at the Temple, the Rabbis looked to revive past practices, including the intimate family groupings originally depicted in the Book of Exodus. In order to keep alive hope for better times, our Sages also developed additional seder rites identifying Pesach with the Jewish dream of messianic redemption. The ultimate sign of rabbinic worthiness connects the collective performance of the *pesach* sacrifice with the defining mark of a single Jew. Our modern politically correct sensibilities notwithstanding, we can still appreciate these words from midrash elaborating on the rite ordered by Joshua during biblical times: "When the Israelites saw that the uncircumcised were disqualified from eating the *pesach* sacrifice, they arose with the least possible delay and circumcised all their servants and sons and all those who went out with them. It can be compared to a king who arranged a banquet for his friends and who said, 'Unless the invited guests show my seal, none can enter.'"

Today, most Jews still recognize male circumcision as a categorical Jewish identification, though our gender-sensitive consciousness more satisfactorily equates doing mitzvot with bringing the Messiah into our midst. Understanding and observing Pesach are guaranteed steps in the right direction.

Our passage through the five special Shabbatot will prepare us by studying ancient texts, anticipating our dream of *L'shanah habaah birushalayim,* "Next year in Jerusalem!"

# PART II

# Our Tradition's Measured
# Passage to Pesach:
# Five Special Shabbatot

Some of us are born planners, organizing ourselves and our households so well that important dates occurring annually, those requiring long lead times, do not catch us unaware. We reach for our lists and effortlessly proceed down each Roman numeral and cardinal number, making slight changes only to improve the event this time around.

And then there are the other 99.9 percent of us who bumble our way through almost everything. Last-minute scrambling is our "m.o.," enabling us to complain quite legitimately about our heightened stress levels and sleep deprivation. No holiday brings out both the worrier and the procrastinator like Pesach. Of course we eagerly anticipate the wonderful family reunions as we gather around the seder table. But many fear the details and the doing, trembling at the mere thought of where and how to begin.

Though relatively few of us are aware of it, two thousand years ago our Sages evolved a way of dealing calmly with Pesach by planning for it well in advance. The Talmud states, "One should raise issues and give expositions on the laws of Pesach from thirty days before the festival." Several hundred years before the Talmud was written, Rabbis codified long-standing oral tradition in the Mishnah and began Pesach preparations even earlier by proclaiming public observance of a series of special Sabbaths. Starting a full six weeks before Pesach, additional Torah and haftarah portions are added to the usual weekly readings. They discuss various aspects, observances, and rituals of the holiday. If understood as deliberate markers in our passage and studied to better appreciate why we do what we do, these added readings can prepare us intellectually and spiritually for our journey.

We learn from *Mishnah M'gillah* 3:4, "When the first day of the month of Adar falls on a Sabbath, they read the section of *Sh'kalim* [Exod. 30:11–16]." Thus this special reading assigned to Shabbat Sh'kalim marks our first stop in our passage to Pesach. Explaining the half-shekel tax imposed on all adult Jewish males, these verses state that the tax was due on the first of Nisan, just two weeks prior to Pesach. Funds collected by this tax were used to maintain the roads leading to Jerusalem and the Temple itself, as well as for other necessary public works projects to be completed right before hundreds of thousands of pilgrims made their way to the Temple to offer the *pesach* sacrifice. The reading associated with Shabbat Sh'kalim is full of things to be counted and attended to, getting us in the counting mode of Pesach, when we focus on four questions, four cups of wine, ten plagues, and fifteen steps through the seder meal.

"On the second [Sabbath, Zachor, they read], 'Remember.'" This Shabbat, occurring nearest to Purim, recalls in three verses from Deuteronomy (25:17–19) how the arch-villain Amalek attacked the last Israelite stragglers leaving Egypt, killing the weakest and most weary. During the seder, we are commanded to recall and relive the torments of slavery our people suffered and the hard-heartedness of Pharaoh. Then we remember the wondrous Night of Watching on the fourteenth of Nisan, when our people marked their doorposts with the blood of the lamb they had sacrificed, the signal to God to pass over Jewish homes when Egyptian firstborn were struck down. And finally, we relive our hasty dash out of *Mitzrayim*, leaving Egypt so quickly that our bread did not have time to rise.

"On the third [Sabbath, Parah, they read], 'The Red Heifer.'" One of the most puzzling parts of Torah, the nineteenth chapter of the Book of Numbers, deals with the laws surrounding impurity from corpse contamination. When a priest sprinkled a concoction whose prime ingredient was ash from the sacrifice of a *parah adumah*, an absolutely red cow, on a person suffering from this most severe impurity, the Israelite was pronounced once again ritually clean. Only those in such a wholly pure condition were permitted to make a *pesach* offering so as not to defile the Jerusalem Temple, which was always in a state of absolute purity. While these laws were meant originally to address cultic, religious aspects of the affected persons, today we also concern ourselves with moral and psychological character improvements as we get ready for Pesach.

"On the fourth [Sabbath, HaChodesh, they read], 'This month shall be unto you.'" Shabbat HaChodesh marks the beginning of the month of Nisan, the first month of the ancient biblical Jewish calendar, by once again turning to the Book of Exodus (12:1–20) for its additional, special Torah reading. This portion records the biblical laws Moses announced to the people of Israel just before they left Egypt, particularly the preparation and eating of the paschal lamb in family groups, suggesting the first notions of the seder that we celebrate today.

Our tradition refers to readings for these four Sabbaths, and thus the sum of the days themselves, as *Arba Parashiyot,* four spring Saturdays singled out to help us begin our Pesach arrangements early. We add to these a fifth Sabbath, Shabbat HaGadol, "the Great Sabbath," which takes place immediately prior to Pesach. Texts assigned to the first four Shabbatot include additional selections from both Torah and haftarah and look to past events anchored by current circumstances. However, on Shabbat HaGadol we imagine our ultimate redemption, guided by prophetic statements from only a special haftarah reading, from the Book of Malachi. At that time, we are promised, the prophet Elijah will come to earth to announce "the coming of the awesome, fearful day of *Adonai,*" a future so joyous and full of wonder that "parents will reconcile with children and children with parents" (3:23–24). During each seder, as the children open the door to welcome Elijah and inspect his wine cup, they look for signs of his presence that will usher in the Messiah. We hope our actions of the past year have made this long-anticipated event draw a little nearer.

Over the centuries Jewish legends have been repeated and mystics have created much literature surrounding these special Shabbatot. The next five chapters often refer to two collections of midrash that are repositories of aggadic, or narrative, works collected specifically for celebrating our Festivals. It is believed that the editor of *P'sikta D'Rav Kahana* compiled his work in the seventh century, and the editor of *P'sikta Rabbati,* a few hundred years later. At about the same time, early medieval poets composed lyrical texts to augment the liturgy in which these additional Torah and haftarah selections were read. Their efforts, called *piyutim,* mystical liturgical texts, were largely excised from Reform liturgy because they were thought to lengthen worship excessively and were considered too otherworldly by nineteenth-century standards of rationalism. By reintroducing a few of these treasures from our tradition that have been removed from most of the prayer books we use, our passage to Pesach will take many previously unexplored avenues, expanding the breadth and depth of our holiday horizons.

But we also want to follow familiar paths. Celebrating Pesach should be an experiential paradise, exciting our senses in a shared profusion of touch, sight, smell, taste, and sound. Each chapter exploring our special Sabbaths is also dedicated to one of our five senses. As we study Shabbat Sh'kalim, our aim is to touch the sacred. We see our defining memories as we reflect on Shabbat Zachor texts. Studying Shabbat Parah, we follow the scent of the mysterious red heifer. We savor the tastes of Pesach when we examine Shabbat HaChodesh. Finally, our passage almost at its destination, we listen to each other to hear the voice of God as we reach Shabbat HaGadol.

Let us begin, together . . .

# Shabbat Sh'kalim: Touching the Mundane, Striving for the Sacred

(Exod. 30:11–16; II Kings 12:1–17)

At first glance, the additional Torah portion for this first of five special Sabbaths leading to Pesach reads like a basic, hands-on instruction manual. It comes from those chapters in the Book of Exodus that describe the building and furnishing of the Tabernacle, the portable sanctuary that the newly freed Israelite slaves carried with them during their post-Egyptian years of wandering. What interests us here are those few verses explaining how the people financed the Tabernacle: "This is what everyone who is entered in the records shall pay: a half-shekel by the sanctuary weight—twenty *gerah*s to the shekel—a half-shekel . . ." (Exod. 30:13).

The extra haftarah portion for Shabbat Sh'kalim also resembles a nuts-and-bolts primer that might have been distributed in a course teaching prudent Temple management. We learn which fund-raising methods worked and which didn't, and how our ancestors accumulated the funds to pay for maintenance items like material and labor.

> [King] Jehoash said to the priests, "All the money, current money, brought into the House of *Adonai* as sacred donations . . . let the priests receive it, each from his benefactor. . . ." And the priest Jehoiada took a chest and bored a hole in its lid. He placed it at the right side of the altar . . . and priestly guards deposited there all the money. . . . (II Kings 12:5–7, 10)

What began as a one-time Tabernacle tax evolved into an annual Temple levy. As *Mishnah Sh'kalim* relates, though the money collected paid primarily for daily Temple sacrifices, these same funds also paid for the repair of roads and the mending of breeches in Jerusalem city walls damaged by severe winter rains. Everything had to be in perfect condition in time for the spring journey taken by hundreds of thousands of Jewish pilgrims, all ascending to Jerusalem for Pesach.

But nothing in Torah remains simple for very long. What begins as a series of practical explanations soon becomes profound, expounding on the most sacred of Jewish beliefs. How do we identify ourselves and our community? How do we relate to each other through both the good and the evil we do? How do we describe the complex relationship between ourselves and our God? And what does all this have to do with Shabbat Sh'kalim, the first benchmark on our journey to Pesach?

## "When You Take a Census . . ." (Exod. 30:12)

The simple act of counting seems as natural to the human condition as breathing. Instinctively, when a mother sees her newborn for the first time, she counts fingers and toes to make sure that her child is "all there." Among her first words to her infant are nursery rhymes involving counting, such as "One Potato, Two Potato," "One, Two, Buckle My Shoe," and "This Little Piggy." Couplets soon give way to counting games such as hopscotch and pickup sticks. Later, we count to keep score in the sports we play and to keep time in the music we make.

The French medieval sage Rashi tells us that those who count give life both to those who literally do the numbering and to those who are being counted. Without the acknowledgment of another, the spark that makes us come to life in someone else's eyes, our lives would be incredibly sad and lonely, barely worth living. Merely existing, not touching the hearts and souls of others, defeats our greater purpose. Those who have withdrawn to the fringes of our spiritual center need to be told how much they "count" in the larger community, how much they are appreciated by family and friends who care.

The practice of Judaism overflows with commandments decreeing exact counts. Traditionally, a Jewish worship service includes a minimum of ten persons at least thirteen years old. Otherwise, essential prayers such as the Mourner's *Kaddish* cannot be recited. Our most important moral values, those that form the basis of our covenant with

God, are first numbered, then named—the *Ten* Commandments. In Hebrew they are referred to as *Aseret HaDibrot,* "the Ten Things," emphasizing not particular labels, but universal, timeless virtues. In a maxim from midrash, our Sages compared the life-giving value of counting to the essential need of natural nourishment: "Just as wheat is measured and stored away, so will Israel be numbered and preserved."

And of course, Pesach begins with one or two nights devoted to counting, evenings spent classifying and categorizing as we recall the many symbols unique to this holiday. We participate in a seder meal, emphasizing the "order" of the rituals we celebrate. Each step follows the other in a sequence put into place hundreds of years ago. We first break the middle of three matzahs and are instructed to hide the larger, not the smaller piece. The youngest person present—and often there is a lively discussion to determine who is "youngest" that year—recites four questions. We sing about four children, drink four cups of wine, recall ten plagues God inflicted upon the Egyptians, and end our night of recounting by asking and then answering the question *Echad mi yodei-a?,* "Who knows one?"

All of us who host or lead a seder know that planning is paramount. That means listing everything needed and then making smaller lists of lists, counting and measuring, checking and double-checking, going over things yet one more time. Using the same logic, the Rabbis designated many weeks of Pesach planning. In ancient times, Pesach preparations began on Shabbat Sh'kalim, the New Moon heralding the Hebrew month of Adar, a full six weeks before the fourteenth of Nisan and the first night of Pesach. Since the annual shekel tax was due at the beginning of Nisan, one of the main purposes of this special Shabbat was to issue the first official tax-due notice, a kind of fiscal "heads-up" to the population. Though the tax was not a large amount, just "a half-shekel by the sanctuary weight—twenty *gerah*s to the shekel" (Exod. 30:13), people often had to plan in order to pay it. The tractate, or book, entitled *Sh'kalim* in the Jerusalem Talmud is even more specific, furnishing a timetable based on distance from the Temple: "On the first of Adar, they announce the collection of the shekel tax. On the fifteenth of Adar, money collectors and changers set up their tables in the provinces of Judah, and on the twenty-fifth of Adar, tables would be erected in the Jerusalem Temple, all to facilitate the paying of the tax."

## "Everyone Who Is Entered, from the Age of Twenty Years Up . . ." (Exod. 30:14)

To most of us today, being counted in a census and paying taxes are somewhat annoying but routine realities of life. Yet biblical commentators have found less innocuous messages in the taking of a census, ones not merely associated with payment of a small tax. Census taking could mean much more—it could in fact be a prelude to conditions of physical danger. According to Rashi, things that are numbered, most particularly human beings, are subject to the influence of the Evil Eye. As if to validate this sinister prognosis, Rabbi Joseph Hertz, the late chief rabbi of Great Britain, connected the counting of all male adults to compiling a list of potential warriors, a type of biblical draft registration. According to Hertz, throughout this period a ruler ordered a census during troubled times, when war threatened. A military commander had to know how many men he could draw from to form his army. Then, as now, the only way to obtain this basic yet vital information was to know of each person capable of serving.

In biblical times, military mustering usually meant that fighting would soon follow and, with that, the real possibility of injury or death on the battlefield. Counting for purposes of taking a martial census could literally be dangerous to one's health and thus was avoided whenever possible. Moreover, the Bible tells us that only God could sanction war; people could be counted and battle each other solely for sacred purposes, not to foment human greed or lust for power. An instance of a nondivinely authorized census during King David's wars of empire building resulted in a horrific epidemic, a plague in which seventy thousand died (II Sam. 24).

Counting is considered dangerous because it is a privilege belonging to and reserved solely for God. A *piyut*, written by the early medieval writer Eliazer Kalir and traditionally said during the Shabbat Sh'kalim service, tells us: "When Moses heard the command to 'count the heads of the Children of Israel,' he exclaimed in fear, 'How can I [a mere mortal] investigate them?'" In fact, a midrash teaches us that it was God, not military commanders or tax collectors, who routinely counted the Israelites. God tallied the people three times in the Pesach story alone. First, God counted the Israelites as they entered Egypt: "The total of Jacob's household who came to Egypt was seventy persons" (Gen. 46:27). Second, God counted them as they were about to leave: "The Israelites journeyed from Raamses to Succoth, about six hundred thousand on foot, aside from children" (Exod. 12:37). Finally, God counted Israel as the people went into the wilderness: "Take a census of the whole Israelite community by the clans of its ancestral houses . . . head by head" (Num. 1:2).

When counting is done by mortals instead of God, it diminishes the spiritual as well as the physical dimension of humanity. To many of us, a number replacing a name instantaneously recalls the insidious tattoos branded on the arms of Nazi concentration camp inmates. Numbering transforms individuals into faceless, anonymous objects. But if we are allowed to reconfigure ourselves by name and cast off the number given by a sinister, external source, we recover individual worth and meaning. All we then need is another caring soul willing to hear our story and be touched by it, welcoming us as valued, strengthening our will to function as a necessary member of the community.

Yet our world demands situations when counting becomes unavoidable. So the Jewish tradition teaches various mnemonic devices that remove physical or psychic harm, neutralizing numbering to a technical, mechanical action. Some engage in a bit of negative wordplay, calling out, "not-one, not-two" when a physical count is needed. An ancient Jewish processing method seems as permissible as it is practical. We learn in the Mishnah that everyone who is entered in a census also has possessions that may be numbered, in this case, animal herds and flocks. All sheep pass under a shepherd's staff, and every tenth sheep is marked. We can also count by reciting a Hebrew phrase composed of ten syllables that is found in every worship service. At the Red Sea, after Israel successfully fled Pharaoh's grasp, Miriam and Moses sang, *Mi chamochah, ba-eilim Adonai?*, "Who is like You, Eternal One, among the gods that are worshiped?" As we praise God, we thus transform evils associated with numbering into sacred deeds.

## "The Rich Shall Not Pay More and the Poor Shall Not Pay Less" (Exod. 30:15)

However we feel about the literal or moral dimensions of calculating, the Bible makes it clear: all Jews had to pay the half-shekel tax, and all

Jews were required to contribute the same amount, regardless of fiscal worth. Since God makes no distinctions between individuals, neither should we. Both the portable sanctuary and the Temple in Jerusalem belonged to every Israelite, irrespective of social status or wealth. Contributing one basic tax helped solidify the Jewish people into a coherent, cohesive community even after Jerusalem's destruction caused our physical dispersion. This spirit of indivisibility continued during the many centuries when the Land of Israel existed only as a fervent dream. Although on occasion we may need to remind ourselves, we are a single people regardless of political, geographic, and ideological distinctions.

In biblical days, the annual payment bonded Israelites together in what was an important indication of inclusive community membership. The Jewish historian Josephus, writing immediately after the Temple's destruction at the end of the first century C.E., describes an incident in which our people actually demanded to pay this tax. Jews living in Ionia, in present-day Turkey, requested an audience with King Herod, the ruler of Judea, when he visited their city. They told him they were being denied the right to send their half-shekel collection to the Jerusalem Temple, thus severing the connection to their spiritual home hundreds of miles away. Herod successfully interceded on their behalf, and Ionian Jews again were permitted to send their tax to their countrymen in Palestine, once more feeling part of the Jewish people.

Aiming at a similar objective, today many synagogues hold community seders. This gives the entire temple family the opportunity to be together at this festive time, encouraging a joyous sense of belonging. Sponsoring a synagogue seder also accommodates those who do not participate in a private, home ritual meal. A midrash puts this nicely. Translating the first part of Exodus 30:12 as "When God lifted Moses' head" (really a more literal translation than "census," since the Hebrew word *rosh*, "head," is used in this verse), *P'sikta Rabbati* continues the metaphor, "now Moses lifted up the heads of all My children." No individual was left out of the group or was lifted higher than any other. An earlier midrashic collection, *P'sikta D'Rav Kahana*, continues this classic theme. It contrasts the one Jewish fee to the many taxes that Rome inflicted upon the conquered Israelite nation: "[Rome] keeps jabbing away . . . 'Bring your head tax, bring your general tax, bring levies upon your crops and herds.' But God makes it easy for

Israel to support God's House, narrowing down the obligations to a single head tax, and even this is not demanding."

## "They Would Deliver the 'Weighed Out' Money to Overseers of the House of *Adonai*" (II Kings 12:12)

Just as we adopt "the more, the merrier" philosophy for our seders, always able to squeeze another person around the holiday table, so our biblical tradition makes inclusivity a priority, allowing as many people as possible to contribute to the Temple's upkeep. The additional haftarah portion for Shabbat Sh'kalim states how easy it was to make a donation: "And the priest Jehoiada took a chest . . . and placed it at the right side of the altar [before] one entered the House of *Adonai*" (II Kings 12:10). Even if someone was ritually unclean, and therefore not permitted to enter the holy area of the Temple, he could still fulfill the mitzvah and contribute the shekel tax.

Since our earliest times as a people, we have all been responsible for putting our houses in order, our personal as well as our sacred dwelling places. The extra Torah selection for this Shabbat, read and studied a full six weeks prior to Pesach, encourages us to do a thorough job. We are placed on notice that our homes require the same type of routine maintenance as do our other prized possessions. Just as our car wheels may need realignment after too many encounters with winter potholes, so too do our gutters need to be cleared of the leftover leaves of fall. And just as we touch up a slight dent in our car that only we can notice, so too do we put another coat of paint on our already shining dining room walls.

Spiritually, we also use this time to begin scraping off collected deposits of ill will and stubbornness, the sticky *chameitz* that has accumulated on our souls as well as in our homes. As we contemplate coming together to celebrate God's passing over the children of Israel, we wonder if we will be judged worthy of receiving such divine mercy. In biblical times, the monies collected through the shekel tax had spiritual as well as literal value. By paying this tax, each Israelite contributed a means of personal purification as an offering to God, the ultimate Judge. We are continually reminded that repentance is not reserved exclusively for Yom Kippur. Derivatives of the Hebrew root כ-פ-ר,

"expiation" or "atonement," are used three times in the five verses comprising the Torah portion of Shabbat Sh'kalim, including twice in the final verse:

> You shall take the expiation money from the Israelites and assign it to the service of the Tent of Meeting. It shall serve the Israelites as a reminder before *Adonai,* as expiation for your souls. (Exod. 30:16)

Expiation money, *kesef hakipurim,* is not just another incidental assessment. It is intended to repair and redeem our troubled selves; it is the outward acknowledgment of our inner determination to rectify sinful deeds. The Hebrew word *shekel* also connotes a lift or balance; in verb form, the root letters ש-ק-ל weigh our acts, tipping the scales first to one side and then the other. Pesach is not a holiday of unrelenting gaiety, like Purim, during which we are commanded to drink until we cannot tell the difference between Mordecai and Haman. During the Pesach seder, the four cups of wine we drink are carefully measured and spaced throughout the meal to avoid a drunken demeanor. Our joy as the holiday commences gradually shifts to a more somber mood. We honor our departed loved ones by saying *Yizkor* in their memories in a worship service specifically named as such as the week of Pesach ends. A well-known story illustrates how God mourns even the slain enemies of Israel, killed at the time of the first Pesach. The angels were about to celebrate the drowning of the Egyptians at the Red Sea by singing psalms of victory. They were quickly silenced by a brokenhearted God, who angrily chastised them, saying, "My creatures are perishing, and you are ready to sing."

## "A Half-Shekel as an Offering to *Adonai*" (Exod. 30:13)

We are told that this shekel payment is no ordinary weight. It is twice as heavy as the usual shekel measure, an indication of its sacred significance and consequence to our people. Yet it came to be considered such a negligible monetary amount that, as a one-time payment by a single individual, the actual amount didn't really matter, least of all to God. What did matter is the spirit in which it was offered. Commenting on a pertinent passage in the midrash collection *Sh'mot Rabbah,* Rabbi

Ezekiel Joseph, a nineteenth-century rabbi wrote, "When You make Israel aware they are in debt to Me, then they shall give, every person, a ransom for their soul to the Lord."

There are several acceptable understandings of the Jewish relationship with God. Some always view our Creator as the Pesach Activist, smiting the firstborn of every Egyptian while allowing all of the Israelite slaves to live and then to escape from the clutches of their masters. They also cite God's dynamic role at the Red Sea, drowning Egyptian soldiers and destroying their chariots. Two parables from *P'sikta Rabbati*, both applauding Israel as the exclusive beneficiary of God's deeds, illustrate this message. "God said to Moses, 'Take special care of this nation. Of all nations that I created in My world, this was the first to proclaim me King, saying at the Red Sea, "This is my God" [Exod. 15:2].'" "A King had many purple cloaks, but He had one in particular about which He always gave orders to His keeper of the wardrobe. When the man asked why, he was told, 'I must take special care of this one, for I had it on when I wed a princess.'"

While these parables may move some of us, others may find them sadly outdated. How can we believe in this kind of superhuman Supernatural, who is able to solve all of our problems? Where was this God during World War II, when God's "first nation," God's "princess," was being decimated? The God many pray to is more self-contained and vulnerable. Our ancient Sages, being realists, also recognized our need for a more exposed, susceptible Presence. "Rabbi Judah bar Simon said in the name of Rabbi Yochanan: From the Divine Power, Moses heard commandments that startled him and made him recoil. God said: 'Let them make Me a sanctuary, and I shall dwell among them' [Exod. 25:8]. In reply Moses said bluntly to the Holy One: 'Master of the universe, behold! The heavens, not even the heavens above the heavens, can contain You.' Thereupon the Holy One reassured Moses: 'It is not as you think; though the sanctuary is to be [small], I shall go down to earth and shrink My Presence into your midst below. . . .'"

This talmudic notion of *tzimtzum,* "contraction," brings with it a sense of theological perspective that resonates with many of us today. Rabbi Mordecai Kaplan, the twentieth-century founder of Reconstructionist Judaism, taught that we do not pray to a distant, transcendent Deity but to a more immanent, personal Source of

Creation. The contemporary commentator Nahum Sarna interprets God as dwelling *among* the people, each individual, equally.

"Rabbi Levi said: Why did God keep counting the Children of Israel? His action may be compared with that of a Roman governor who had charge of so many treasures that he would not take the trouble to count them all. But he had one small chest filled with gold pieces, which he used to take up all the time, count the pieces in it, then put it aside, only to bring it forth after a few days, and count the gold pieces again."

Like the Roman governor, we have to touch something continuously to make it ours. So we participate in a Pesach seder year after year after year and always manage to find something distinctive about each one that strengthens its meaning and heightens our joy.

We do not need to be apprehensive about leading a seder or concerned that we'll do something wrong or leave something out. We begin at our current comfort level and proceed at our own rate, adding whatever prayers and rituals speak to us at every step along our personal journeys. We grow in Jewish understanding. A middle-aged Jewish woman, recently widowed, described her anxieties as she faced her first Pesach without her husband: "Each year I face the same question: Who will lead the seder? I am building the courage to do it myself. But to do this, I would have to make time to study. . . . Now that I stand alone, can I make further changes on my own? Can I fully take charge as I have in other areas of my life? And if not now, when?"

By starting our passage to Pesach at the New Moon of the month of Adar, during Shabbat Sh'kalim, we join with our Divine Partner who leads us to redemption: "As for myself, how precious to me are those who are assembled and counted."

## From Our Tradition

*Several short texts that explain the themes of each chapter from a storytelling perspective appear in this section. They further examine and reflect upon the many meanings of Pesach.*

The Holy One said: It is foreseen by Me that whenever a census of Israel is taken, their numbers will be diminished. And so this is what I shall do: I shall prepare a remedy for them, so that they will have a means of expiation. The giving of shekels for the daily offering was the means of expiation. (*P'sikta Rabbati* 10:1)

"Moses was commanded to take a census." To what may this be compared? To a flock that is dear to its Owner, upon which fell a pestilence. As soon as it ceased, the Owner said to the shepherd: "I beg of you, count my sheep and ascertain how many of them are left." He did this to show that the flocks were dear to Him. (Rashi, *Commentary to Exodus,* 172a)

"Yet the number of the Children of Israel shall be as the sand of the sea, which cannot be measured nor numbered" (Hos. 2:1). What is the meaning of this passage? God let Hosea see what He had let Abraham see, when God said, "Look now toward heaven, and count the stars, if you are able to count them" (Gen. 15:5). (*P'sikta Rabbati* 11:4)

Rabbi Yudan, citing Rabbi Samuel bar Rav Nachman, told the parable of a king who had a particular undergarment concerning which he kept giving commands to his servant, saying: Shake it out; fold it up; give it constant care. The servant said: Of all the undergarments you have, you keep giving me commands only about this one. The king replied: Quite so, because this is the undergarment I wear close to my body. Likewise Moses spoke to the Holy One: Master of universes, of the seventy nations that are Yours, it is only concerning Israel that You continually command me. The Holy One replied, I keep commanding you concerning them because Israel cleaves close to me. (*P'sikta D'Rav Kahana* 2:7)

# 4

## Shabbat Zachor: Seeing Our Memories as They Define Us Today

### (Deut. 25:17–19; I Sam. 15:2–34)

The ability to remember is the theme of this second special Shabbat before Pesach. The act of remembering—*zachor*—seems congenitally ingrained in all of us. We don't know exactly how the process of memory works, but we have all experienced the rush of feelings when our memories are triggered. The novelist Jonathan Safran Foer elevates the ability to remember until it becomes the defining quality of the Jewish soul: "Jews have six senses: touch, taste, sight, smell, hearing . . . memory. . . . The Jew is pricked by a pin and remembers other pins. . . . When a Jew encounters a pin, he asks: *What does it remember like?*" Sometimes it seems as if our recollections form our essence, dictating our movements as we go about our daily routine and invading our thoughts even as we sleep. When we are awake, if a particularly troubling memory plagues us, we often try to substitute a more pleasant one. We flip through our emotional Rolodexes as we search for happy times, when our family would reconnect and celebrate together. As we replay our favorite *simchah*s—a bat mitzvah, a special birthday, a Pesach seder—our fondest moments are vividly recalled.

But sometimes darker thoughts force their way into our consciousness. Sometimes none of the mental tricks we use to beat back bad memories work. We find ourselves needing to revisit them in order to disengage their hold on us. Both the additional Torah and haftarah portions that we read on Shabbat Zachor immediately before Purim speak of this grim aspect of memory. Our haftarah portion saddens and mystifies us as we read the travails of Saul, the first king of Israel, in the Book of First Samuel. Though he successfully conquers Amalek, the traditional Jewish foe, Saul is punished by God for not following the divine commandment to decimate completely the dreaded Amalekites and for keeping the best Amalekite sheep and cattle for himself. Our immediate response is to question both the severity of Saul's punishment and the very reading of these verses at this time. Isn't *Adonai* chiefly concerned with saving lives, not destroying them? Why did the Rabbis assign precisely this haftarah portion just before Purim, the most decidedly joyous holiday of the Jewish year?

The special portion from the Torah read on Shabbat Zachor only adds to our bewilderment. In three verses from the Book of Deuteronomy, God twice orders us to dredge up terrible memories, the massacres inflicted upon our people by the ancestors of those Saul battled.

> Remember what Amalek did to you on your journey, after you left Egypt . . . he surprised you on the march, when you were famished and weary, and cut down all the stragglers in your rear. . . . Do not forget! (Deut. 25:17–19)

Once we remember this horrific event, we are given an additional task:

> . . . you shall blot out the memory of Amalek from under heaven. . . . (Deut. 25:19)

These verses raise additional questions. Why are we first commanded to relive such a dreadful tale, only to forcibly remove it from our memories immediately afterward? Exactly who is Amalek in the Book of Deuteronomy, and what is his connection to the enemy of King Saul in the Book of Samuel?

## "Remember What Amalek Did to You on Your Journey, after You Left Egypt . . ." (Deut. 25:17)

We all know the Pesach story by heart. Through God's continued intercession, Moses led the Israelites out of Egypt to freedom. As they were hotly pursued by Pharaoh's army, the former slaves were given a sec-

ond victory when God parted the Red Sea. The last people to escape
were the most vulnerable, the sick and the elderly. Exhausted by their
ordeal, they walked more slowly than the healthier, younger Israelites
and became separated from them. It was these stragglers whom Amalek
attacked. A midrash describes how Amalek isolated the weak and the
infirm: "Amalek got into Egyptian archives and found the names of all
of the Israelites. Amalek stationed himself just beyond God's cloud of
glory, which protected the people, and called out—'Reuben! Simeon!
Levi! Judah! I am your brother. I want to transact business with you.'
As they came forward, Amalek slew them."

Our Sages also tell us that Amalek devised this despicable deed long
in advance; he did not come upon the debilitated Israelites by accident
or make a decision on impulse. "Rabbi Yose ben Chalafta says: 'He
came with a plan.' Amalek assembled all the nations and said, 'Come
help me against Israel.' But they said, 'We will not be able to stand
against Israel. Pharaoh could not stand against them.' Amalek said to
the nations, 'If they defeat me, you flee; if not, then you come and help
me against Israel.' Rabbi Judah says: 'Amalek had to make his way
through five nations to come and wage war against Israel.'"

Since Amalek was the very first foe to attack Israel after they were
freed from Egyptian bondage, Amalek and all of the generations that
succeeded him became God's eternal enemy. Instead of offering food
and drink to a people who were weary from the effects of a long journey (as we do during a Pesach seder evening), Amalek sought to destroy
them.

## "King Ahasuerus Promoted Haman" (Esther 3:1)

Our tradition connects several of the Jews' most heinous opponents
through the Amalekian hereditary line. Though many hundreds of
years separate Amalek from the Persian court of Ahasuerus, his beautiful Jewish queen, Esther, and his diabolical prime minister, Haman,
we discover that Amalek and Haman are directly related. Of all those
who tried to do away with Israel, Haman is the only Amalekite who
attempts to exterminate every Jew in the kingdom in a single day. The
midrashic anthology *P'sikta Rabbati* warns that if we fail to read this
passage containing God's two admonitions to remember every year,

God will return Israel to the slavery of another Egypt. Although we have survived countless enemies, we certainly would rather not tempt fate, so we obediently read Deut. 25:17–19 on every Shabbat Zachor.

## "Remember What Amalek Did . . ." (Deut. 25:17)

Just who was the first Amalek, the man with the demonic determination to destroy our fledgling people? We first encounter him in the Book of Genesis (36:16) as one of many names in a genealogical list of the descendants of Esau, the patriarch Jacob's twin and, according to our tradition, the ancestor of the Arab peoples. Biblical scholar Nahum Sarna has determined that, of the entire list, only Amalek is identified as the son of a concubine rather than an official wife, a direct indication of his lowly birth. Thus biblical interpreters tagged Amalek as a potential problem to Israel right from the start. Later, Rabbis used his name synonymously with first Esau and then Edom, two of Israel's most ancient enemies. During rabbinic times they were stand-ins for the dreaded Roman conquerors, destroyers of the Temple in Jerusalem and responsible for exiling Jews from their hereditary land.

Because of Amalek's crimes against the stragglers leaving the Red Sea and what we are commanded to remember, *zachor,* our Sages have used about every conceivable invective to describe this venal human being. "Marauder," "archenemy," "lacking even the most elementary decency," "devoid of pity and fundamental humanity," and "impervious to morality"—not a venomous branding has gone unuttered.

Why are Amalek's deeds considered so dastardly? A clue can be found in the biblical verses that immediately precede God's injunction to remember.

> You must have completely honest weights and completely honest measures if you are to endure long on the soil that *Adonai* your God is giving you. For everyone who does those things, everyone who deals dishonestly, is abhorrent to *Adonai* your God. (Deut. 25:15–16)

The struggle between Israel and Amalek is not about material possessions, but about moral acts and religious obligations. While the following midrash was more relevant to a time quite different from our own, when it was believed that rewards and punishments automatically followed good and evil, it goes a long way to explain rabbinic reasoning. "As R. Banai, citing Hua, said, When you see a generation whose measures and balances are false, you may be certain a wicked kingdom will come to wage war." Or, as the medieval sage Rashi relates, "If you use false weights and measures, you must expect the provocation of an enemy." Everyday transactions must be carried out virtuously. Otherwise, Jews run the risk of returning the Amalekites to the Land, repeating the history of death and devastation aimed precisely at those least able to defend themselves.

## "Remember . . . after You Left Egypt" (Deut. 25:17)

Our tradition has always singled out Amalek as our most feared enemy, rather than the dastardly Pharaoh, the Egyptian god-on-earth-king. But doesn't Pharaoh, rather than Amalek, merit this title? After all, a willful Pharaoh consistently refused Israel freedom until God killed every Egyptian firstborn, including the royal prince. Especially since Pharaoh is so much better known to us, why shouldn't he, rather than Amalek, assume the title of "Public Enemy Number One," the chief foe of the Jews?

Our commentators have wrestled with this problem as well and have come up with several interpretations. First is the economic argument. "The Israelites had done Moses' bidding and borrowed from the Egyptians objects of silver and gold and clothing" (Exod. 12:35). The late chief rabbi of Great Britain, J. H. Hertz, explains that while Moses had given this command to the people some time before their departure, Israel did not exit Egypt penniless. Second is the political argument. Scholar Benno Jacob bases this understanding on the first chapter of the Book of Exodus, concluding that Pharaoh's oppression of Israel was motivated by a concern for Egypt's national survival, even if it was misguided.

> "Look, the Israelite people are much too numerous for us. Let us deal shrewdly with them, so that they do not increase; otherwise, in the event of war, they may join our enemies in fighting against us." (Exod. 1:9–10)

We are then told that the Egyptians' usual methods of controlling a foreign, potentially troublesome people living in their midst were not working.

> But the more they [the Israelites] were oppressed, the more they increased and spread out, so that the Egyptians came to dread the Israelites. (Exod. 1:12)

Though the Israelites were consistently starved and persecuted, they still were able to bear many children who survived until adulthood. Thus, hypothetically, they would be able to help defeat the militarily mighty Egyptians in battle by joining forces with her other historic enemies.

And finally, there is a moral argument that shifts the title of most feared foe of the Jews from Pharaoh to Amalek. Although the people of Israel suffered greatly under the Egyptian taskmasters, our tradition removes some of the onus of their deeds. Jews are admonished not to hate the Egyptians, "for you were *gerim* [strangers] in the land of Egypt" (Exod. 23:9). Jews have long known feelings of isolation and persecution as members of a minority, beginning with the time they spent in Egypt. Perhaps God placed the Jews there precisely to teach this lesson. The Bible teaches that Jews, of all people, must be sympathetic to the plight of others who are also different from the norm. Welcoming those who might be ill at ease is a basic Pesach theme and a cherished Jewish value.

## "Remember . . . Do Not Forget!" (Deut. 25:17, 19)

Remembering the terrible things Amalek did to the Jewish people is but one example of how the special Torah portion for Shabbat Zachor focuses our thoughts on past events. Because remembering our history is such a timeless concern, contemporary thinkers still grapple with it. Essayist Roger Rosenblatt puts it quite well: "Memory! An impossible subject. One remembers too little or too much, and we are never sure which is worse. . . ." On the one hand, we dread the irretrievable loss of memory attached to effects of aging such as Alzheimer's disease, for its appearance can bring on a withering loss of self, preceding physical death by years. On the other hand, remembering too much, without the ability to compartmentalize horrific past events and move on, is a recipe for personal emotional collapse and destruction. A midrash tells us to "remember with utterances of your mouth"; perhaps if we force ourselves to give voice to the unspeakable we can finally let go of our terrible anguish and be done with it. Certainly proponents of talk therapy proclaim this to be true. This is one of the reasons we read the Haggadah out loud at the Pesach seder every year. Not only must we never forget what happened, we must ensure that the generations coming after us remember as well. The great medieval commentator Nachmanides said that Deut. 25:17, the single verse from the Shabbat Zachor portion describing the evil Amalek did to us, requires continuous public reading.

Not only must the Jewish people remember, but God must remember, too. The covenant made on Mount Sinai, taking place a little more than three months after the Israelites left Egypt, is mutually binding. Just as the former slaves are admonished never to forget the many commandments they are about to receive, God pledges to uphold God's part of the pact. A midrash tells us: "God will remember you again and again. Why does Scripture refer to successive acts of remembering? Because there will be a remembering in Egypt and a remembering at Sinai, a remembering at Nisan and a remembering at Tishrei . . . a remembering in this world and a remembering in the world-to-come." As lofty and as spiritual as memory can be, it also serves a quite practical function. "Rabbi Berechiah Berabbi said: A king had an orchard and also a dog that guarded it. When the son of the king's friend came to steal from the orchard, the dog set upon him and bit him. Whenever the king wished to remind the friend's son of his attempt to steal, he would say—Remember what the dog did to you!"

## "*Adonai* Will Be at War with Amalek throughout the Ages" (Exod. 17:16)

While in the Torah we don't hear the specifics of Amalek's crime against Israel until the Book of Deuteronomy, the first battle between these two archenemies is actually recounted earlier, in the Book of Exodus. The Bible tells us that just weeks after leaving Egypt, Israel fought its first military engagement as a free people in the wilderness of Rephidim against the army of Amalek. Biblical scholar Rabbi W.

Gunther Plaut says it was the memory of this first battle that stamped Amalek as Israel's most feared enemy.

As we did with the passage from Deuteronomy that comprises the additional Torah reading during Shabbat Zachor, we must also look at the verses that immediately precede this reading from the Book of Exodus. Rather than referring to the site as Rephidim, the biblical name, Rashi explains that "the place was named Massah and Meribah, 'trial' and 'quarrel,' because the Israelites quarreled and because they questioned *Adonai*'s commitment to them, saying, 'Is *Adonai* present among us or not?' (Exod. 17:7)." Rashi asks us to "think of a mighty man who was walking along the road with his son perched on his shoulders. Whenever the son saw something he wanted, his father would stoop down, pick it up, and give it to him. This happened over and over again. Then they met someone in the road. The son, who was still on his father's shoulders, asked him, 'Have you seen my daddy?' The father said, 'Do you not know where I am?!' And he threw his son off—and a dog came and bit him."

The medieval midrashic anthology *P'sikta Rabbati* provides an even simpler understanding: God's call to remember Amalek is not uttered in a spirit of revenge, but to remind Israel of its own sin at Rephidim, when Israel doubted God's presence. Another, somewhat earlier anthology, *P'sikta D'Rav Kahana*, relates that the name Rephidim can be broken down into two Hebrew roots: ר-פ-ה, "let go," and י-ד-מ, "hands," that is, literally and figuratively losing touch with divine purpose. "Before Amalek's attack, Israel's hands let go of Torah and the commandments."

## "The Lord Said to Moses: Write This in a Document as a Memory" (Exod. 17:14)

Doesn't it seem strange—the first mention of writing something down in the Bible documents what happened at Rephidim, a vaguely remembered battle in our people's history! Later, Israel fights countless times against innumerable foes. Yet the fledgling nation is not commanded to create a book describing her many battles against other traditional, better-known enemies, like the Philistines, the Moabites, or the Midianites. But here, in the middle of the desert, from among this ragtag bunch of former slaves, a scribe is ordered to find a bit of parchment, some dye or other ancient form of ink, and a writing utensil. An anonymous person then puts to paper what the people had just experienced—their first military testing and subsequent victory as a unified group of free men and women.

Perhaps this written artifact was the "official" version, to make sure everyone remembered "seeing" the same sights, a necessary exercise when establishing an institutional memory. We see what our minds expect us to see and can be reminded of it by repeatedly reading it. The philosopher Nachmanides refers to an actual memorial book containing the Rephidim narrative and other ancient military victories, *The Book of Wars of the Eternal*. But how many ancient Israelites were literate enough to read this book, or any other? A more accessible remembrance was needed, an instantaneously recognizable visual cue that connects the victorious Israelites with the true Victor at Rephidim.

## "And Moses Built an Altar . . ." (Exod. 17:15)

And Moses built an altar and named it *Adonai-nisi,* [*Adonai* is my banner]. He said, "It means, Hand upon the throne of *Adonai!*" (Exod. 17:15–16)

From the time of our biblical Patriarchs, Jews have been thanking God for helping them to find a safe haven by erecting a tangible place to praise God, either a stone or a pillar that immediately becomes sacred or a simple altar of offering. Some of us today believe we can dispense with this visual connection, that a mere physical memory jog cannot stand for a deeper spiritual understanding. But then we remember that among Pesach's most powerful symbols are a bit of dry, flat cracker, a small bone, and a simple roasted egg. Would we remember all of the details of our escape to freedom without them? Two thousand years ago, our brightest Sages required their use. The entire seder is a magnificent sight poem filled with drama that transforms the usual into the sacred and rekindles memory anew every year.

In recent times, we have commemorated the unspeakable horror of the Holocaust by building monuments to the memories of six million Jews whose actual places of rest are unknown. It is no accident that Yom HaShoah, our annual Holocaust commemoration, comes ten days after the conclusion of the weeklong Pesach celebration. In the years following World War II, some survivors began to remember their murdered relatives and friends by marking the date of the Warsaw Ghetto uprising. As Pesach approached in the spring of 1943, several hundred young Jewish men and women still alive in Warsaw somehow conducted a makeshift seder and then fought for every building and alley in the ghetto, knowing they had no chance to win. Nevertheless, they were able to hold out for weeks against the trained German army, then considered the mightiest military apparatus ever created.

As time went on, the Warsaw Ghetto uprising came to commemorate the entire Holocaust. Now Jews and non-Jews all over the world gather on Yom HaShoah in museums and sculpture gardens built especially to remember this tragedy. In one such place, after almost sixty years of silence, the people of Austria erected a large, ultramodern monument in what had been Vienna's ancient Jewish ghetto. But some survivors attacked it as inappropriately "abstract art." They wanted something simpler and better defined, for they reasoned that Jews didn't die "in the abstract," but as real flesh-and-blood individuals. The memory of those who perished had to be seen as more realistic. For many, the most poignant visual reminder of the *Shoah* is a huge pile of small shoes in the National Holocaust Memorial Museum in Washington, D.C., a speechless testament to the million and a half Jewish children who wore them on the last days of their lives.

## "Saul Went to Carmel, Where He Erected a Monument for Himself" (I Sam. 15:12)

Finally, on Shabbat Zachor, we revisit poor, hapless, tragic Saul. We are commanded to remember what can happen when God's commands are not obeyed precisely. Chosen by God, anointed by the prophet Samuel to be Israel's first king, Saul never understood that one doesn't build structures to honor one's own achievements, especially when the failure to follow God's instructions is what sparked that dubious act. After accepting kingship, Saul became military as well as political commander-in-chief and was soon embroiled in endless wars of conquest. Ordered to "attack Amalek, and . . . spare no one, but kill alike men and women, infants and sucklings, oxen and sheep, camels and asses" (I

Sam. 15:3), Saul could not bring himself to destroy the enemy totally, though God explicitly commanded this to be done. The prophet Samuel had to finish the job himself and personally killed Agag, the enemy king. Our story comes full circle when we learn that Agag was a direct descendant of Amalek, the man who ambushed our ancestors soon after they left Egypt.

Thus we find the connection between the story of Saul in the special haftarah portion for Shabbat Zachor and the additional Torah portion for this Sabbath from Deuteronomy, in which we are reminded what Amalek did to the Israelites just after the Exodus. In both narratives, God demanded a total annihilation of the Amalekites and all of their possessions. Saul just didn't see what God expected of him. He thought his military victory, "destroying Amalek from Havilah all the way to Shur, close to Egypt" (15:7), earned him the right to alter the final outcome, stopping short of fulfilling God's take-no-prisoners command. Finally, having seen his victory turned into a terrible tragedy, Saul fell on his own sword, a devastating, humiliating end.

Our Sages have grappled for centuries over the meanings and lessons of Saul's downfall. One scenario punishes Saul for acting more devout than God, for Saul spared Amalek's animals instead of killing them, as God had required.

> Samuel said to Saul, "Why did you disobey *Adonai* and swoop down on the spoil [not destroy it all], thereby doing what was evil in the sight of *Adonai*?" [I Sam. 15:19]. Saul responded, "I understand how humanity has sinned, but what have Amalek's beasts done amiss?" A *bat kol* [heavenly voice] said, "Be not more righteous than your Creator." (Eccles. 7:16)

According to this interpretation, Saul was reprimanded for following the general spirit of one law while ignoring the precise letter of another.

Another textual clue provides a simpler, more obvious explanation.

> Saul said to Samuel, "I did wrong to transgress *Adonai's* command . . . but I was afraid of the troops and I yielded to them." (I Sam. 25:14)

At one time or another, all of us have done the same, losing our high resolve and breaking under the pressure of the moment, taking the easy way out. Hopefully we realize the sin we have committed, and seek forgiveness from our peers and our God. *T'shuvah*, "repentance," is one of our most important Jewish virtues, accepted in all but the most extraordinary cases, like this one. For Saul was not your average citizen, but king of an entire people. And not just any people, but those chosen by God to be God's *am s'gulah*, God's treasured possession. Saul's fatal, pathetic flaw was also his most human one. He chose the love of the people over the commandment of God.

Rabbi W. Gunther Plaut sees another understanding. A close reading of the Hebrew in this passage reveals that Saul obeys the wrong commandment for the wrong reason.

> "The troops spared the choicest of the sheep and oxen for sacrificing to *Adonai your* God." (I Sam. 15:15)

Not "our God" or "my God," but "your God," just as, three verses earlier, "Saul erected a monument *for himself*" (15:12). Like the wicked child in the Pesach seder, Saul denies the existence of a personal God whom he must obey. Instead of listening to the commanding voice of God, speaking through the prophet Samuel, Saul elevated his own human achievements, in effect committing idolatry by worshiping a god of his own making.

## "Remember What Amalek Did . . . Undeterred by the Fear of God" (Deut. 25:17–18)

Though vastly different in intention, scope, and execution, Saul and Amalek committed similar transgressions—each did not hold God in the respect and awe that God demands from all of us. This primary idea of Shabbat Zachor helps keep our Purim revelry and our Pesach industriousness in proper perspective. An important lesson in the Bible teaches that any mortal king serves at the prerogative of the heavenly Ruler. This was God's war against the Amalekites, not Saul's. When Saul "rejected *Adonai*'s command, *Adonai* rejected [Saul] as king over Israel" (I Sam. 15:26). God's judgment, untempered by the option of divine mercy, swiftly disciplined Saul when fear of losing his people's love overshadowed his obedience to God.

God's treatment of Amalek and his descendants is much more understandable. No other nation is described in Torah by the phrase "he feared not God" (Deut. 25:18); such outright condemnation of an entire people does not occur elsewhere. For Amalek and his people, no act was too repugnant, not even slaying those too weak and old to resist. Amalek's actions testify to his lack of God fearing. Far from being an outmoded turn of phrase, this ancient precept also serves as an ultimate motivating force for decent behavior today.

## "The Midwives Feared God" (Exod. 1:17)

There is another memory that comes to mind as we approach Pesach. In direct contrast to the sins of the evil Amalek, whose deeds occur at the end of the Exodus narrative, two paragons of correct moral action who ensure the survival of the Israelites in Egypt appear early in the Exodus story. Unlike both Amalek and Saul, these two women did "fear God." The midwives Shiphrah and Puah resisted a direct command of Pharaoh, that, when helping deliver Jewish baby boys, they kill them. "The midwives, fearing God, did not do as the king of Egypt told them; they let [Hebrew infant] boys live" (Exod. 1:17).

The midwives are not portrayed as other than ordinary citizens whose personal standards demanded they do the right thing, even though they might have been killed by Pharaoh for doing it. "Because the midwives feared God, [*Adonai*] established households for them" (Exod. 1:21). We remember these defiant acts of moral certainty every Pesach as we recall and revere the One who first gave us our freedom. By remembering everyday exemplars of extraordinary courage, we are more clearly able to see the paths we should follow, the passage leading to the sacred.

## From Our Tradition

Remember the Amalekites . . . who flew like locusts to destroy my portion, to smite the mighty in everyone's sight and to eliminate Me. (*Piyyutim,* trans. Marmorstein and Marmorstein, 109)

Amalek made you lukewarm, like water that had cooled off. Rabbi Huna said, a pool of scalding water, at first so hot everyone drew back from it. One man came, jumped into it, and made it lukewarm. Thereupon everyone came and bathed in it. When the Israelites came out of Egypt, nations drew back in fear from them. But Amalek came and made Israel appear lukewarm. (*P'sikta Rabbati* 12:13)

The ancient Amalek has appeared . . . in Jewish history in many forms and guises: he wore the signet ring of the king as Haman; the royal crown as Antiochus; the general's uniform as Titus; . . . the priestly robe as Torquemada; the cossack's boots as Chmielnitzki; or the brown shirt as Hitler. (W. G. Plaut, *The Torah: A Modern Commentary*, 514)

## 5

# Shabbat Parah: Following the Scent of a Red Heifer

### (Num. 19:1–22; Ezek. 36:22–38)

More than two thousand years ago, our ancestors chose a cow, then as now among the most common of domestic animals, to serve in an inscrutable religious ritual. Known in Hebrew as a *parah,* the feminine form of *par,* "bull," this legendary animal represents our third special pre-Pesach Sabbath, Shabbat Parah. Now this was no ordinary cow, but a rarity: a completely red heifer, a *parah adumah*. Legend has it that only nine such cows played a role in Jewish tradition from the time of Moses to the destruction of the Second Temple, a period of almost one thousand years. And the tenth red heifer, it is believed, will not appear until the time of the Messiah.

It was not the cow herself, but the use of her ashes once her body had been completely burned that heightened the sense of mystery surrounding this ritual. A major function of ancient Jewish priests was to ensure the constant purity of the most sacred places, first the portable wilderness Tabernacle and later the permanent Temple structures built in Jerusalem. Because ritual impurity could spread from individuals to these holy Jewish sites, priests devised an elaborate way to rid unclean persons of their contamination.

> Instruct the Israelite people to bring you a red cow. . . . Give it to Eleazar the priest. . . . The cow shall be burned in his sight. . . . The priest shall take cedar wood, hyssop, and crimson stuff and throw them into the fire consuming the cow. . . .

> He who touches the corpse of any human shall be unclean for
> seven days. He shall cleanse himself with [the ashes mixture,
> mixed in water] on the third and seventh day. Then he shall be
> clean. (Num. 19:2–3, 5–6, 11–12)

This rather bizarre ritual applies to the Pesach story because only
ritually pure persons could eat from the paschal lamb that was sacrificed at the Temple on the fourteenth of Nisan, immediately before the
holiday began. Thus the description surrounding the ritual of the red
heifer has a compelling correlation to ancient ways of celebrating
Pesach. It focuses on ritual purity, the many ways of becoming ritually
unclean, and how the ashes of a red heifer helped to regain purity.
Today we commemorate the sacred obligations Jews performed while
the Temple still stood by studying the text about the red heifer during
Shabbat Parah, as Pesach approaches.

But we must first mention the most famous cow in the Torah, which
almost doomed our people in their first months of freedom, the Golden
Calf. In a *piyut*, we see a direct connection between this blasphemous
idol and the purifying red heifer. "God told Moses, . . . Why do you
weary yourself investigating? It is deeper than an abyss. The ashes of
the heifer whiten the stain left by the Golden Calf, atonement for those
who strayed." Usually our tradition calls for children to bear the onus
for the sins of their parents. Prominently displayed in the third of the
Ten Commandments, we read:

> For I *Adonai* your God am an impassioned God, visiting the guilt
> of the parents upon the children . . . of those who reject Me.
> (Exod. 20:5)

Yet the special Torah reading for Shabbat Parah implies that here a
"child," the calf, actually causes the sin that its "mother," the red
heifer, will remove. Since everything else about the red heifer is topsy-
turvy, why not a generational reverse as well?

One midrash implies a maternal relationship between the two animals, the Golden Calf and the red heifer. "Rabbi Aibu said, A hand-
maiden's son polluted a king's palace. The king said, let his mother
come and clear away the filth. In the same way, the Holy One said, let
the heifer atone for the incident of the calf." Other human familial relationships are drawn into the idolatry of the Golden Calf. The chapter

from the Book of Numbers that we read on Shabbat Parah explicitly tells us that Eleazar, and not his father, the High Priest Aaron, supervises the slaughter of the red heifer (Num. 19:3). Commentators look upon this as just judgment brought on by Aaron's complicity in the creation of the Golden Calf while Moses, his brother, climbed Mount Sinai to receive the Torah from God.

## "Instruct the Israelite People to Bring You a Red Heifer . . ." (Num. 19:2)

Our Sages placed impossibly strict demands on what constituted a *parah adumah,* a red heifer. Just two non-red hairs sprouting anywhere on her hide would be enough to disqualify the heifer from consideration. Of course, she had to be physically perfect, without blemish, a typical sacrificial criterion. She also had to be an animal "on which no yoke has been laid" (Num. 19:2), a law singular to the red heifer. She could never have been worked in the field "or ridden on, or leaned on, or hung on her tail, or used by one to cross a river, or put one's cloak on her [even for an instant]."

From conception, the red heifer had to be wholly dedicated to God, a *kadeish,* or holy animal, in every meaning of the term. Though today we tend to emphasize the term's legal connotations, the primary meaning of *kadeish* is to make separate and distinct, creating a holy barrier between the profane aspects of our world and the higher authority of our Higher Authority. A *parah adumah,* pure and sanctified, could never be yoked to the mundane tasks of a workday existence. A *parah adumah* was born to submit solely to the yoke of Heaven, used only for Israel's ritual cleansing. Ancient Sages have written that God first told our patriarch Abraham of this important distinction. When Abraham "ran to the herd to fetch a heifer" (Gen. 18:7) to feed his heavenly visitors, God was in fact showing him that his descendants would be purified by this exceedingly rare animal.

## "The Priest Shall Be Unclean until Evening" (Num. 19:7)

But there is an unfathomable enigma concerning the red heifer. This critical bestower of purification rendered her human purifiers, the holy priests, impure by doing the very acts that purify others! The priest who burned the red heifer, the priest who prepared the mixture made from her ashes, and even the one who took the unconsumed ash "garbage" outside the camp, all became ritually unclean until after sundown of the day they performed these acts. The clothes the priests wore while performing the ritual also became unclean. They had to be washed at the same time the priests washed their bodies to rid them of ritual uncleanness (Num. 19:7, 9–10, 19, 21).

> Whatever that unclean person touches shall be unclean; and the person who touches him shall be unclean until evening. (Num. 19:22)

Even King Solomon, reputed to be the wisest person in the ancient world, could not solve this conundrum: "I succeeded in understanding the whole Torah. But as soon as I reached the chapter about the red heifer, I searched, I probed, I questioned. I said I will get wisdom, but it was far from me." The late chief rabbi of Great Britain, J. H. Hertz, wrote in his Torah commentary that this mystery indicates a basic attitude of Judaism: "We shall never know why such defilement should be removed in this specific manner."

Yet today, many of us may be more accepting of this story than our rationalist ancestors, who believed it possible someday to find a definitive answer or solution for even the most perplexing problem. We now realize that the wonders of science can only go so far in revealing the basic components of nature. And though we have made giant strides in vast areas of technology, we still cannot fully comprehend the forces that surround the mysteries at the beginning and end of life. Some call this awareness the attainment of heightened spirituality; others speak of this fundamentally indefinable process as simply faith.

## "This Is the Statute *Adonai* Commanded . . ." (Num. 19:2)

Rabban Yochanan ben Zakkai's faith was quite matter of fact. "He said to his disciples, no matter how it appears, a corpse does not defile, nor does an ash and water mixture cleanse. The Holy One has set down a statute, issued a decree. You are not permitted to transgress." By placing this widely quoted midrash in the voice of the prominent first-century Rabbi who transformed Judaism after the destruction of the Temple, our ancient Sages put forth Yochanan Ben Zakkai's legislation as unquestioned and absolute. We are forbidden to use reason when confronted with the rite of the red heifer. It must be observed because it is divinely commanded.

As liberal Jews, we may chafe at the notion of a divine command, especially something as otherworldly as this enigmatic procedure. Obviously we are long past invoking heifer burnings and ash sprinklings. And we don't like to be told what to do. After all, we have been taught that from talmudic times questioning and debating have always been commendable Jewish styles of learning. We even begin our Pesach celebration by asking four specific questions and follow these with many more questions that we expect to be answered forthrightly. Why on earth must we still bother with *parah adumah*?

For the last thousand years, Jewish scholars have attempted to answer these questions. The eleventh-century French scholar Rashi puts a decidedly contemporary twist on that ageless dilemma "What will the neighbors say?" "Because other nations taunted Israel, saying, 'What is this command and what reason is there for it?' Torah uses the Hebrew term *chukah* [statute] which implies, 'It is an enactment before God—you have no right to criticize it.'" A later, Chasidic response warns from another point of view why we cannot fathom the meaning of the red heifer ritual: "You have no right to investigate it, because if you investigate the law and try to find reasons for it, that in itself may lead to your violating it."

## "*Adonai* Spoke to Moses and Aaron . . ." (Num. 19:1)

But we moderns can't help ourselves. We believe there is something almost sacred about revisiting and questioning these quirky issues for ourselves, searching for solutions. We endlessly pursue possible understandings as we probe our tradition for meaning. By exploring the meanings and uses of several objects discussed in the Shabbat Parah Torah text—cedar, the hyssop plant, "crimson stuff," and blood—we may be able to bring at least a little clarity to our confusion and understand how Shabbat Parah relates to our upcoming Pesach celebration.

## Cedar, Hyssop, and Crimson Material

According to the Torah portion, a priest adds "cedar wood, hyssop, and crimson stuff" (Num. 19:6) ingredients to the fire already consuming the red heifer, thereby creating the ashes that purify those made impure by coming into contact with a dead body. Elsewhere in the Bible, the same King Solomon who cannot decipher the meaning of the red heifer impresses his royal associates by discoursing on a variety of subjects, including trees "from the mighty cedar in Lebanon to the lowly hyssop that grows out of a wall" (I Kings 5:13). In the Book of Kings, these two widely disparate plants mark the wide boundaries of Solomon's brilliance. Here in the Book of Numbers, the special Torah portion for Shabbat Parah, they reveal extremes that balance each other to create a concoction potent enough to diminish corpse contamination, the most severe of impurities. They also refer to the same ingredients a priest uses in his sacrifice to thank God for healing the physical infections of leprosy.

> If a priest sees the leper has been healed of his scaly affection . . .
> he takes the live bird, along with cedar wood, the crimson stuff,
> and hyssop, and dips it . . . and sprinkles it seven times on him
> who is to be cleansed. (Lev. 14:3, 6–7)

It takes both the lowliest shrub as well as the mightiest tree to purify spiritual and physical ailments. So too do we blend the sharp taste of horseradish and the sweetness of *charoset* in the same bite during the Pesach seder. We temper our current freedom with the reminder of our cruel former slavery, knowing that today millions of people still suffer under the bitterness of slavery's yoke.

## Blood

While cedar and hyssop may be secondary ingredients in the purification ritual of the red heifer, blood is of primary importance in this and other Jewish rites of cleansing. It surely accounts for the red color of the very material connecting the cedar and hyssop, the "crimson stuff," as well as the color of the purifying animal, the red heifer. Several hundred years ago, inquisitive individuals discovered that blood was the conduit of life's essential nutrients as it travels through our bodies. In ancient times, people knew that a clear sign of a dead body was the white color of a human corpse, indicating that blood no longer provided life-giving essentials.

Before using blood's magical powers to purify tainted humans or their dwelling places, the High Priest ritually cleansed God's residence.

> Eleazar the priest shall take some of the blood [of the red heifer] and sprinkle it seven times toward the front of the Tent of Meeting. (Num. 19:4)

As the *parah adumah* attends to the yoke of heaven, so ancient Jewish holy men first addressed sacred needs of purification before attending to mundane, human ones.

Because blood was thought to be synonymous with life, healers determined that it could serve as the paramount "cleanser of choice," the ritual detergent *par excellence*. But because blood was thought to be synonymous with life, too much of it marked an object as sinful. And that notion has lasted throughout time. Someone referred to as a "scarlet woman" is one who gives too bountifully of herself to too many men. The color "blood red" is so strong and bright that only the most confident like to use it.

Blood also figures prominently in a verse several lines before the additional haftarah portion for Shabbat Parah, from the Book of Ezekiel. These verses discuss one traditional Jewish aspect of blood most modern Jews disdain: the association of women's monthly menstrual cycles with ritual impurity.

> When the House of Israel dwelt on their own soil, they defiled it with their ways and their deeds; their ways were in My sight like the uncleanness of a menstruating woman. (Ezek. 36:17)

And, while liberal Jews cannot generally countenance this idea, we can lessen its sting through a close reading of the text. In both the haftarah and Torah selections, the Hebrew word *nidah* is used, normally associated with the impurity of a menstruating woman. However, in the Torah verses, the phrase *mei nidah*, "water for sprinkling" (Num. 19:9, 13, 20), refers to blood's vibrant, healing function. The powers of blood are indeed so enormous, they point to both the best and the worst humanity is capable of. On the one hand, only a woman who regularly bleeds can give life to a child. On the other hand, if someone causes another to lose too much blood, those actions take life away. No wonder this most potent symbol is also the most dangerous, reserved for the most sacred acts of God.

# "Put Some Blood on the Doorposts . . ." (Exod. 12:7)

A sign made in blood was the singular marker deciding who would live and who would die in ancient Egypt at the time of the Exodus. When biblical interpreters wrote down our most memorable tale of freedom, they described how the Angel of Death distinguished between the houses in which Israelite slaves resided and the homes of their Egyptian taskmasters by

> the blood on the lintel and the two doorposts. And *Adonai* will pass over the door and not let the Destroyer enter and smite your home. (Exod. 12:23)

The daubing of blood simultaneously provoked the deaths or saved the lives of the firstborn in every family in the land. As the last and most sinister of God's Ten Plagues against Pharaoh, this distinct marking even led to the death of the young Egyptian crown prince. In his grief, the despairing despot freed his slaves. As a sign of life, the daubing of blood ritualized the birth pangs of a free Jewish people, becoming critically important as we remember our ancient story of Pesach.

# "This Is the Ritual: When a Person Dies . . ." (Num. 19:14)

To the best of our knowledge, humankind is the only species that is aware of its inevitable mortality. But awareness and understanding are quite different concepts. Many of us find the mystery of death as unexplainable as a faultless red cow. For all our ancient ancestors knew, perhaps a person could indeed die merely by touching someone already dead. In fact, modern medicine has taught that some of the most deadly diseases are indeed contagious. So a highly developed fear of death was anything but irrational. The Jewish general Josephus, who switched sides and fought with Rome during the destruction of Jerusalem almost two thousand years ago, wrote several histories of the Jews. In the *Jewish Antiquities,* he tells how his near contemporary, King Herod, had to force people to move to the new harbor town he built in Tiberias because much of it had been constructed over a massive graveyard.

But others say it is the Jewish sense of reality and perspective, our determination to live in the present, here-and-now world, that has kept our focus on life rather than death. The ancient Egyptians worshiped their dead rulers as departed gods. They constructed massive pyramids as royal tombs and filled them with luxuries to make eternal life as pleasant as possible. We Jews show our love of God by performing daily deeds of loving-kindness for the living while never denying or dishonoring the sacred memories of our dead. In fact, some commentators have said that the reason impurity caused by corpse contamination became the most severe form of uncleanness was to make sure that mourners did not dwell too long with the bodies of their loved ones and did not grieve in excess. Our tradition constructs a careful balance between celebrating the living and remembering the dead by making Pesach one of several *chagim,* Jewish holidays during which we hold a *Yizkor* service honoring our departed relatives.

## " . . . His Uncleanness Is Still upon Him" (Num. 19:13)

Death has a smell about it all its own. In our present sanitized, civilized circles, we obsess over the faintest whiff of body odors that might cause others to shun us. Our forebears were more tolerant of the obvious smells of the living. But they, too, found it hard to abide the scent of life decomposing. The hyssop plant, one of the objects used in the ritual of the red heifer, was well-known for its clear, sweet smell, which was quite effective in countering unpleasant odors. Perhaps, in addition to its symbolic presence, priests threw hyssop into the pyre of the burning red heifer to make this important ritual more palatable to ancient sensitivities.

Since we mortals don't like offensive odors, biblical writers deduced that God had the same reaction to noxious smells. We learn in several places in the Torah (Gen. 8:21; Lev. 1:9; 17:6) that God accepted the offerings of burnt sacrifices, in some ways similar to those of the red heifer, because they brought *rei-ach nichoach l'Adonai,* "smoke as a pleasing odor to *Adonai.*"

In our own idiomatic English, the reverse is also true; if something "smells fishy," it has a bad moral aroma and we'd better steer clear of it. In addition, researchers have associated our sense of smell with emotional well-being. They hypothesize a direct link between the ability to detect odors and the ability to relate to others. Most of us can understand this problem. When we complain of being "stuffed up" other senses don't work well either. It becomes difficult to concentrate; we tend not to find things located right under our noses. If we are unable to savor the sweet smell of God's gifts to us, such as the scent of flowers or freshly baked bread, our mood may turn sullen and our reasoning may become muddy. We long for the cleansing powers of natural things, for a return to an unpolluted, purer time.

## "An Unclean Person . . . Defiles *Adonai*'s Sanctuary"
### (Num. 19:20)

While the Torah portion for Shabbat Parah addresses itself to individual impurity, the haftarah portion, from the Book of Ezekiel, defines Israel's collective impurity as widespread. Thus God banishes the entire people from the land since it is God's dwelling writ large. The place that God permitted Moses only to view from afar, the place where the Israelites could live permanently as a free people, had become polluted, not from massive corpse contamination but from "the blood they shed upon their land, and for the fetishes with which they defiled it" (Ezek. 36:18).

The prophet Ezekiel lived during the sixth century B.C.E. He was part of the generation exiled to Babylonia after the First Temple was destroyed. Ezekiel tried to make some sense of what had befallen his country. He believed there had to have been a reason his people were scattered. According to Ezekiel, that reason had to do not with their physical but with their massive moral impurity: "I punished them in accordance with their ways and their deeds" (Ezek. 36:19). We see this same cause-and-effect understanding hundreds of years later, after Rome destroyed the Second Temple. Trying to rationalize the horror of being forced to watch Jerusalem in flames and the people once again dispersed and enslaved, our Sages decided that the Jewish people's own evil deeds caused their calamity.

In his commentary to the Shabbat Parah haftarah portion, the contemporary scholar Rabbi W. Gunther Plaut gives this passage a postmodern interpretation. Discussing the verse "But when they came to those nations, they caused My holy name to be *diminished*" (Ezek.

36:20), Plaut notes that the Hebrew root ח-ל-ל usually is translated "to profane." The people thought so little of God they made God seem ordinary. For all intents and purposes, the God of Israel appeared to be just like one of the many gods prayed to by the idol worshipers Israel lived among and emulated. By their impure acts and immoral conduct, the people violated the sacred, holy otherness of God as surely as if they had physically tainted the Temple through corpse contamination. Defiling God's name was tantamount to defiling God's Being, negating the first two of the Ten Commandments:

> I *Adonai* am your God who brought you out of the land of Egypt, the house of bondage: You shall have no other gods besides Me. (Exod. 20:2–3)

So God had to act, "not for your sake, O House of Israel, but for My holy name . . ." (Ezek. 36:22). To recover God's "godliness," God's distinctiveness, God had to purify Israel and thus regain divine honor. And what was the sacred elixir, the holy remedy? It was the ability to recognize Israel once again as God's holy treasure, becoming a people who pledged fidelity to the One, forsaking the many. Ezekiel recalls the language of the Book of Exodus, when God describes the rescue of the Hebrew slaves from Egypt: "I will free you . . . and deliver you . . . and take you to be My people" (Exod. 6:6–7). So Ezekiel describes similar holy actions: "I will take you . . . gather you . . . bring you back to the land. . . . I will deliver you from all your impurities" (Ezek. 36:24, 29). To Ezekiel, cleanness is clearly equated with godliness. It is the holy restoration itself, returning the people to the land, and God to the glory of the faithful.

We end our Pesach seder by proclaiming "Next year in Jerusalem" as our messianic charge. Ezekiel returns Israel not only to the physical land for final redemption, but to that first place of lush, fertile soil, the place where God was both sacred and accessible. "That land, once desolate, has become like the Garden of Eden . . ." (Ezek. 36:35). Israel becomes as innocent as Adam and Eve before eating that infamous fruit. In the words of Rabbi Akiva: "Happy are you, O Israel! Before whom are you cleansed and who is it that cleanses you? . . . God is Israel's *mikveh*. Just as the *mikveh* cleanses those who become defiled, God cleanses Israel."

## From Our Tradition

Said Rabbi Acha in the name of Rabbi Yose bar Chanina: As Moses went up on high, he found the Holy One busy, absorbed in His book. God was busy reading this very passage dealing with the red heifer . . . "I am busying Myself with nothing other than the means of purifying Israel." (*P'sikta Rabbati* 14:6)

The cedar alludes to haughtiness, while the hyssop implies humility. Every person must have a note in one pocket that states, "I am but dust and ashes," while in the other pocket he must have one that states, "The world was created for me." The wise person knows when to use which. (Rabbi Simchah Bunim of Pshischa)

The mixture of water and ashes of the red heifer remind [humanity] of what elements they consist, for knowledge of oneself is the most wholesome form of purification. (Philo)

Who can bring forth a clean thing out of an unclean thing? Is it not the One? (Job 14:4)

Who other than the One can do so?
Who other than the One can so ordain?
Who other than the One can so decree?
Is it not the One?
Is it not the Unique One of the world? (*P'sikta D'Rav Kahana* 4:1)

# Shabbat HaChodesh:
# Tasting Pesach in Public Places,
# in Private Spaces

### (Exod. 12:1–20; Ezek. 45:16–46:18)

Food, glorious food! We salivate at the mere thought of Pesachs we've celebrated in years gone by, remembering brisket and homemade chicken soup with matzah balls, *tzimmes,* and seemingly endless kinds of kugels. The early twentieth-century French Jew Marcel Proust relived poignant childhood experiences by evoking the pastries he called *petites madeleines.* We re-create all the meals we've ever eaten at this special holiday every time we taste our beloved traditional dishes. My husband's elderly aunt will not come to the seder table unless she sees a bottle of the sweetest, most syrupy kosher wine we can find, because as a child she was permitted to taste wine only on Pesach. For her, it's not Pesach without it. The recent surveys reporting the seder meal to be the most celebrated Jewish ritual in America reveal our identification of specific food or drink as "being Jewish," equating repast with religion.

Though the current American multicultural lifestyle has made much traditionally "Jewish" food ubiquitous—you can get a bagel just about anywhere—we Jews tend to look at our normative dishes as defining. The commemoration of Pesach, which gives us so much of our cherished cuisine, has become the quintessential Jewish holiday; it marks our birth as a free people. It is something we don't often think about but a truism nonetheless: in freedom, people can choose what they eat. This is exactly what the additional Torah portion we read on Shabbat

HaChodesh, the fourth of our specially named Sabbaths, is saying. It is chock full of commandments, relating to what we must and must not eat at Pesach. In fact, this additional Torah reading from the twelfth chapter of the Book of Exodus, following the narrative of Genesis and the preceding chapters of Exodus, contains the very first biblically given mitzvot found in Torah.

## "*Adonai* Said to Moses and Aaron in the Land of Egypt"
### (Exod. 12:1)

We know that our additional Torah portion is special for another reason. It specifies a foreign country, not the Land of Israel, as the location in which God spoke. Though mere slaves turning out bricks and mortar for the glory of Egypt's Pharaoh, the Jewish people were reminded when they heard God's words that their Creator had not forgotten them. This portion is filled with vital information the people needed once they were free. There was so much they had to remember that they never had to deal with before. Today, we do much the same thing when those we love are about to travel to distant, unfamiliar places. We remind them to bring along passports and plane tickets. And if we remember the apt maxim "our hearts are led by our stomachs," we may even prepare something special for them to nibble during their journey.

When we read the HaChodesh Torah and haftarah readings in our synagogues, Pesach is only about two weeks away, and it is time to begin planning our seder menus. We find it quite gratifying that the Book of Exodus solves an important taste-oriented problem: When exactly can we prepare all of the marvelous food we are commanded to eat? We learn we may indeed cook that day's Pesach meals on the holiday, a quite different ruling from a similar one regarding Shabbat. On Pesach, we are told:

> You shall celebrate a sacred occasion on the first day, and a sacred occasion on the seventh day; no work at all shall be done on them; only what every person is to eat, that alone may be prepared for you. (Exod. 12:16)

An account written in medieval times gives us a rather fanciful depiction of thousands of holiday sacrifices being offered. Jewish commentator Solomon ibn Verga describes trumpeters playing instruments made of silver to announce the day, accompanying dozens of priests whose sole function was to catch the blood of just-killed animals in silver and gold basins. Ibn Verga also tells us what the priests wore, not to supply a fashion statement but to show how practically the men were garbed: "During the service the priests dressed in scarlet, that the blood which might accidentally be spilled on them should not be noticed. The garment was short, reaching only to the ankle. The priests stood barefoot, and the sleeves reached only the arms, so they should not be disturbed during the service." Jews by the tens of thousands crowded into Jerusalem to celebrate Pesach by sacrificing at the Temple. Our Rabbis indulged in more than a bit of hyperbole in estimating the festive throngs: "King Agrippa once wished to count the hosts of Israel. After he told the High Priest, 'Number the paschal lambs,' he took a kidney from each, and 600,000 pairs of kidneys were found, twice as many as the number of people who departed from Egypt."

## "Do Not Eat Any of It Raw . . ." (Exod. 12:9)

Our three-thousand-year-old biblical recipe offers a choice of meat, depending on market availability and the pocketbook of the person wishing to make the sacrifice. And only prime quality product is allowed:

> Your lamb shall be without blemish, a yearling male; you may take it from the sheep or from the goats. (Exod. 12:5)

The preferred method of cooking is clearly stated:

> Do not eat any of it raw, or cooked in any way with water, but roasted—heads, legs, and entrails—over the fire. (12:9)

Attention to spoilage in this Mediterranean country, millennia before electric refrigeration, merits a five-star rating:

> They shall eat the flesh that same night. . . . You shall not leave any of it over until morning. If any of it is left until morning, you shall burn it. (12:8, 10)

Tradition from Mishnaic times tell us the people roasted the offering over a spit of pomegranate wood, basted it in fruit juices, and served it with a fruit-spice sauce made of finely ground fruit and nuts mixed with wine, an early version of today's delectable *charoset*.

Of course, all of this detail was not included to enhance Jewish prowess in the ethnic cuisine of the day. It was supplied to begin the arduous task of creating Jewish distinctiveness, molding a band of slaves into a God-chosen people by first honing their simple, everyday routines, such as preparing a meal. In that springtime so long ago, our people had endured more than four hundred years of bondage. Since the pagan peoples who lived alongside them often ate their sacrificial meat raw, Jews were deliberately commanded to cook their offerings until the meat was thoroughly done. But meat left too long in a fire tends to fall apart. This most important of dishes must be served whole, a harbinger of the unified nation the former slaves now sought to build with God's help.

In the HaChodesh reading, the community of Israel is instructed to choose the lamb to sacrifice on the tenth of the month, but to refrain from slaughtering it until the fourteenth of the month, a long time to be forced to listen to the bleating of a tethered, frightened animal. Why cause further commotion during this already stressful period? Here is the answer given in our traditional texts. Egyptians worshiped the lamb as one of their most important gods. Believing the astrological signs of the zodiac to be divine, they celebrated the thirty-day interval that includes Pesach by worshiping the constellation Aries, depicted as a ram. Just imagine the audacity of slaves who took their masters' "gods," tied them to bedposts or doorknobs for three days, and then roasted and ate them! God commands this downtrodden people to thumb their noses at their taskmasters by slaying Egyptian deities in public and celebrating the spectacle at an equally public feast. And God demands that this take place on the fourteenth of the month, in the middle of the Egyptian month Aries, nearing the height of the Egyptian ram's ascendancy.

## "This Month Shall Mark . . . the First Month of the Year for You" (Exod. 12:2)

HaChodesh, the name of this special Shabbat, translates as "the month," from the first words of *Adonai*'s message. It is read on the

Saturday closest to Rosh Chodesh, the beginning of the month of Nisan in the Jewish lunar-based calendar. While Jews announce every new month in synagogue on the Sabbath prior to it, only the month of Nisan begins by a special Torah reading specific to that celebration. Its biblical Hebrew name is Chodesh HaAviv, the month of spring. At some point during the Babylonian exile, more than six hundred years after the Exodus, the name Aviv changed to Nisan, the Akkadian word for "first fruits," which is linked to Nisannu, "to start," the first month in the Babylonian calendar. Later still, talmudic Sages called the first day of Nisan the "new year for kings and festivals," alluding to the custom of biblical kings to reckon all other months from Nisan.

According to a midrash, God decided to cede the whole business of calendar creating to the people during the same month in which God freed Israel. "During each of the 2,448 years before the Children of Israel went out of Egypt, the Holy One used to sit, thinking out the calendar . . . making changes . . . proclaiming the days on which the new years were to commence, and announcing the beginning of months. But when Israel went out of Egypt, then God turned these matters over to them." Slaves must do what they are told without taking much notice of the changing days or seasons. Assigning the task of noting distinct time changes lends a whole new awareness to routine. Assuming responsibility for the structure of time, the free people Israel became aware of each day's differences and opportunities.

Seminal Jewish events seem destined to happen during Nisan. Of course we all know how the Israelites were freed on *Pesach Mitzrayim*, the first, Egyptian Passover. We are also told that the wilderness Tabernacle was erected on Rosh Chodesh Nisan. Going backward in time, Abraham and Isaac made their fateful three-day journey to Mount Moriah during Nisan. A *piyut* links the lamb sacrificed by Abraham in lieu of Isaac to "the lamb offered up in time of trouble as a gift to the Lord. . . . The devotion of Abraham, who bound his son for a whole offering, was remembered in Egypt and stood by us." Because of Nisan's special status, fasting is not permitted (with the exception of the day preceding Pesach) during the entire month. The thirteenth-century commentator Nachmanides gives a spin to this most honored of Jewish months. Because, he says, we begin counting all months with this one, we immediately remember the great miracle that happened during Nisan whenever we say its name; in Hebrew, *neis* can be translated as "miracle." To bestow further respect on Nisan, other months discussed in the Torah are not named as proper nouns, but only as numbers ("e.g., in the seventh month").

## "Speak to the Whole Community of Israel" (Exod. 12:3)

Like the other special Sabbaths, Shabbat HaChodesh has an additional haftarah portion assigned to it. Like Shabbat Parah, which immediately precedes it, the section of haftarah read at HaChodesh comes from the Book of Ezekiel, the first prophetic book to emphasize messianic themes. Ezekiel was a member of a priestly family exiled to Babylonia around the time of the destruction of the First Temple, in the sixth century B.C.E. Though usually remembered for his magical visions, he describes a quite sensible scene in our Shabbat HaChodesh verses. A prince sacrifices in a newly restored, futuristic Temple. A priest applies blood to the Temple doorposts and the four corners of the Temple altar (Ezek. 45:19), an intentional replication of the similar scene from our Exodus verses.

> They shall take some of the blood and put it on the two doorposts and the lintel of the [Israelites'] houses. (Exod. 12:7)

While we are told that the prince "provides the passover sacrifice; during a festival of seven days unleavened bread shall be eaten" (Ezek. 45:21), specific data such as the name of the prince and his connections to the restored sanctuary remain deliberately undisclosed. The entire lives of slaves are predestined, unchanging. In contrast, those who live in freedom really cannot predict what the future holds. True, at times boundless choice can be disconcerting. But it is vastly preferable to endless toil for the sake of others.

We read another Exodus theme in the Book of Ezekiel. After describing the Temple offering of the prince, God issues an additional command.

> In this contribution, the entire population must join with the prince in Israel. (Ezek. 45:16)

This prophetic charge of unity underscores a responsibility shared by both the people and their ruler, an identical goal, whether portrayed in the Babylonian exile of Ezekiel's time or the earlier, Egyptian exile. The message is clear. Only if we work together can we accomplish our desire for cohesion, melding perfectly with the wish of *Adonai*. The contemporary theologian Irving Greenberg elaborates this point: "The primary hallmark of freedom is this capacity for solidarity. A slave thinks only of himself and his next meal." It is difficult for disconnected, passive individuals to achieve anything worthwhile and permanent. Joining together, with God's help, we can do almost anything, even successfully rebel against Pharaoh, the most powerful human on earth.

## "Each Shall Take a Lamb to His Family . . . to a Household" (Exod. 12:3)

Contrary to the title of the well-known best-seller, it really doesn't "take a village" to raise a child. We know that a single family's daily love and nurturing devotion to this most important undertaking (plus a whole lot of luck) can bring forth a splendid adult, a true community asset. When we examine the biographies of our first ancestors, we are heartened to see that Abraham and Sarah, Isaac and Rebekah, and Jacob, Leah, and Rachel were not saints. In so many ways they were just like us, living imperfect existences in an imperfect world.

But we also have to take into account a major difference between biblical and modern family structures—their respective size. The great medieval sage Rashi explains that a family exiting Egypt included children, multiple spouses, and offspring of a common grandfather, people we refer to as our uncles, aunts, and cousins. Loosely related individuals stayed together and lived interconnected lives. No single couple bore the huge responsibility of child rearing by themselves. As the many Genesis narratives relate, this arrangement was not foolproof. Yet it encouraged familial bonding and loyalty to the same God-centered, moral ideals.

In our time, folks try to re-create a similar sense of caring community by the phenomenon of the block party. People living close by gather together; each family brings a designated dish and swaps stories, eating and celebrating in a peculiarly American brand of secularized religion. Who would have guessed that this practice was born not in 1950s suburbia but several thousand years earlier in the middle of Hebrew slave quarters! The contemporary American block party tradition shares a biblical objective.

> Let him share [a lamb] with a neighbor who dwells nearby, in proportion to the number of persons: you shall contribute for the lamb according to what each household will eat. (Exod. 12:4)

The ideal Jewish nation is composed of families living near one another, worshiping the one God together.

## "And the Blood on the Houses . . . Shall Be a Sign"
### (Exod. 12:13)

The *pesach*, the paschal lamb, symbolizes the sacrificial meal Jews ate as they prepared to leave Egypt. An additional understanding points to God's compassion, protecting the Children of Israel from the awesome power of God's acts. Even as God "went forth among the Egyptians, [killing] every firstborn in the land of Egypt" (Exod. 11:4–5), God skipped those houses where Jews resided, "seeing" fresh animal blood smeared prominently on the outside. Thus in Rashi's eleventh-century France, the Old French meaning of *pesach* refers to a "springing offering," God's movement from house to house. Another definition also highlights the skipping act itself, mimicking the hesitant, jerky gait of a still immature, yearling lamb. The prophet Isaiah emphasizes the caring nature of God's Pesach deed: "Just like the birds that fly, even so will *Adonai Tz'vaot* shield Jerusalem, shielding and saving, protecting and rescuing" (Isa. 31:5). Taking leave of this majestic vision of God's redeeming Israel, we have a description of a dapper, lighthearted *Adonai* leaping lithely like a gazelle "from Egypt to the Red Sea and from the Red Sea to Sinai," so effortlessly does God redeem Israel.

Several commentators connect paschal blood and blood shed during the other primal rite distinguishing a Jew: the ceremony of *b'rit milah*, circumcision. Rashi notes that the number of days the Jews waited between choosing a lamb and slaughtering it, four, is the same length of time it takes a circumcision wound to heal. He implies that the Israelite slaves had not maintained this defining observance; God commanded them to circumcise themselves in Egypt before granting them their freedom. An anonymous sage put it even more bluntly: "The time has come for the foreskin to be cut; the time has come for the Egyptians to be cut down; the time has come for their idols to be cut out of the world."

## "Eat It Hurriedly" (Exod. 12:11)

On that first fourteenth of Nisan, the soon to be former slaves not only (1) sacrificed a *pesach* offering to God, (2) roasted and ate it, (3) dabbed their doorposts and lintels with its blood, and (4) recovered from *b'rit milah*. They also (5) quickly organized provisions for their open-ended journey. They were very, very busy and did not have the time to prepare for a feast, which usually involves chopping, sautéing, and baking for hours. Since slaves didn't maintain overflowing kitchen pantries, they hastily concocted a staple food using the few provisions they already had, what the Haggadah calls "poor person's bread," a "bread of affliction." The end result—matzah, a mixture of slightly baked grain and a little water shaped flat and cracker-like—had to suffice.

According to Chasidic Rabbi Tzadok HaKohen of Lublin, a hurried, harried departure for the glory of God is preferable to calm forethought: "When a person decides to serve God, he should do so in haste, like the paschal sacrifice eaten in haste. Once he has begun to serve God, he may act with moderation." Even the Talmud suggests a person "on the lamb" should reduce the quantity of food consumed: "One who is taking a journey should not eat more than the customary amount during years of famine," in order to remain free of what the Rabbis delicately refer to as "disorder of the bowels." Yet our Sages promised a much more sanguine entry into the world of eternity. "Rabbi Samuel bar Nachman said: Seeing that in this world, you had to eat the roasted flesh in haste, what is said of your deliverance in the world-to-come? 'For you shall not depart in haste, nor shall you leave in flight; for *Adonai* is marching before you, and the God of Israel is your rear guard.'" (Isa. 52:12)

## "It Is a Passover Offering to *Adonai*" (Exod. 12:11)

The editors of the Book of Exodus introduce matzah into their narration without explaining exactly what it is. The ingredients and consistency must have been so well-known to their contemporaries that no clarification was necessary. Redactors also rather inelegantly combine two ancient holidays: a shepherd's festival, whose main event entailed sacrificing a lamb in gratitude for the protection of the flock; and a farmer's sacred ritual, a seven-day celebration of the barley harvest. The Israelite flight from Egypt was tacked onto these two pagan holidays, creating the week of Pesach we commemorate today. However, we must never forget to whom we owe our salvation: "It is My will that in this month you shall be redeemed."

Any holiday celebrated over the course of several thousand years is bound to change, modified by shifting cultural and political influences. So it is amazing how many rituals associated with Pesach from ancient times still resonate with us today, a tribute to our continued faith and hefty doses of Jewish perseverance. Our tradition gives the term *Pesach Dorot*, "the Passover for the Generations," to all Pesachs following that first night in Egypt. While the Temple in Jerusalem stood, Pesach was celebrated in the very public manner already described. It became the most popular of the three annual Pilgrimage Festivals, the calendar's first mass convergence of Jewish humanity, all going up to the Temple.

But once the Temple was destroyed, outdoor festivals were forced to modify and privatize. Whereas Jews previously celebrated their historic deliverance by coming to Jerusalem and sacrificing to God, now a display of matzah by a far smaller group gathered around a festive table inherited the same emotional appeal. The three designations of biblical Jews—priests, Levites, and Israelites—transformed into the three symbolic matzot we use in seder rituals. The convenience food Hillel was credited with inventing, substituting *charoset* and *maror* for paschal lamb "sandwiched" between two pieces of matzah, was actually created several centuries post-Hillel. And several thousand years ago, Jews asked each other Three Questions, including one alluding to the roasted offering. These became our traditional Four Questions, which eliminated references to the sacrifice and added dipping and reclining queries.

### From Temple Sacrifice to Greco-Roman Banquet
*The large room is elegantly but sparsely furnished with a number of stone and wooden couches, strategically clustered into subgroupings to encourage conversation. Tastefully dressed guests enter the room, greet each other, and slowly sink into deep cushions. Soft music puts*

*them at their ease. Servers offer the first of several glasses of wine to each guest and pass light finger foods. The host rises to his feet—the symposium has begun.*

*In Roman times as in today's cosmopolitan world, assimilated Jews greatly outnumbered their observant counterparts. Not wanting to completely forego their cherished Pesach traditions, Jewish men and women transformed the secular formal banquet in order to celebrate Pesach in a way their non-Jewish friends and neighbors would find familiar. We're told that the typical meal consisted of three courses: hors d'oeuvres, entrée, and dessert, easily translating into a Pesach menu of karpas and charoset appetizers, two meat dishes, and the final sweet, or afikoman. However, food and ambiance were not the evening's prime considerations. As at any assemblage of thoughtful Roman citizens, conversation and instruction functioned as the raison d'être of early Jewish seder participants.*

## "A Festival to *Adonai* throughout the Ages" (Exod. 12:14)

Even as Pesach was being celebrated elegantly and secularly on select Roman verandas, other Jews experienced a more solemn, faith-oriented observance. The first Jewish philosopher, the Egyptian-born Philo, describes a quite different atmosphere: "The whole nation performs sacred rites, acting as priests; every home is invested with the outward semblance and dignity of the Temple."

God's place of residence thus extended from what had been the public Temple to the private domain. Already in the days of the first generations of Rabbis, eating, sanctifying, and remembering were utterly linked. "If three persons have eaten together and did not discuss Torah, it is as though they had eaten of the sacrifices to the dead. . . . But if three persons have eaten together and have spoken words of Torah, it is as though they had eaten from God's own table." By performing ancient rituals, believers view the Exodus as both a past and future event. In contemporary times, the relevance of naming the most famous ship to bring Holocaust survivors to Israel *Exodus '47* does not go unnoticed.

Thus Pesach fuses food, table, and observance into an eternal coming of spring. Pesach, like Shabbat, gives us a brief glimpse into that time of never-ending prosperity and happiness. "It can be compared to a king who betrothed a woman and at the time, promised her just a few presents, swearing to give her many more gifts when they actually wed. This world is like a betrothal. The actual marriage ceremony between God and Israel will take place in messianic days." A talmudic statement places this marriage in our special *chodesh*. "Rabbi Joshua says: In Nisan they were redeemed and in Nisan they will be redeemed in the time to come."

## From Our Tradition

"Arise, my beloved,
My fair one, come away.
For now the winter is past,
The rains are over and gone.
Blossoms appear on the earth;
The time of singing is here,
And the song of the turtledove
Is heard in our land."
(Song of Songs 2:10–12)

When they arrived at the mountains which surround Jerusalem, the multitude was so great that grass was not seen any longer, as everything turned to white by reason of the white color of the wool. . . . And the Jews made an ordinance, that when going [out to buy or sacrifice the paschal lamb], no one should say to his neighbor, "Step aside," or "Let me pass," even if the one behind was King Solomon or David. [The priest said this was so ordered] to show that there is no rank before the eyes of God . . . more especially at the service itself; at that time all were equal in receiving God's goodness. (Solomon ibn Verga)

*This month shall be to you.* A slave has no time he can call his own. He is totally subservient to his master, who decides how his time shall be used and controls his days and months. Therefore freedom would grant Hebrew slaves mastery over their days and months. They themselves would decide how to use their time. (Sforno)

The Holy One wrapped Himself in a prayer shawl with woolen fringes and placed Moses on one side and Aaron on the other. Then God summoned Michael and Gabriel who, as if they were messengers dispatched by an [earthly] court, were to report when they witnessed the arrival of the new moon. . . . In such a manner shall My children on earth reckon the calendar throughout the year: in the presence of an elder, of witnesses, and wearing a prayer shawl with woolen fringes. (*P'sikta D'Rav Kahana* 5:15)

# 7

## Shabbat HaGadol: Hearing One Another to Listen for God's Voice

### (Mal. 3:4–24)

With this Sabbath immediately preceding Pesach, our "passage" approaches its conclusion. Preparations for the holiday engulf us. We need some sane study time to center ourselves, to act as a shield of reflection to ground and give focus to our frenetic activity. For while the Talmud suggests, "One should raise questions and give explanations on the laws of Pesach from thirty days before the festival," we admit to postponing our intellectual duties, just as, year after year, we procrastinate doing the ever-increasing number of Pesach tasks that by now should be routine. We seem to forget (or deny) all of the cleaning and cooking, the special ordering and buying that we know need to be done every year, leaving few leftover moments to step back and contemplate more profound meanings.

But when we are able to take time for thought, it is disconcerting to discover no mention of Shabbat HaGadol, "the Great Sabbath," perhaps the one special Sabbath many have heard of, in either the Mishnah or the Talmud. The Mishnah, compiled around 200 C.E., and predated by a much older oral tradition, only discusses four, not five "special *parashiyot*": "If the first day of the month Adar falls on the Sabbath, they read the Pentateuch portion 'Shekels.' On the second [special Sabbath] they read the section 'Remember what Amalek did.' On the third they read 'The red heifer.' On the fourth, they read 'This month shall be for you. . . .'" Because talmudic Sages are silent as well about the existence of Shabbat HaGadol, twentieth-century commentator Solomon Zeitlin assumes its observance began only at a later, post-talmudic time. The mystery deepens when *Machzor Vitry,* an early prayer book dating from the twelfth century, notes: "The people call the Sabbath before Pesach the Great Sabbath, but they do not know why, since it is not greater than other Sabbaths." Other scholars maintain that until well into the Middle Ages, Jews kept no "Great Sabbath" at all.

Through the centuries, commentators and academics have offered various explanations. The most literal one refers to the amount of time people spend in synagogue on this day, listening to the rabbi expound upon the many laws pertaining to Pesach, making the day seem especially "long," *gadol.* Another view puts forth the notion that "HaGadol" might merely be a mistranslation of "Haggadah," since a long-standing custom in traditional synagogues requires reading large sections of the Pesach Haggadah on this Sabbath. Yet another determination has Jews countering the Christian practice of reading from the New Testament, from the Book of John (calling the day after the crucifixion of Jesus "a Sabbath of very great solemnity" [19:31]) on Palm Sunday, the Sunday before Easter. This reasoning assumes a balancing Jewish need to create a formal beginning to the week before Pesach, which usually occurs at about the same time as Easter. Thus, in this understanding, Jewish sages took their cue from the surrounding Christian community and created a seminal Sabbath we may claim as a "great day" of our very own, a Shabbat HaGadol.

A more frequently championed assumption goes back to biblical roots by addressing the "great miracle" that took place right before the Exodus from Egypt, when each family of Israelite slaves sacrificed a lamb to God. Though Egyptians considered lambs to be important deities, they were helpless to stop what in their eyes was deicide on a grand scale. Since the Israelites were able to offer paschal sacrifices without Egyptian interference, commentators connect the miracle of this event with the Exodus, the wondrous physical redemption that took place on the very next day, the fifteen of Nisan.

# "I Will Send the Prophet Elijah to You before . . . the Great and Awesome Day" (Mal. 3:23)

The most obvious explanation for the name Shabbat HaGadol comes from the extra haftarah section, read as part of synagogue worship only on this day. Unlike all of the other special Sabbaths we have discussed, the readings associated with Shabbat HaGadol do not include an additional Torah portion. Instead, our focus concentrates on twenty quite powerful verses from the Book of Malachi. Much of the haftarah portion recounts a vision for the future, when the prophet Elijah will appear to announce the coming of the Messiah.

Our Sages introduced Elijah at this time to make at least three important points. First, this selection cements and expands his unique role in the ultimate redemption of the Jewish people. We will say much more about this ninth-century B.C.E visionary later on when we discuss the cup of wine dedicated to Elijah that appears on the seder table. Here, we want to note how his role has developed in Jewish thought. In the Second Book of Kings we are told that Elijah did not die in the usual fashion. Rather, "a fiery chariot with fiery horses suddenly appeared and separated . . . and Elijah went up to heaven in a whirlwind" (II Kings 2:11). As the centuries passed following the canonization of the Bible, Elijah became the symbol of healing and support, reconciliation and peace. His special status as the harbinger of the Messiah was confirmed by this prominent mention in the Book of Malachi.

Second, by evoking Elijah as we celebrate becoming a free people, we connect our collective, physical redemption with our individual, spiritual one. Each year on Pesach we have another opportunity to begin our personal journey anew. And as a group, we annually celebrate our beginnings as a free people and all that nation-building entails. Both goals, to grow as individuals and to achieve unity as one people, are enhanced as we mark our redemption from Egypt. During our annual reliving of the initial Pesach, we focus on not only our past traditions and our present endeavors. We also look ahead to the time when Elijah heralds the ultimate time of peace and understanding. So each year we look for the arrival of Elijah at our seders, hoping that we have made a little progress in our efforts to make our world a better place, making us whole both as individuals and as a people.

Finally, invoking Elijah enables us to anticipate and specify our ultimate mission. On Shabbat HaChodesh we took note of the special month of Nisan: "This month shall mark for you the beginning of the months; it shall be the first of *months* . . ." (Exod. 12:2). Now, on Shabbat HaGadol, God promises to send Elijah on that "great and awesome *day*" (Mal. 3:23). Just as we designate a month during which we prepare, commemorate, and discuss the miracles of the Exodus, so we further understand how God plans for the exact day of our final judgment by sending Elijah, God's designated emissary.

## "Behold, I Am Sending *My Messenger* to Clear the Way before Me" (Mal. 3:1)

Though the above verse appears right before Shabbat HaGadol's haftarah portion, we cannot make sense of what we are hearing without first referring to these words. And, in typically Jewish fashion, they simultaneously clarify and confuse. On the one hand, we learn that, indeed, we will have some inkling when God's "great and awesome day" will occur, since we've been put on notice of a prior sighting of a celestial herald, who we assume will be Elijah. On the other hand, we really don't know the exact identity of this "messenger" spoken of in Mal. 3:1. Some claim him to be the biblical scribe Ezra; others say he is Mordecai, cousin of Esther, heroine of the Purim story. Yet if either man authored this work, why wasn't his name used as the title of this final prophetic book, rather than what most modern interpreters agree is an anonymous term, universally translated from the Hebrew as "My messenger"?

While we don't know the specific identity of the author of Malachi, we do have a fair idea of when he lived and the financial, ethical, and moral status of those Jews he addressed. Word clues from the book itself and later talmudic writings indicate the prophet described conditions in Jerusalem soon after the Temple was rebuilt, dating the work between 500 and 450 B.C.E. At this historical period, Judea was a rather backwater province of the Persian empire, ruled by a political appointee who served himself and the distant Persian potentate, with the people's interests ranking a distant third. The times were tough. The prosperity spoken of so glowingly as sure to follow the rebuilding of the Temple by Haggai and Zechariah, whose books immediately precede Malachi, never materialized.

One modern commentator offers a fitting subtitle to the biblical book: "A Message for an Age of Discouragement." The people's crops were destroyed by locusts; the soil was so infertile that "vines in the field had no grapes growing from them" (Mal. 3:11). The Jews who returned from Babylonia with such high expectations experienced a harsh dose of reality. The land of their fathers was not flowing with milk and honey but had become a wilderness. Malachi offers what biblical editors considered an appropriate explanation for these troubles: the people brought the terrible conditions on themselves by their immoral conduct and blasphemous attitude. They are

> practicing sorcery, committing adultery, swearing falsely . . . and subverting [the cause of] the widow, orphan and stranger. . . . (Mal. 3:5)

> [They also] have said: "It is useless to fear God. What have we gained by observing God's service or walking mournfully before *Adonai Tz'vaot*?" (Mal. 3:14)

According to Malachi, the Israelites not only did bad things, committing foul acts toward the most defenseless in their midst. They also had the colossal cheekiness to blame God for their abysmal situation, saying that *Adonai* caused their insolence by rewarding the wicked and punishing the obedient.

## "Yet You Say: 'In What Way Do We Need to Return . . . How Have We Cheated God?'" (Mal. 3:7, 8)

These Jews are not respectfully challenging the Eternal. Even our patriarch Abraham humbly begged God's pardon when he dared to speak up, fighting for a few righteous souls in the wicked cities of Sodom and Gomorrah. Abraham prefaced his requests by respectfully saying: "Here I venture to speak to my Lord, I who am but dust and ashes . . ." and "Let my Lord not be angry if I speak but this last time" (Gen. 18:27, 32). Far from using suitably obsequious language, the people of Israel as described by Malachi engaged in defiant verbal jousting with the Divine.

And yet, how modern this disputational speech sounds to us! While we may not have heard Malachi's specific words, the tone and message of the squabbling he recorded suggest contemporary sparring we've heard all too frequently. Recall overheated conversations in the local supermarket between crabby kids and their pushed-to-the-brink mothers, or the constant combat pitting parents against perpetually sullen teenagers playing out nightly in our living rooms.

When we read these confrontations in Malachi between God and the people of Israel, it almost seems as if we are eavesdropping, silently observing an early therapy session. Though allegedly "hearing" each other, very little actual listening occurs, at least by our ancestors. But soon the scene shifts from the aggrieved to the faithful. After listening to the "hard words against Me" (Mal. 3:13), God then gives attention to the speech of the righteous, those "who revere *Adonai* and esteem God's name" (Mal. 3:16). God promises to inscribe this second, morally upright group in "a scroll of remembrance" (Mal. 3:16). This document is similar to the Annals of the Kings of Media and Persia described in the Book of Esther (6:1, 10:2), and gives a further justification to a Persian setting for Malachi, the Shabbat HaGadol haftarah reading.

The unidentified person who writes in the name of Malachi is the very last to have a biblical book dedicated to his pronouncements. As the Talmud teaches, "Haggai, Zechariah, and Malachi are the last prophets. When they died, the spirit of prophecy departed from Israel." To take their place, conscientious administrators like Nehemiah and efficient scribes like Ezra handled the problems of the people, assiduously recording life-cycle events, carefully monitoring, as did Malachi, who married whom, in order to prevent Jewish men from marrying non-Jewish women.

But the issue of intermarriage, important as it is, doesn't concern us as we prepare for Pesach. What does concern us is the series of dialogues that marked the final days before the Exodus and how these words affect us today as we relive the first Pesach, several millennia later.

## "But First I Will Step Forward . . . I Will Act as a Relentless Accuser" (Mal. 3:5)

The verbal dueling discussed in the text thus far points to a distinctive feature of Malachi. We read several sets of questions and answers, forming a running dialogue between God and the Children of Israel. We listen to a debate with cosmic consequences as we witness the spectacle of "The Divine said; Israel said."

The brief bits of conversation we hear in Malachi echo the extended verbal confrontations between the King of Egypt, enshrined on his throne and worshiped as a god, and the scruffy shepherds Moses and Aaron. Pharaoh took the words of these two Jewish slaves about as seriously as did the disdainful Jews who bait God in the Book of Malachi. In the Exodus story, Aaron and Moses returned to Pharaoh after each plague occurred and spoke the same direct demand from God: "Let My people go!" Though he might have heard the words, Pharaoh certainly did not comprehend their meaning. So the confrontational battles continued, bringing successively harsher punishments to the people of Egypt.

In his discussion of the Ten Plagues, "R. Levi bar Zechariah taught: God first shut off the Egyptian water conduits. Then God brought up loud voices to confuse them . . . the croaking of frogs, which, according to Rabbi Yose bar Chanina, was harder for Egyptians to bear than their disgust at the sight of them." We understand how these unbearably loud, unceasing sounds might drive a whole nation to distraction. Yet Pharaoh repeatedly turned a deaf ear to the pleas of Moses and Aaron.

Pharaoh did not hear God's words. He could not comprehend the horrific consequences of his entrenchment. Louis Ginzberg, collector of Jewish midrash, offers a scenario that depicts the Egyptian monarch merely going through the motions of doing God's bidding: "Moses said to Pharaoh, 'Raise your voice and say, Children of Israel, you are your own masters. Prepare for your journey.' . . . Moses made him say these words three times, and God caused Pharaoh's voice to be heard throughout Egypt. . . ."

Finally Pharaoh heard the horrible sound of death in his own household, the killing of his eldest son, his firstborn. The early medieval poet Yannai describes the tormented timbre: "There were corpses as if they had been strangled in every house in Noph (Egypt); everywhere the groans of the dying [could be heard]. . . . Wailing took hold of them; stunned, they rose and ran out of their homes in the night."

# "I Will Be as Tender toward Them as a Parent Is Tender toward a Child" (Mal. 3:17)

For thousands of years we have tried to picture what happened during that dreadful night, the "night of watching" on the fourteenth of Nisan, as Jews huddled together, hoping the lamb's blood on their homes would spare them the awful fate of the Egyptians. Several versions of the following legend have come down to us, which describe not the *how*, but an underlying response to the *why* of the particular punishment defining the tenth plague. Sages call attention to a usually overlooked agenda: the fundamental breakdown of the Egyptian family. "When Jews took the firstborn lambs, Egyptians asked, 'What is the purpose of this?' The Jews replied, 'These animals are being prepared as *pesach* offerings to God, who will then slaughter all firstborn of Egypt.' Upon hearing this, the firstborn went to their fathers and beseeched them to petition Pharaoh to send Israel from the land. 'Since all that Moses has predicted concerning the Egyptians befell us, we must get these Hebrews out of our midst.' But their fathers would not comply. They replied, 'Each of us has ten sons. Let one of them die, just so Hebrews are not permitted to get out.' The firstborn then went and slew sixty myriad of their fathers."

Of course, we all rush to say, no Jew would ever act like that. No Jewish parent would ever treat his or her child like that. Surely, we resolutely maintain, this could never happen to the Jews. Just remember how carefully the Rabbis recount the legend of the four children in the Pesach Haggadah. Even the wicked child, the child who denies his own birthright by sneering, "What does all this mean to you?" is answered graciously, if somewhat abruptly. The Haggadah instructs us to make him feel merely uncomfortable and respond, "It is what God did for me, not for you."

And yet we've all heard of cases in which members of Jewish families turned against each other, harboring bitter resentments that lasted for decades, sometimes not having the chance to reconcile before the feuders die. We snicker when we read accounts of very public lawsuits in which children sue parents and parents sue children if one of them perceives family fortunes being divided inequitably or otherwise "misused." These spectacles have occurred, apparently, ever since courts of law were established. "A woman was about to bring charges against her son because he kicked her when he was in her womb. The judge asked the mother if her child, already grown to manhood, had done anything against her since that time. She replied that he had not. Whereupon the judge proceeded to rule that there was no offense in what the child did." A Yiddish proverb bittersweetly notes another classic generational conflict: "Once parents used to teach their children to talk. Today children teach their parents to keep quiet."

## "[Elijah] Shall Reconcile Parents with Children and Children with Parents" (Mal. 3:24)

During at least one or two nights each year, parents and children make special efforts to bridge the generation gap peacefully. At Pesach, the evening is designed to be a loving, family affair. The whole idea behind the several question-and-answer exchanges in the Haggadah is to keep the children from getting bored, to sustain children's curiosity and parents' eagerness to respond. As Jonathan Sacks, chief rabbi of Great Britain, explains, a primal purpose of Pesach is to hand down the story of our journey to the next generation. People really do want to converse with each other, especially if they are related (though they might be reluctant to admit it). The elder generation proudly expounds its own story; the younger generation eagerly anticipates being considered mature enough to find their role in that particular story while spinning a particular twist on the tale to make it theirs.

One need not be a biological parent to act as a major presence in the life of a child. The Talmud commends a person who teaches Torah to his friend's offspring, regarding the child as being born to him. Closer to our own time, American school boards once would hire only unmarried women as teachers. For many women only a few generations ago, being married meant almost constant pregnancies. It may have been thought impossible for women to impart instruction successfully both inside and outside the home at the same time. Of course, our tradition does not address the modern quandary of trying to balance motherhood and career. However, our Sages heaped praise on those who contributed financially to the next generation's welfare, especially if they were not religiously obligated to do so. "Rabbi Tanchuma discussed an unmarried man who, of his own accord, without being required (because he lived in a rural place without schools) or specifically commanded, paid the fee in another location for teachers of Scripture and Mishnah. Because he made it possible for children to study . . . God deemed this act equivalent to the act of creation."

A recurrence of God's creation blesses us every spring. For those of us who barely survive cold, stormy winters, the promise of warm, sunny days when trees bud and flowers blossom reinvigorates our bodies and renews our spirits. Depending on when Pesach falls in our secular calendar, crocuses have already bloomed and maybe even a tulip or two has joined them. As it happens, one of several names our tradition calls Pesach is *Chag HaAviv*, "the Holiday of Spring." A biblical connotation adds a second derivative from nature. Referring to the fresh young ears of barley sprouting across the fertile land of Israel, we learn that the word *aviv* also recalled "the month of ear-forming, or of growing green." It's not much of a stretch to connect the ear-forming we observe whenever we stop to admire a field of grain waving in the sun to the ear-forming development of listening skills in our growing children. What better time to take note of their progress than on Pesach, when their ears perk up in anticipation of proudly reciting the Four Questions or running through the house in search of the *afikoman*? What better time to reconnect with our cousins, nieces, and nephews as we open the door to welcome Elijah, who brings us all together once again?

## "On the Day I Am Preparing, They Shall Be My Treasured Possession" (Mal. 3:17)

Many of us admit to picturing God occasionally as a kindly grandparent, smiling benevolently from the heavens. It is a comforting and satisfying image. A basic psychological motivation impels our need to be cared for, to feel part of a group that values each individual contribution and cherishes the loving protection of a Holy One who guides us through life's capricious paths.

We can think of few things more dismal than spending Pesach alone. Surely, someone will always beckon us genuinely, with the compassion of a loving parent, showing concern by caring for us unreservedly. On this day, of all days, a Jewish soul should not feel abandoned. And it never is. Whenever we perform mitzvot, study Jewish books, or observe our ancient rituals through our time-honored liturgy, we indeed become the focus of God's unconditional love. As Malachi proclaimed:

> *Adonai* has heard and noted . . . those who revere *Adonai* and esteem God's name (3:16).

As parents tenderly embrace their child as a *s'gulah*, a most revered gift, so *Adonai* is ever attentive to each one of us. "One who looks at his father is like one who sees God, because he can look beyond his father to creation. And one who looks at his children sees God, because he can look beyond his children through the generations to the Messiah."

ᔆᔆ Thus we come to the end of our study of "this great and awesome day," Shabbat HaGadol. We have finally arrived at the "great day" of Pesach, our destination. Our passage *to* Pesach has concluded as the day itself fades, as we gather around the festive table, laden with Pesach adornments . . . as we begin once more. . . .

## From Our Tradition

When [Israel] the bride received news of her coming exaltation, she arrayed herself with her perfumes . . . appeared in the full glory of her beauty. When [Egypt] the oppressor saw her, she was astounded—is not this a despised and insignificant people? . . . Pharaoh roared and hardened his heart, afflicting the bride with hard servitude, hoping she would grow ugly. . . . At last Pharaoh released the oppressed. . . . The All-Perfect will again dwell with me, whispered the bride in her delightful voice. (Benjamin ben Zerach)

Pharaoh rose in the night of smiting. . . . He didn't know where Moses lived and [had problems finding the right house]. Hebrew lads he asked . . . played practical jokes on him, misdirecting him. . . . Meanwhile Moses, Aaron, and all Israel were at the paschal meal, drinking wine

. . . leaning to one side, singing *Hallel*, songs in praise of God that they were the first to recite. (Louis Ginzberg)

Rabbi Menachem, citing Rabbi Mana, said: No creature in the world is able to distinguish between the seed of the firstborn and seed that is not of a first birth, only the Holy One. As for me, said Moses, it was too difficult. (*P'sikta Rabbati* 17:1)

Jews who long have drifted from the faith of their fathers . . . are stirred in their inmost parts when the old, familiar Passover sounds chance to fall on their ears. (Heinrich Heine)

# PART III

## Pesach as Passage:
## Cups of Wine, Biblical Promises

> A man is commanded to make his children and his wife happy on the holiday. With what does he make them happy? With wine, as it is written, "and wine gladdens the human heart" (Ps. 104:15).
>
> *(Tosefta, P'sachim* 10:4)

Its delicate bouquet and its wonderfully smooth taste make wine the perfect brew to "gladden the human heart." On Pesach, as on other holy Jewish occasions, "ordinary" wine is made sacred by saying the *Kiddush* blessing over it, thanking God for bringing us fruit from this particular vine. Custom has it that since we are no longer slaves, forced to do the bidding of others, we should not pour our own wine at seder. We allow ourselves the small luxury of being served by a person sitting near us, and then we serve a neighbor in return. We accept this modest perk of freedom that speaks volumes of nuanced cordiality and graciously accept assistance as a token of mutual respect.

The many seder civilities we practice extend to all Jews. In the Mishnah we are instructed that drinking four cups of wine to commemorate the Exodus from Egypt is not an option reserved for the rich and powerful. "Even the poorest in Israel must not be given less than four cups of wine, even if it is from a [pauper's] dish." Wine is more than just a good drink. At Pesach it becomes a key participant in holiday rituals, infusing the redemptive narrative with moments of both gravity and glory. But we are also cautioned that drinking wine with a solemn demeanor does not satisfy the obligation either. To fulfill the requirement completely, we must enjoy the drinking and savor the tastes of freedom to its fullest. Of course, this includes spacing our wine consumption as the Haggadah mandates, to avoid the drowsiness and light-headedness that might come from enjoying too much of a good thing too quickly!

Various answers have been given to the question of why four was chosen as the obligatory number of wine cups to be drunk at the seder meal. Some point to the four fringes at the corners of the *tallit* and the four sections of Torah comprising the prayers found in *t'fillin*. Others cite the four types of vegetation composing the *lulav,* which is used in the celebration of Sukkot, or the four world empires that conquered the Jewish people and our land—Egypt, Babylonia, Persia, and Greece— only to be destroyed in turn. Or, the four wine cups could correspond to the four Hebrew letters of the name of God, *yod-hei-vav-hei.* More particularly to Pesach, the historian Chaim Raphael dedicates each cup to a Pesach toast of health and hope, offering wishes "To life! To freedom! To peace! To Jerusalem!" as the seder progresses. The social activist Leonard Fein relates the four cups of wine to acts of memory and reverence, continuing the journey of our ancestors, but never completing it: "We remember not out of curiosity or nostalgia, but because it is our turn to add to the story."

I am partial to yet another explanation, that the four cups of wine correspond to the four biblical promises of redemption God gives to the Hebrew slaves to strengthen their resolve, even as Pharaoh makes their tasks more onerous. In the Book of Exodus, God pledges to Israel to achieve these four deeds:

> *v'hotzeiti*—"I will bring you out from under the burden of the Egyptians";

> *v'hitzalti*—"I will deliver you from their bondage";

> *v'gaalti*—"I will redeem you with an outstretched arm and with great judgments";

> *v'lakachti*—"I will take you to Me as a people." (Exod. 6:6–7)

Archeologists working in the Mideast have unearthed evidence that these four verbs of action resemble ancient covenant language between a ruler and his vassals. Even as kings of yore promised basic security to those who pledged their loyalty, so God promised to protect Israel in return for their vows of love and trust. On Pesach we review this sacred bond and seal each promise with a glass of wine.

After exploring the history of the Haggadah, our addition to the Pesach story transforms the four cups of wine into basic symbols of the seder, viewing the promises made by God to Israel in an ascending order. In the chapters that follow, the "First Cup—*V'hotzeiti*" describes matzah and discusses the various dimensions of the holiday's foremost food in the context of God's first gift, the physical act of freeing our people as a measure of justice. How does a simple cracker and the few words "I will bring" combine to represent the most important journey ever undertaken in the history of the Jewish people? The "Second Cup—*V'hitzalti*" explores the several items on the seder plate and points to God's moral, compassionate nature. Actually "delivering" an entire nation from slavery to freedom involves a complex series of steps. Each item can be named, from *charoset,* the sweet nut and apple mixture, to *z'roa,* the shank bone, and personally involves us in our timeless story.

As God "brings" and "delivers" us, the distance between us contracts. Only God's direct involvement, in the form of both the plagues God inflicts on the Egyptians and the miracles God performs for Israel, sets the people free. These examples of divine intervention bring families together as well. They grow closer as they taste the cup of "redemption," the "Third Cup—*V'gaalti,*" with special notice of our most precious miracle, our children. The "Fourth Cup—*V'lakachti*" of our passage expresses our most intimate emotion, love. We recite the *Hallel,* psalms of praise to God, and sing our final songs of devotion to God's eternal oneness and might, to the One who "took" us into our own land.

Two additional "cups" conclude our "wine passage." Though the fifth cup is indeed filled with wine, we do not drink from it. The sixth cup is a quite recent addition to the seder and contains not wine, but water, the most elemental liquid of all.

In the center of the table sits a cup to honor the prophet Elijah, the harbinger of world peace and understanding. An ancient folktale tells us that Elijah will grace our seder to announce the coming of the Messiah, when all doubts will disappear and disputes resolve. We will know the prophet has entered our home because the children will notice less wine in Elijah's cup than before they opened the door to welcome him, since he is the sole drinker from the cup named in his honor. But words of a decidedly different mood accompany this family activity. For hundreds of years, the traditional Haggadah has included several biblical verses that foresee wreaking havoc and vengeance on the enemies of Israel as a prelude to the prophet's arrival. A troubling transformation from messianic mercy to unblinking justice, at least in contemporary eyes, serves as the "Fifth Cup" of wine—*V'heiveiti.*

Our "Sixth Cup" presents no such ambiguities. We fill a goblet with water to suggest the legendary wells of the prophet Miriam, remembering her ability to find life-sustaining sources of water wherever Israel wandered in the wilderness after leaving Egypt. We will focus our final Pesach passage on feminine themes of affirmation, as Jewish women come out of the kitchen to celebrate freedoms particular to their own dreams and identities.

So, if a little wine is spilled, causing the seder tablecloth to stain or a page or two of a Haggadah to blur, consider these a part of the festivities. The process of passing from slavery to freedom finds added meanings with every sip of wine we drink, with each new association we bring to familiar Pesach observances. *L'chayim*!

# 8

## History of the Haggadah: Telling the Pesach Story through the Ages

And you are to tell your child on that day, "It is because of what *Adonai* did for me, when I went out of Egypt." (Exod. 13:8)

I never learned how my father came upon *New Haggadah,* Mordecai Kaplan's Reconstructionist offering that was as much a Pesach staple in our home as my mother's chicken soup. Perhaps it was recommended to him by Jacob Weinstein, prominent rabbi of K.A.M., the South Side Chicago congregation my parents joined soon after coming to America. The themes of *New Haggadah,* justice for all of God's creatures and giving special attention to the poor and the neglected, jibed with the thinking of Rabbi Weinstein, an exemplar of Reform Jewish ideals and activist deeds. He defined mid-twentieth-century Judaism for my parents, European refugees trying to figure out what remained of their faith in God and humanity after the Holocaust. *New Haggadah*'s light blue cover and distinctive bold black lettering always signaled an extended night of family visits and exotic foods. Yet, seeing my father pull out this particular book meant something even more precious to me. I loved what I now realize was the intellectual preparation we shared, just the two of us sitting together a few days before Pesach began with the Haggadah opened between us, deciding which readings best related the Exodus story to current world conditions and family happenings.

The Haggadah, "the telling" of our most important story, is not about the arrival, but about the journey of the Jewish people. It chronicles the single event within the Jewish calendar that remains with us throughout the year, involving each individual's memories and experiences. The Haggadah, a manual for home education and observance of Pesach, provides precise sets of written instructions that direct us through the evening. Built into its fixed agenda is a very clear understanding that some deviation from it is not only permitted, but expected. The seder leader assumes a role similar to that of a game show host, adding family jokes and events as recent as last night's news to enliven the meal and involve all participants. While some consider the Haggadah to function almost as a prayer book for a specific home-based holiday, it is better understood as a study guide for a learning experience geared to a specific time and place. This learning experience must be fresh and inviting to make real the presumption that each of us was a slave in Egypt. So Haggadot have come to serve as social and political barometers registering the mood of particular Jewish communities in defined historical periods. Reviewing the development of the Haggadah over the centuries reflects the many historical, political, and economic shifts Jews themselves have survived.

This explains why several Haggadah readings were originally written in Aramaic, not in Hebrew. Aramaic was the everyday language spoken by Jews at the time the Haggadah was being compiled. Aramaic was the first lingua franca of the long Jewish dispersion, from the time of the Babylonian exile in the sixth century B.C.E., well past the destruction of the Second Temple in 70 C.E. Today Aramaic is still used in prayers as significant as the *Kaddish* and *Kol Nidrei* and as the passage-defining words from the marriage *ketubah*. In his *Passover Haggadah,* Elie Wiesel relates a story from Kabbalah explaining why it was important for the text to be widely understood. God likes to hear Jews recount the story of the Exodus. So, much of the Haggadah is written in Aramaic, which the angels do not understand, and speaks directly to God without intermediaries.

The most ancient part of the Haggadah may well be the passage in Aramaic calling matzah "the bread of affliction," *ha lachma anya.* It is thought that the oldest Haggadah passages in Hebrew formed part of the ceremonial prayers when the Temple still stood and included several of the Psalms composing the *Hallel* and at least three of the Four Questions.

While most authorities agree that the basic elements of the Haggadah were fixed in place by the end of the second century C.E., one scholar has pushed for a significantly earlier date. Louis Finkelstein, head of the Jewish Theological Seminary in the middle decades of the twentieth century, believed large chunks of the Haggadah were written before the Maccabean revolt, as early as the third century B.C.E. He finds hints in the text of a political struggle between the Egyptian Ptolemys and the Syrian Seleucids for control of Judea, as Palestine was called at the time. Much of the Jewish establishment of the day supported the Egyptian leaders. Thus Egypt was downplayed as the enemy of the Jews. "Once we were slaves to Pharaoh in Egypt, and *Adonai* our God brought us forth *from there*" (italics added). According to Finkelstein, the Haggadah chooses its words carefully, referring to Egypt as an indefinite place "from there" so as not to offend the Egyptian rulers who were friendly with prominent Jewish families. The lengthy elaboration on Deut. 26:5–8, which forms the bulk of the *Magid,* or narrative section of the Haggadah, is another case in point, says Finkelstein. The verse beginning "My father was a fugitive Aramean" (Deut. 26:5) can also be interpreted, "Look what Laban the Syrian tried to do to our father." Finkelstein believes that this is a direct reference to the Syrian king of the third century B.C.E. who was trying to wrest power from the Egyptians. The Jews put their allegiance with the contemporary Egyptian rulers and so described the Syrians as more cruel than Pharaoh at the time of the Exodus.

Finkelstein's quirky interpretation notwithstanding, written proof of the Haggadah's slightly later beginnings is documented in the Mishnah, the legal code edited in Palestine around 200 C.E. The tractate called *P'sachim* devotes its tenth and last chapter to a detailed rundown of the events of the fourteenth of Nisan, night of the first seder. In the Mishnah we have instructions explaining when we drink the four cups of wine, what foods we dip and when, questions a child asks (still three, not yet four), and Rabban Gamliel's edict requiring the explicit explanation of *pesach*, matzah, and *maror* as being mandatory to the proper observance of the holiday. The ten Rabbis specifically named in the Haggadah were all involved in the writing of the Mishnah. The word *haggadah* is not used until the Talmud, in *P'sachim* 115b, compiled several centuries after the Mishnah, and recalls the biblical pronouncement from the Book of Exodus that began this chapter, requiring parents to tell their children how God redeemed Israel from Egypt.

Several centuries after the Talmud was completed, in the eighth and ninth centuries C.E., the heads of the Jewish community in Babylonia, called *gaonim,* compiled the first actual Haggadah, quite similar to what we use today. About 850 C.E., Amram Gaon included a Haggadah as a section of the prayer book he edited. The earliest complete Haggadah text that still exists today comes from the tenth-century prayer book of Saadyah Gaon, who was both in charge of the Babylonian academy at Sura and the most important Jewish scholar of his day. In eleventh-century France, students of the great commentator Rashi included a Haggadah in their prayer book, *Machzor Vitry.* More than one hundred years later, the famed commentator Maimonides dedicated one of his books in the comprehensive *Mishneh Torah* to the Haggadah, *Hilchot Chameitz Umatzah,* "Instruction Concerning *Chameitz* and Matzah." In it Maimonides states that reading the Haggadah is a positive commandment incumbent on all Jews.

By the thirteenth century in Spain and the fourteenth century in France and Germany, the first Haggadot manuscripts to stand separately from either prayer book or study guide were being created. Also about this time, the biblical verses beginning *Sh'foch chamat'cha,* "Pour out Your wrath," were added to the Haggadah, which also introduced the prophet Elijah to the seder. This was the period of the Crusades, when Christian soldiers killed thousands of Jews in Rhineland communities while on their way to do battle in Jerusalem against the Islamic rulers of the Holy Land. The added biblical verses from Psalms and the Book of Lamentations cry out against these massacres and demand divine retribution against the marauders. In the late thirteenth century, Samuel ben Salomon of Falaise developed the fifteen "seder steps" (*kadeish, ur'chatz* . . .) we chant as the seder begins, to give those without the text of the Haggadah in front of them the ability to remember the order and contents of the many seder observances. With the inclusion of *piyutim,* medieval liturgical poetry forming the last songs of the seder, and the folkloric nursery songs "Echad Mi Yodei-a?" (Who Knows One?) and "Chad Gadya" (An Only Kid) in the fifteenth century, the Haggadah as we know it today was complete.

For almost two hundred years prior to the invention of movable type, unique illuminated Haggadot were created, one laborious copy at a time. These beautifully illustrated works of art were frequently fashioned by non-Jews in Germany, France, Spain, and Italy. Several factors contributed to their development. The growth of towns, as opposed to isolated agricultural communities, fostered the rise of urban craftsmen, some of whom were dedicated to book manufacturing and developing improved techniques for the preparation of parchment, ink, and gold leaf. An increased interest in learning led to the establishment of the great medieval universities, located in urban environments. And, perhaps most important, greater political and economic stability led to the rise of Jewish as well as Christian entrepreneurs with the desire to commission textual works of art, and the means to pay for them.

Around 1300, an illuminated Haggadah manuscript was created that depicted Jews with the heads of birds and so became known as *The Birds' Head Haggadah,* the oldest such surviving Ashkenazi work. We know the figures to be Jewish because on the male birds' heads appear the trademark conical "Jews Hat," which were mandatory in Christian lands. It is also assumed that the avian-like head was substituted for a more human one to get around the edict of the Second Commandment, which many Jews interpreted to forbid any representational art in human form. So in *The Birds' Head Haggadah* we see Moses, sporting a head of a bird, receiving the two tablets of the Law. The patriarchs Abraham, Isaac, and Jacob are led into paradise by an angel—all four figures look as might be expected, with the exception of each of their heads.

A famous fourteenth-century illustrated Spanish Haggadah has recently gained new life and added prominence after being thought a casualty of a late twentieth-century war. Known as the *Sarajevo Haggadah,* this masterpiece contains thirty-four pages of miniature paintings displaying well-known stories from the Jewish tradition, beginning with the creation of the world. Other drawings represent the Jerusalem Temple and Pesach preparations. The Haggadah received its name when it was purchased by the Sarajevo Museum in 1894, after a child from that city's Sephardic Jewish community brought it to school to sell it. More than a century later, after most of Sarajevo was destroyed in the devastation of the Bosnian war, the Haggadah miraculously survived, hidden by a non-Jewish museum official.

The magnificent illustration gracing the cover of *Passage to Pesach,* as well as those throughout the book, come from *The First Cincinnati Haggadah,* one of several antique masterpieces owned by Hebrew Union College–Jewish Institute of Religion and displayed at its Cincinnati campus. In the last decades of the fifteenth century, a scribe named Meir ben Israel Jaffe of Heidelberg created this work. The many illustrations vividly depict Pesach preparations and seder scenes. Most pages of *The First Cincinnati Haggadah* are wine-stained. This Haggadah, like its medieval cousins, was created not to be collected, but to be used and reused at countless Pesach celebrations.

The first known printed Haggadah came off a Hebrew press in 1486, published by the distinguished Soncino family in Guadalajara, Spain. It was not a separate text, but still part of a bound prayer book. We find it significant that, only twenty years later, the first commentary on the Haggadah appeared. Its author, Don Isaac Abarbanel, was a highly ranked advisor to the Spanish king Ferdinand and his queen Isabella. Tragically, not even entreaties from Abarbanel deterred the monarchs from expelling the Jews from their kingdom, and he was forced to flee as well. Thus his masterpiece, *Zevach Pesach* (Pesach Sacrifice) was printed in Venice in the beginning of the sixteenth century.

With the advent of printing and more advanced artistic techniques, illustrated Haggadot became more plentiful. What is amazing is that the first printed illustrated Haggadah, produced in 1512, was published by Christians and translated into Latin! The Franciscan friar Thomas Murner printed the book to advance the cause of Christian, not Jewish, Hebraism, at a time when other Christian clergy were trying to end this academic discipline.

A Jewish printer, Gershon ben Solomon HaKohen, published the *Prague Haggadah* in 1526. The noted twentieth-century scholar Yosef Hayim Yerushalmi calls it one of the greatest Haggadot ever printed. The language was not Hebrew (or Latin), but Yiddish, the vernacular of Ashkenazic Jews printed in Hebrew script. Among the sixty woodcut illustrations is one that began as a misapplied Pesach scene, but nevertheless was replicated in Haggadot for the next several hundred years. The Hebrew phrase that begins a Saturday night seder has the acronym *YaKenNeHaZ,* which German-speaking Jews mistakenly turned into the German word *Jagen-has,* a "hare hunt." The *Prague Haggadah* was the first to feature hunters in hot pursuit of a ritually *treif* rabbit, this new "traditional" Jewish activity. Another illustration first found in the *Prague Haggadah* and recurring in Haggadot until contemporary times represents the "evil" of the four sons as a soldier, confirming the ageless Jewish connection between wickedness and war.

Several other Haggadot first printed during the late Renaissance introduce distinctive details. In the *Mantua Haggadah* (1560), pudgy *putti*, distant cousins of the friendly cherubs we associate with today's sentimental Valentine cards, dance inside highly decorative borders that surround traditional seder text. An illustration of the "wise son" copies Michelangelo's prophet Jeremiah in the Vatican Sistine Chapel. Haggadot printed in Venice in the beginning of the seventeenth century appeared in editions of three different languages: Judeo-German (Yiddish), Judeo-Spanish (Ladino), and Judeo-Italian. At the end of the seventeenth century, a former Protestant pastor who converted to Judaism first used the technique of copper engraving to illustrate another priceless work, the *Amsterdam Haggadah*.

While these are examples of illustrated texts, most Haggadot that have appeared since the invention of printing have not contained any pictures at all. As befits "the people of the Book," visual images were considered until quite recently to be secondary to the words they occasionally adorned. One such Haggadah was printed in its entirety in the pages of *The London Times*. Its appearance sent a message of compassionate solidarity in the wake of a mid-nineteenth-century accusation of ritual blood libel. In the spring of 1840 in Damascus, Syria, a Christian monk was murdered. Eight Jews from the community were arrested and brutally tortured, charged with killing the monk in order to use his blood to make matzah for Pesach. By printing a complete English translation of the Haggadah, this most prestigious British newspaper sought to "repel strongly the barbarous notion that human blood, or blood of any kind, is essential to its [Pesach] celebration" (August 17, 1840).

The first Haggadah to be printed in the United States was published in New York in 1837 in Hebrew and English. For the next several decades, a fair number of American Haggadot were printed in German, reflecting the large immigration from Germany during this period. None is better known than the Haggadah printed in the 1858 German-language prayer book *Olath Tamid,* which was written by Rabbi David Einhorn, the German-born champion of Reform Judaism. This edition dispenses with any mention of wine, candles, and the traditional seder plate. No singing at all was sanctioned in this seder, not the *Kiddush,* which traditionally begins the seder, nor "Dayeinu" (even one of God's Exodus miracles "would have been enough"). A German rendition of "Adir Hu" (Mighty Is Our God), was spoken, not sung, to end this austere seder. In a later edition of his Haggadah, Einhorn does mention *maror,* the bitter herbs traditionally representing the hard labor Hebrew slaves were forced to perform in Egypt. But Einhorn uses *maror* to symbolize "the never-ending task of waging hard and bitter combat on behalf of God's doctrine and law among the nations of the world," the classic nineteenth-century Reform message of universal justice as transmitted through Jewish moral law.

In 1892, the Central Conference of American Rabbis, the rabbinic arm of American Reform Judaism, included a Pesach seder service in its first edition of the *Union Prayer Book.* The CCAR published its first official Haggadah in 1908, the *Union Haggadah: Home Service for the Passover Eve.* In it, a child asks only one question, not four: "What is the [defining] characteristic of this Seder Haggadah?" The response from the *Union Haggadah* continues the sweeping Reform doctrine of Einhorn's day: "The delivered became the deliverers, when Israel was appointed the messenger of religion unto all mankind." A later, 1923 edition still excludes the Haggadah's traditional concluding words "Next Year in Jerusalem," recitation of the Ten Plagues, and the vengeful phraseology "Pour out Your wrath" that immediately precedes the opening of the door for Elijah. This befitted the then-widespread Reform philosophy of anti-Zionism and properly transcendent decorum. Fifty years later, reflecting the shift in observance toward more traditional text, the *New Union Haggadah* restores these passages while adding quite beautiful watercolor illustrations by the artist Leonard Baskin. The Reform Movement has recently published *The Open Door: A New Haggadah,* filled with additional readings and meditations that speak to the liberal Jew of the twenty-first century.

Of course, other American Jewish denominations published Haggadot as well. Mordecai Kaplan's Reconstructionist *New Haggadah* was first published in 1941. A second Reconstructionist Haggadah, *A Night of Questions,* was published in 2000. While some think of the 1959 "Silverman Haggadah" as the first Conservative effort, the first Haggadah to be produced by an official body of the Conservative Movement was edited by Michael Strassfeld in 1979. Writer Esther Broner and several other of her "Seder Sisters" (among them the late New York politician Bella Abzug, writer Grace Paley, and activist-author Gloria Steinem) put together an early Jewish feminist Haggadah in the 1970s. Twenty years later, Debbie Friedman, the "poet laureate of Reform Judaism," and others created a tremendously successful seder for women living in the New York area that was repeated all over the country. Many of these women's seders use a specially written Haggadah called *The Journey Continues: Mayan Passover Haggadah*. All told, more than four thousand different editions of Passover Haggadot have been published, with new ones coming out every spring.

Two special Haggadot reflect the triumph of the human spirit as our true ultimate redemption. In March 1945, while still fighting in Germany, Jewish soldiers from the U.S. Army Rainbow Division celebrated Pesach with a small Haggadah printed for their use; it was probably one of the first Hebrew books printed in Germany since World War II had begun. One year later, right before Pesach 1946, Holocaust survivors in displaced persons' camps in Munich created a Haggadah commemorating their first Pesach after liberation. In a combination of Hebrew and Yiddish, the text connects the ordeal of Jewish slaves in Egypt with the hell of the Holocaust. Simple border etchings recall those earliest illustrations created by medieval artisans several hundred years before. But mixed with traditional drawings of matzah and *maror* are pictures of flames and chimneys, horrific illustrations signifying the ordeal they had just survived.

That Pesach, in a seder using this Haggadah, the time approached to ask the Four Questions. The people suddenly became aware that no children were present to recite them. The group fell silent, then wept as one. Finally a single voice found the words he needed and the courage to speak them. He was soon joined by the entire gathering, demanding to know, "Why is this night different . . .?" In this Haggadah of the liberation, the message is loud and clear—that none of us forget!

# The First Cup—*V'hotzeiti:*
# Matzah, Soul Food of Freedom

Say, therefore, to the Israelite people: I am *Adonai.* I will bring you
out from the labors of the Egyptians. (Exod. 6:6)

It is a simple concept, really. Just a physical shift, picking up and moving from point "A," regrouping at point "B." But specifying a "from"
does not also automatically frame a "to." Assembling six hundred
thousand Israelites, most accompanied by spouses, children, and animals, must have tested the patience of even God. Taking on the additional tasks of actual movement, lugging enough supplies for a forty-
year passage, and collecting last-minute items given to the Israelites by
their former Egyptians taskmasters defines a logistical nightmare. And
have we mentioned food?

Whatever sustenance was deemed suitable had to be portable and
impervious to desert elements. It had to be light, compact, and just
about indestructible. Most important, it had to be something that could
be prepared in a jiffy. For the Torah tells us:

The Egyptians urged the people on, impatient to have them leave
the country. (Exod. 12:33)

We all know what came next.

And they baked unleavened cakes of the dough they took out of
Egypt, for it was not leavened, since they had been driven out of
Egypt and could not delay. (12:39)

Matzah was the perfect travel food—flat, filling, never going stale. And if it broke, who cared? It was a simple means to fend off hunger. To paraphrase the sixteenth-century Italian sage Obadiah Sforno, matzah was the original "fast food," the bread of a tight schedule. Its recipe is simple, calling for just two ingredients, flour mixed with cold water. The most primitive of ovens could handle its baking. For the first Pesach, the Exodus from Egypt, no food topped it.

But something that starts out simple seldom stays that way for long. As the celebration of Pesach evolved from Temple sacrifice to home seder meal, matzah took on more complex, conflicting roles. The holiday table typifies one such tension. In front of every seder attendee, dry, flat matzah and moist, volatile wine compete for attention, engaging in what one modern scholar has deemed a "dialectical relationship." Ancient custom has evolved a fairly equitable truce between these two key Pesach elements. Whenever we raise our glasses of wine, we must first cover the matzah. And we must empty our glasses of wine prior to picking up and raising the matzah. This stems from an offbeat allegory, instructing that, since matzah assumes the role of bread during Pesach and bread is regarded as the most important food, the matzah would take umbrage at the honors being bestowed on the wine. To spare the matzah's "feelings," it is covered whenever the wine is emphasized. Since the Jewish tradition normally does not animate its food with feelings or emotions, we can infer from this exception the importance of matzah to the understanding of the Pesach narrative.

## "Let All Who Are Hungry Come and Eat"

Another primal dichotomy shows itself at the very beginning of the *Magid,* or lengthy story section that forms the bulk of the premeal seder observance. Quite generously, we issue an expansive dinner invitation: "Let all who are hungry come and eat." But seconds later, we admit, "Now we are slaves." How can people who are slaves, with no control over their own supply of nourishment, at the same time magnanimously feed others? The mystery is compounded by the seder leader's action while reciting these words, for she or he holds up a *broken* piece of matzah, the smaller half, having just hidden the larger section as the *afikoman*. This doesn't auger well for a welcoming or filling repast to follow, especially to a genuinely hungry person.

The medieval commentator Ibn Ezra may have uncovered a clue to solving this problem. His extended travels once took him to India. There, he observed that prisoners were fed something similar to matzah for a brutally practical reason. Because this matzah-like substance was difficult to digest, it remained in prisoners' digestive systems longer, lessening their hunger and requiring fewer meals for their jailers to prepare. Ibn Ezra presumes Egyptian taskmasters followed a similar practice when feeding their Israelite slaves. Matzah is the dietary staple of those not free to determine the composition and frequency of their meals, or much of anything else in their sad lives. Thus matzah becomes a symbol, not of freedom, but of slavery.

Yet it is important to remember how the Pesach passage ends, with Israel's escape from her Egyptian masters. During the seder, we move back and forth from memories of past servitude to dreams of future redemption, from "now we are slaves" to "next year, may we live in freedom." Rabbi Richard Hirsh refers to this as the "already/not yet" Jewish syndrome, as we simultaneously celebrate our freedom and redemption while reminding ourselves we are neither wholly free nor redeemed, even today. Similarly, matzah can also symbolize a situation we may not feel prepared for, but we have to contend with anyway. When the Jewish people faced the swirling waters of the Red Sea on one side and the advancing troops of Pharaoh on the other, no one knew what to do until Nachshon, one of the leaders of the tribe of Judah, bravely took his first steps into the water. This courageous act rid the people of their paralyzing fear. Matzah thus represents determination, calling forth the need for action in the present as well as recollection of the past.

Interestingly, the first recorded uses of matzah in the Bible occurred not during the Exodus, but long before. Our earliest ancestors served matzah as they opened their homes to strangers in gestures of hospitality. When our patriarch Abraham was resting in his tent, still recuperating from circumcising himself at the not very youthful age of ninety-nine, he entertained three persons unknown to him with cakes of matzah, which had been quickly prepared by his wife Sarah. Next, Abraham's nephew Lot also fed the same men matzah in Sodom, even as they told him and his family to flee the town, just before God destroyed it and its wicked inhabitants.

Today we follow centuries-old Jewish tradition and contribute to community collections during the weeks before Pesach to provide *m'ot chitim,* "wheat money," to those who otherwise would not be able to afford matzah and the many other special Pesach foods needed to celebrate the holiday properly. Nobel laureate Elie Wiesel remembers how *m'ot chitim* was administered in small towns of pre-World War II Hungary. "One by one, [people] would enter a room in the community house. There they would find a dish filled with money. Those who had money left some; those who needed money took some. No one knew how much was given or how much was taken. Thus, the needy were taken care of with dignity."

The Pesach invitation to help the needy can be traced to the Talmud, to a good deed performed by the third-century Sage Rav Huna. He called out to all those who passed his house when he was about to sit down for a meal, opening his door and saying, "Let all who are hungry come in to eat." Today, few of us act this spontaneously. But we recognize how our homage to liberation loses meaning unless we seek to free the downtrodden who suffer injustices: the poor, forced to work long hours for little pay; those subjected to mental or physical abuse; or tragically, even those who labor today in conditions similar to slavery. Helping to relieve deprivation wherever it appears, with Pesach on our minds, adds to the understanding that freedom's struggle is not yet complete. An engaging language game heightens this connection of word to deed. Without vowels, the Hebrew words for "matzah," מצה, and "mitzvah," מצוה, look almost exactly alike. Just as we can transform the food of "matzah" to a sacred commandment, "mitzvah," by changing a few vowels, so should eating the food of liberation be our first step to performing acts dictated by God, doing all we can to free those still enslaved.

## "We Start with Disgrace and End with Praise"
### (*Mishnah P'sachim* 10:4)

Some commentators ascribe the Hebrew word *g'nut,* customarily translated as "disgrace," with a moral overtone. In this understanding, the Israelites brought their problems on themselves by their idolatrous behavior, leading to their exile in Egypt and subsequent enslavement.

Others more matter-of-factly point to slavery as a political and economic state for which our predecessors bear no blame. Whichever comprehension one leans toward, its explanation begins with matzah.

Another Hebrew "word game," matzah as "poor person's bread" versus matzah as "bread of answers," builds on the complexity of this seemingly simple food. Once again, we leave the Hebrew consonants intact and maneuver only the vowels, changing עוֹנִי, *lechem oni,* "poor person's bread," to עוֹנֶה, *lechem oneh,* "bread of reciting or answering." Each year we begin the seder with a declaration over matzah, "This is the bread of affliction," making clear that the entire Haggadah is dedicated to reciting our passage to freedom in its name. Matzah becomes the ubiquitous food supplying all of the answers, cataloguing our quite human humiliations, numbering their remedies, and singing our praises to *Adonai,* our Redeemer, past, present, and future.

Matzah didn't always look like the nondescript cracker that now graces our seder tables. In the days of the Talmud, through most of the Middle Ages, some Jewish bakers etched doves and fish, animals and flowers into their matzah dough, creating edible works of art. Instead of relegating its storage to a cupboard, Jews living in Germany in the fourteenth century hung their matzah on a wall of the synagogue for all to see. Only in the sixteenth century were all such designs banned. Perforations were the only markings allowed, and their purpose was not to beautify, but to prevent matzah from rising during baking.

In the mid-nineteenth century, an enterprising Austrian Jew invented the first matzah-making machine. Some Orthodox rabbis strongly praised it because, in their opinion, it guaranteed more scrupulous supervision and cleanliness. Other religious leaders just as vociferously opposed it because it threatened to eliminate the livelihoods of so many Jewish bakers right before Pesach, since other usual baking stops for the duration of the weeklong holiday. Down to contemporary times, rigorously observant Jews still eat only handmade matzah called *sh'murah* because it is "guarded" from the time its grain still grows in the fields, through harvesting, grinding into flour, and making of the dough. Then *sh'murah* matzah dough is carefully placed into closely watched ovens, removed after precisely eighteen minutes, the length of time at which flour mixed with water will begin to ferment or, as our tradition tells us, the length of time it takes to walk a (Roman) mile!

## "*Kadeish, Ur'chatz, Karpas, Yachatz*" (Order of Seder)

We have determined that matzah is vital to the seder meal, indeed, to the whole commemoration of Pesach. But what is so magical about the number "three" that only this number of especially designated matzot can move us along through the seder observance? (Obviously many more "ordinary" matzot are consumed as we pass through the evening.) One answer from our tradition assumes that, during Pesach, a third "loaf of bread" was added to the standard double portion of manna. This is the breadlike food that fell from the sky for the forty years the people of Israel wandered in the wilderness. Early practice in Palestine mandated only two pieces of matzah, not three. Somewhat later, the Babylonian custom of including one additional matzah on the seder plate became standard throughout the Jewish world. Still, the Jewish philosopher Maimonides used only two pieces in twelfth-century Egypt. And there were holdouts as recently as two hundred years ago. At the end of the eighteenth century in Lithuania, the scholar known as the Vilna Gaon placed only two pieces of matzah on his seder plate.

Today, three whole pieces of matzah are used in our Pesach celebration. The first, uppermost matzah has been called "Kohanim"; the second, "Levite"; and the third, "Israel," for the three classes of Jews in ancient Judea. Others, alluding to the matzah/mitzvah wordplay referred to earlier, say these matzot represent the three mitzvot of the seder: (1) matzah—Torah—learning; (2) pesach—*avodah*—worship; and (3) *maror—g'milut chasadim*—human relations of loving-kindness. Rabbi Sherira Gaon, a medieval Babylonian sage, named the matzot after the three biblical Patriarchs: Abraham, Isaac, and Jacob. Whatever the three pieces are called, since all Jews are to be treated equally, especially during Pesach, everyone at seder eats from all the matzot.

There is another question about numbers and matzah. If three pieces of matzah are essential, why is the middle piece, and only the middle piece, "*yachatz*ed," broken in two, just as the seder is getting started, creating in essence a fourth "official" matzah, the *afikoman*? Perhaps because four is the same as the number of seder questions, wine cups, and archetypal children. Most commentators associate breaking this piece of matzah with the slavery of Israel in Egypt or the historical poverty of Jews in general.

Egyptian masters sought to deplete the Jewish population in their land through starvation and overwork, frequently withholding even the meager slave rations. Therefore, to lengthen survival, a slave would not eat a complete matzah at one time. Instead, he would hoard part of it, turning this scrap into a meal when given no food at all. The sixteenth-century Bohemian rabbi known as the Maharal also observed this among the poor of his area, who divided their meager bread into many smaller portions. So afraid that there won't be any more, a person accustomed to poverty doesn't dare eat all the allotted food at once. Much closer to our time, World War II concentration camp survivors have described similar behavior.

## "*Sour Dough* Must Be Burned, and One Who Eats It Is Subject to Penalty" (*Mishnah P'sachim* 3:5)

This text from the Mishnah does not use the familiar Hebrew word for fermented bread, *chameitz* (leaven), but introduces a new word, *s'or* (sour dough), the precursor to modern-day yeast. Those of us who bake our own bread know that yeast is a critical ingredient. It makes bread rise, "leavens" it. Today, prepackaged yeast is easy to obtain, purchased at any grocery store. But before this convenience was invented, our ancestors used another leavening agent—*s'or*. This sour dough was a portion of the previous week's dough that had been saved, unbaked, and allowed to ferment. It was then used to start the leavening process for a new batch of bread, with the process repeating over and over again. In our Hebrew tradition, *s'or* refers to the old leavening enabler, while *chameitz* refers to new dough to which *s'or* had been added. This combination, in turn, is called *lechem chameitz,* "leavened bread." As it says in Torah: "This offering, with cakes of leavened bread [*lechem chameitz*] added . . . " (Lev. 7:13). For Pesach, though, the rules changed. Both categories, leavening agents and leavened bread, had to be discarded or burned in order to establish the purity of the holiday, as this reading from the Book of Exodus describes:

> Seven days you shall eat unleavened bread [*matzot*]; on the very first day you shall remove leaven [*s'or*] from your houses, for whoever eats leavened bread [*chameitz*] from the first day to the seventh day, that person shall be cut off from Israel. (Exod. 12:15)

Right after Pesach's conclusion, having rid ourselves of old fermentable substances the week before, we start fresh. Pesach as a period of transition is pivotal to our genuine efforts to separate the old from the new. Hopefully we have gotten rid of everything we let stand around, including the moral and emotional rot that puffs us with pride and self-absorption. Thus leaven stands for all of our selfish tendencies, which left to their own devices, proliferate into humanity's evil inclinations, *yetzer hara*. To counter baseness, the third-century Palestinian Sage Rabbi Alexandri ended his daily silent devotions with the following prayer, naming *s'or* as the obstacle forestalling more God-inspired personal behavior: "Sovereign of the universe, it should be quite evident to You that our will is to do Your will. What impedes us? The yeast, *s'or*, in the dough. . . ."

What other "yeasts" obstruct our finer moments by their prideful pufferies? Uncontrollable feelings of possessiveness, which make us take things we don't even want? Uncontrolled competitiveness, which promotes a winner-takes-all mentality? Raging jealousy, so unrestrained that it threatens to damage our closest relationships? Whatever label we put on it, leaven, the unnecessary yeast making up our emotional DNA, lacks qualities of discipline and consistency. Unstable, subject to radical change, both *s'or* and leaven are missing matzah's defining elements—immutability, stability, quiescence.

## "These Things Fulfill the Pesach Obligation"
### (*Mishnah P'sachim* 2:5)

But before we cast matzah into the figurative role of the greatest Jewish symbol, let us remember its literal essence, grain and a little cold water. And not just any grain, but one or more of the exact grains that causes dough to swell in the first place: wheat, barley, spelt, rye, and oats. Thus another perplexity surrounds matzah! Only what can become *chameitz* may be used to make it. Only something that has both the potential for evil as well as the potential for good, *yetzer hara* as well as *yetzer hatov*, can become a genuine matzah. What determines the tilt one way or the other, for good or for evil, is the mysterious intangible we call faith. A talmudic tale describes this concept. Moses and the angels were involved in a dispute. The angels argued that humanity was unworthy of receiving Torah. Moses' triumphant rejoinder was that heavenly hosts, lacking the negative emotions of jealousy, temptation, or evil inclination, had no need for Torah. It is plainly meant for mortals, waging their constant battle between good and evil.

This taste of reality we call matzah is the bread of both slavery and liberty, the essence of life for poor and rich alike. It is the basic kernel of hope at the heart of our transitional state, a continual becoming in the soul of Judaism. Because matzah is so primal, it grounds the very centers of our lives.

After the Temple was destroyed more than two thousand years ago, Jewish leaders had to redirect Judaism for a scattered people lacking a pivotal shrine. Gone was the pageantry of dozens of priests in richly designed raiments, assisting ordinary Jews to offer sacrifices to God. Now all Jews had to learn how to become their own priests. Guided by rabbinic teachings, each could access the Divine directly, without needing a human intermediary. The scholar Moshe Greenberg believes that, even when sacrifices still connected mortals to God, they were offered in their least altered state, closest to the manner in which God created them.

Ultimately, this ideal of simplicity was transferred to the absence of leavening, correlating the symbolic purity of the food we eat to the miraculous power of the sacred. Complicated, elaborate bread is not appropriate for Pesach, which celebrates one fundamental action— God's redemption of Israel. Today, many of us search for things "naturally" organic, seeing additives as intrusions to our basic needs and goals. Matzah, the first wholly natural prepared food, perfectly represents our passage from the everyday to the sacred. The Jewish thinker Philo, living in the last days of the Temple and strongly influenced by the flourishing Greek philosophy of his day, described matzah, unleavened food, as a gift of nature, and thus serving as the highest form of praise on the path to perfection.

> The bread is unleavened . . . because during springtime, when the feast is held, the fruit of the corn has not reached its perfection. . . . It was the imperfection of this fruit which belonged to the future, though it was to reach its perfection very shortly. Food, when unleavened, is a gift of nature, when leavened, is a work of art. . . . Art for the sake of pleasure has no place, but only nature, providing nothing save what is indispensable for its use. So much for this.

## From Our Tradition

You shall observe the [Feast of] Unleavened Bread, for on this very first day I brought your ranks out of the land of Egypt; you shall observe this day throughout the ages as an institution for all time. (Exod. 12:17)

You shall observe the Feast of Unleavened Bread, eating unleavened bread for seven days as I have commanded you, at the set time in the month of Aviv, for in it you went forth from Egypt. . . ." (Exod. 23:15)

It was only a few days before Passover, when a man entered the home of Yosef Dov HaLevi Soleveitchik of Brisk, known as the Bais Halevi. "Rabbi," he pleaded, "I have a very difficult question. Is one allowed to fulfill his obligation of the four cups of wine with another liquid? Would one be able to fulfill his obligation with four cups of milk? "My son," the Bais Halevi said, "that is a very difficult question. I will look into the matter. But until then I have an idea. I would like to give you some money in order for you to purchase four cups of wine for you and your family." The Bais Halevi gave the startled man far more than necessary. The man took it with extreme gratitude and relief. When his disciples questioned this act, saying he had given enough for an entire meal with meat, the rabbi smiled. "That is exactly the point! If he cannot afford wine, he cannot afford meat. So not only did I give him money for wine, but for meat as well." (Mordechai Kamenetzky)

# The Second Cup—*V'hitzalti*: Seder Plate Objects, Sacred Symbols

I am *Adonai*. I will deliver you from the bondage of the Egyptians. (Exod. 6:6)

The *k'arah*, the seder plate our family uses each Pesach, is a work of art. A treasured gift my father and stepmother brought from Israel, its place of primacy on our seder table is an instant reminder of past holidays and the people who made them so special. Taking the plate out of the china cabinet and dusting it off a few days before Pesach has become one of my favorite personal rituals. It brings me satisfaction to know that soon each slight hollow will be filled with its very own object. For the seder cannot proceed without the several traditional symbols, each in its proper spot, indispensable to our annual Pesach passage.

As Elie Wiesel has noted, the entire story of the Haggadah is contained in the seder plate. Everything on it symbolizes an aspect of the Exodus. The seder plate takes a theoretical story, beloved as it might be, and turns it into a lived experience. This night is transformed into a magical excursion back in time, to glimpse our beginnings. And because of our interaction with these seder items, each of us also moves forward in journeys of personal Jewish affirmation. We discuss, point, raise, lower, dip, and of course sample the textures and tastes that define our redemptive saga, adding to the story by performing it.

The seder plate simultaneously defines formal boundary and free movement. Each object is placed in its own space, calling attention to a distinct milestone on our passage from slavery to freedom. At the same time, the roundness of the plate itself reflects the endless, universal themes of Pesach, reminding us of the Jewish people's various stages from subjugation to liberty, and hints of the ease with which we may slide back and forth between them.

Each object represents several different aspects, sometimes opposing its neighbor above or below it, sometimes containing conflict within itself. For example, *karpas,* the green vegetable on the plate, recalls verdant renewals of nature and faith. Yet we dip it in salt water to remember the sadness of Egyptian slavery. On most seder plates, *karpas* sits alongside *maror,* the symbol of the harsh labor that the Israelites were forced to endure. Also not far away on the *k'arah* is delicious *charoset,* mixing soft, sweet fruit and the spices of life with hard nuts and dark wine, contrasting life with the inevitability of mortality and death.

While each seder plate "prop" contributes to the Pesach story, individual items may be positioned differently, depending upon the artistic or philosophic bent of the plate designer. Or we may not use a plate at all, preferring the Sephardic tradition of keeping everything in a seder basket. The first mention of the arrangement of seder symbols comes from writings of the Maharil, a thirteenth-century sage. He lined up the symbols in two vertical columns, the left side designating (from top to bottom), egg, *charoset,* and salt water; the right side *z'roa* (shank bone), *maror,* and *karpas.* His rationale follows the talmudic dictum "One does not bypass an obligation." The accessories were placed on the left, with Pesach staples placed on the right, in the order of use. The Haggadah mandates *karpas* as the first seder symbol. Thus, in this sequence, *karpas* is conveniently (and halachically) located at our fingertips, on the lower right. The Vilna Gaon, who lived at the end of the eighteenth century, favored an alternative seder plate design. He placed *charoset* and the egg to the left, *maror* and *z'roa* to the right, and two matzot in the middle of the plate.

Today, most of us follow a seder plate arrangement created by the sixteenth-century mystic Isaac Luria, the Ari. He placed the six objects in two inverted triangles. The first one assigns the egg to the left, *z'roa* to the right, meeting *maror* in the middle. The second triangle has an order of *karpas* and *charoset* connected to *chazeret,* or lettuce, a second type of *maror* not found on many plates today. The top triangle contains objects mentioned in the Torah; items appearing in the bottom triangle were added later by the Rabbis as they finalized the seder ritual. According to Lurianic Kabbalah, the six seder plate objects symbolize the middle six emanations, or *s'firot,* that God used to create the world. The two-triangle Star of David design used on many contemporary seder plates works as a modern interpretation of kabbalistic mysticism.

For most of us, though, it is the objects rather than their order that spark our curiosity and imagination. Their meanings can be grouped into three categories: their appearance as discrete, individual objects; the broader interpretations they assume for the Jewish community; and their sacred symbolism representing God's direct action, a major Exodus theme. A Mishnah text grounds this chapter of our Pesach passage: "They brought before him [the participant at the table] unleavened bread, lettuce, fruit-spice sauce, and two cooked dishes [stand-ins for the two holiday sacrifices]. And when the Temple existed they used to bring before him the bones of the *pesach* offering."

## *Karpas*—Vegetable of Spring

Sharp-eyed readers will note that a seder plate item *not* alluded to in the Mishnah quoted above is the one that begins our seder—*karpas,* spring's signature. *Karpas* was a late rabbinic addition to the seder ritual, a custom, not a commandment like matzah or *maror.* It is the simplest symbol on the seder plate, least changed from its natural state. An important purpose of eating *karpas* is simple as well—to hush our grumbling stomachs, at least for a little while, so we can proceed comfortably through the Haggadah, concentrating on its many lofty messages instead of those tantalizing aromas coming from the kitchen. However, we only eat a bit of *karpas,* and even that is dipped into salt water or vinegar, serving as a reminder of the Jewish slaves' constant hunger in Egypt. The word *karpas* originates either from the Greek *karpos,* "fruit of the soil," or the Persian and Aramaic *karafas,* "celery." In Eastern Europe, spring food such as green vegetables arrived late and was quite expensive. But potatoes were plentiful, and to this day many of us with Eastern European roots put a spud on the seder plate, though we may dip and eat parsley or celery. The nineteenth-century legal interpreter Solomon Ganzfried suggests yet another food as *karpas*: "Many are accustomed to take parsley, but it is best to take celery, which also has a good taste when raw. And it is best of all to take radishes."

While *karpas* took its place relatively late in the establishment of Pesach observances, its inclusion in the Haggadah may hearken back to cultural habits of Temple times. Then, as now, much of Jewish practice was influenced by the manners and lifestyles of our non-Jewish neighbors. All upper-class Greek and Roman banquets began with palate-tempting hors d'oeuvres, tastefully passed on special plates. On this night of contrasts, we imitate aristocrats by eating something raw and uncomplicated as our first ritual food. We take our time making the transition from the common to the more exotic with this first fresh food of the season. Since no specific Pesach story is associated with *karpas,* we can develop our own, creating distinctive Pesach associations for this seder plate symbol.

Just as we are not alone when we observe the Exodus from Egypt but are instructed to celebrate with a group of happy Jews, *karpas* is not eaten by itself. We dip it as a partial answer to question number three of the Four Questions: "On all other nights we do not dip even once, [why] on this night do we dip twice?" Since dipping is not done at a usual dinner party, this rather self-conscious action marks the night as different from its start. The search for meaning takes us back to the very first "night of watching," in Egypt (Exodus 12). God told Moses to make sure each Jewish household marked its doorposts. To do this, a readily available green plant, hyssop, was dipped into animal blood, not for eating, but to make a sign in blood that alerted the Angel of Death to pass them by. Today's more innocuous re-creation, *karpas* submerged in salt water, still lends a somber tone to the festivities of the evening.

As we begin our seder meal, we also remember a more ancient, more guilty dipping, a cruel act involving twelve biblical brothers that resulted in the appearance of a Jewish presence in Egypt. Rabbi Menoah of Narbonne, a medieval sage, connected *karpas* with *k'tonet pasim,* Joseph's beautiful coat of many colors, which was covered by goat's blood and displayed by Joseph's vengeful brothers to their grieving father, Jacob. With one gruesome act of sibling rivalry, when Joseph was sold to slave dealers bound for Egypt, we began our descent into bondage.

But also with one small act, eating *karpas,* we begin our ascent back to freedom. Our people's humble roots as shepherds in Canaan focus our thoughts. As the classical commentator Yismach Yisrael relates, these modest origins are mirrored in the unassuming *karpas*. Though it takes root beneath the ground, it sprouts through the earth and proceeds to shine as the very first symbol on the splendorous seder plate. Similarly, on this night we witness God's compassion as Jews celebrate God's direct action, raising us from the depths to our promised redemption.

## *Beitzah*—the Egg Begins It All

Though every seder plate has a place for *beitzah,* a hard-boiled or roasted egg, it is not mentioned at all in the traditional Haggadah. My family, whose roots began in Central and Eastern Europe, mash eggs in small bowls of salted water as the first appetizer course of the meal. This observance is largely absent from the Sephardic ritual of those who honor their North African or Middle Eastern beginnings. *Beitzah* serves as another contrast on this night of differences. The egg, which symbolizes birth, is the first food offered to mourners returning from the cemetery, a sign of life and death as one never-ending cycle. *Beitzah* gives spiritual comfort as it provides the physical nourishment needed to begin the period of grieving.

A midrash uses the egg as a symbol of both mortal beginnings and endings, justifying why we eat it at our seder meal. Rabbi Yehoshua relates in the Talmud that our Patriarchs were born and died on Pesach. The Sages teach that perfectly just persons die on the day of their birth. So we eat hard-boiled eggs this Pesach evening, noting their endlessly oval shape, to remember the lives and deaths of our own first ancestors, Abraham, Isaac, and Jacob. A Jewish maxim notes that, though most food becomes softer the longer it cooks in hot water, eggs become harder. Jews have gained a tough edge through our unfortunately long exposure to persecution and pogroms. The hotter life is made for us, the stronger and more vigorous we become.

The presence of an egg on the seder plate also reminds us of sacred occasions at the Temple in Jerusalem. More than two thousand years ago Jews gathered in the most holy city to mark the harvest of Nisan, the first month of the year and the first of the three annual Pilgrimage Festivals, commemorated by bringing a special sacrifice, the *chagigah*. Over time, the sacrifice of *chagigah* was transformed into *beitzah,* the roasted egg sitting on the seder plate. It serves as a reminder of the sacrifice Jews are no longer able to make. Since the destruction of the Temple, the egg has become another example of a sad memory in the midst of our happy Pesach celebrations.

## Z'roa—the "Pesach" of Pesach

So *karpas* and *beitzah,* while important enough to merit seder discussion and some ritual activity, are not on the seder plate as a result of biblical commandments. *Karpas* was a rabbinic *minhag,* or custom, and *beitzah* evolved from a Temple sacrifice. But the third symbol, *z'roa* or shank bone, appears on the seder plate as a mitzvah, a biblical commandment dating from the first Pesach.

> Speak to the whole community of Israel and say . . . each of them shall take a lamb to a family. . . . Your lamb shall be without blemish, a yearling male. . . . You shall keep watch over it until the fourteenth day of this month, and all the assembled congregation of the Israelites shall slaughter it at twilight. . . . They shall eat the flesh that same night. . . . (Exod. 12:3, 5–6, 8)

Because of its prominence in the Pesach narrative, the *z'roa* is located in the most favored seder plate position, the upper right, in the most common configuration. While vegetarians may substitute a raw beet, and a chicken drumstick will also suffice, the traditional *z'roa* is the lower leg of a young lamb, preferably with a little roasted meat still left on it. Its hardness, wholeness, and durability make the shank bone the symbol of hope, representing the Jewish slaves' devotion and trust that God would spare them, even as God's messenger, the Angel of Death, was methodically slaying every Egyptian firstborn.

When the Haggadah makes reference to the *z'roa,* it is called *pesach* for the following reason:

> It is the passover [*pesach*] sacrifice to *Adonai,* because God passed over the houses of the Israelites in Egypt when God smote the Egyptians, but saved our houses. (Exod. 12:27)

The Bible thus describes both the act that inspired the first Pesach and the rationale for continuing this commemoration in all Pesachs that follow. Rabban Gamliel, one of the most important early Rabbis, is credited with transforming Judaism after the destruction of the Temple. He thought so highly of the *z'roa/pesach* mitzvah that, in the Haggadah, he named it first among three seder commandments ("Whoever has not explained the following three things on Passover has not fulfilled the purpose of the seder, namely: *pesach* . . ."). And yet, the *z'roa* is neither raised nor lowered from the seder plate. In traditional Haggadot, the leader does not even point to the shank bone when asking, "What is the meaning of this *pesach*?"

The answer to this question is there for all to see, making any further gesture superfluous. The *z'roa* embodies the holiday in seasons past, present, and future. Symbolizing the first, Egyptian Pesach, the shank bone stands for those Israelite slaves who led their households to freedom. The Pesachs that ensued are remembered by the biblical commandment from Exodus, reinforced by the Mishnaic edict of Rabban Gamaliel.

In Temple times the *pesach* was an animal specifically chosen for its sacrificial suitability, without blemishes of any kind. After Temple priests slaughtered it, Jews took the offering back to their homes and roasted it whole, making sure that none of its bones were broken in the cooking process. In our time, the Jewish people stand united in basic beliefs that defy bone-crushing divisiveness. Our future redemption is contingent on our unflinching understanding of *z'roa* as symbolic of the strong, outstretched arm of God, *z'roa n'tuyah*. We endeavor to renew our Mount Sinai covenant with God, pledged barely three months after God led us out of Egypt. Trying to be godlike in our dealings with others will surely help to bring ultimate deliverance. God's hand extends everywhere to guide our moral strivings.

## *Maror* and *Chazeret*—Horseradish or Lettuce?

Each year, after cleaning my seder plate before Pesach began, I would stare at one of its symbols, confounded by its meaning. I presumed I had at least a passing knowledge of Pesach and its observances. But an understanding of *chazeret* completely escaped me. I had never encountered an explanation of *chazeret*, so I willed it into oblivion, covering its designated place, and my ignorance, with additional *karpas* or *charoset.* Only a close reading of reference books and traditional Haggadot led me to learn about *chazeret.*

I soon discovered that *chazeret* is not explicitly mentioned in the Bible. The Rabbis meant *chazeret* to be included in the more familiar, generic term *maror,* or bitter herbs. According to both the Babylonian and Jerusalem Talmuds, the preferred *chazeret* is called *chasah,* a form of lettuce closely related to the romaine or escarole varieties we know today. The Mishnah describes sharp-tasting green vegetables variously translated as endive, chervil, pepperwort, dittany, snakeroot, or sea holly. I also learned that in antiquity, lettuce was used for medicinal purposes and was quite different from our current salad mainstay, made much milder by two thousand years of cultivation. When it first sprouts, *chazeret* has soft leaves and a sweet taste. If allowed to grow until it begins to flower, the leaves harden and become bitter. It is this bitter *chazeret* that adorns some seder plates. "Rabbi Shmuel ben Nachman said: How is Egypt similar to *chazeret?* Just as when it first grows it is gentle but turns harsh and bitter, exile in Egypt began gently and ended harshly."

By late medieval times, when Jews moved east and north to Poland and Russia, lettuce was a difficult commodity to come by, especially in the early spring. They began to substitute the much more biting horseradish root as *maror,* called *chrein* in Yiddish. Ira Steingroot, author of *Keeping Passover,* philosophically reasons that *chazeret* is missing from some modern seder plates because it may have become redundant, given our modern upbeat attitudes. Prosperous, assimilated American Jews no longer feel the need for a double dose of suffering.

A clue to the tradition of two seder plate spaces for *maror* may come from the Mishnah. This legal code, known for its brevity, nonetheless mentions two Pesach actions done with *maror* that we continue to practice at our seders today: "They served him—he dips lettuce before he reaches the 'bread condiment,'" and "They served him unleavened bread and lettuce and *charoset.*" A second hint can be seen by studying our familiar seder plate configuration. *Maror* is situated in the middle, central position, connected to both *beitzah* (egg) and *z'roa* (shank bone), the prime Temple sacrifices of Pesach. The contemporary Jewish scholar and psychologist Reuven Bulka defines *maror* as the central feature and theme of the seder plate. Our Sages doubled its role and highlighted its importance through its prominent seder placement.

A third, psychological rationale resonates today, with so many of us seeking a heightened spiritual understanding of Judaism. Perhaps because of the almost unbearable amount of pain and suffering Jews have been forced to endure, bitterness has become endemic in the Jewish psyche. Zalman Schacter-Shalomi, a creator of the Jewish Renewal Movement in America, explains that this doesn't have to be viewed as totally bad. *Maror* reawakens the pain and bitterness that define parts of everyone's life. We try to work our way through the pain. Sometimes we learn from it, sometimes we do not. With its harsh, biting taste, *maror* recalls pain's reality.

Even when we are prosperous and happy, we remember bad times. Even when living in freedom and well-being, we must remember that our condition was not always thus. That is why, says Israeli scholar Menachem Kasher, we eat matzah before we eat *maror* in the seder ritual. Only after the Israelites had a tantalizing taste of freedom as represented by the matzah did they begin to understand and feel the full bitterness of their exile in Egypt. Slaves become used to their condition. If they are fortunate enough to escape their ordeal, they appreciate freedom more than the rest of us, who tend to take our liberty for granted.

But does this mean that we can appreciate what we have only after we lose it? A large part of the maturation process teaches us the wisdom to distinguish good times from bad, to appreciate the good times as we experience them. Turning to the rhythms of the Pesach seder affords us the opportunity of many "'Dayeinu' moments." Sharing bittersweet memories with family and friends helps us to appreciate our fortunate circumstances together. A short memory of complacency often has bitter consequences. Eating *maror* at seder gives us back our lengthy pasts, reminding us of our substantial, solid history.

We have referred to the first-century Jewish philosopher Philo several times in these pages. His quiet sense of the ideal focuses a search for peaceful order in the mad frenzy of existence. Here is what Philo had to say about *maror*: "[Bitter herbs] are manifestations of a psychic migration, through which one removes from wickedness to virtue. Those who naturally and genuinely repent become bitter toward their former way of life. We who desire repentance eat . . . bitter herbs. We first eat bitterness over our old and unendurable life, and then [we eat] the opposite . . . through meditation on humility, which is called reverence."

*Chazeret* may also be related to the Hebrew word *lachzor*, "to return," signifying God's compassionate freeing of Israel from Egyptian slavery, bringing Israel back to serve the Divine after the long sojourn among Egyptian idolaters. As noted earlier, in the Aramaic vernacular of ancient Jewish life, the word for bitter herbs is *chasah*, which, according to the talmudic Sage Rava, also suggests compassion "because *Adonai* had compassion upon the Children of Israel and redeemed them." Our eating of bitter herbs on Pesach transmits divine tenderness in its many marvelous complexities.

## *Charoset*—Recipes for Judaism

Our last seder plate symbol activates taste buds just thinking about it. There are as many varieties of *charoset,* a mixture of fruit, nuts, and wine, as there are distinct Jewish practices on Pesach. Several ingredients of *charoset* are compared to themes of love in the Song of Songs, the sensual biblical saga we read on this holiday.

> The green *figs* form on the fig tree,
> The vines in blossom give off fragrance.
> Arise, my darling;
> My fair one, come away! . . .
>
> My beloved has gone down into his *nut-garden,*
> To the beds of *spices*. . . .
>
> Let me climb the *date-palm* . . .
> Let your breasts be like clusters of *grapes* . . .
> Your breath like the fragrance of *apples,*
> And Your mouth like choicest *wine*. . . .
> (Song of Songs 2:13; 6:2; 7:9–10)

Two of Judaism's most erudite medieval philosophers could not resist offering their own recipes for *charoset* in their otherwise abstract writings. In his chapters of *Mishneh Torah* devoted to Pesach, *Hilchot Chameitz Umatzah,* Maimonides explains: "Take dates, dried figs, or raisins, and crush them. Add wine vinegar, and mix with shredded cinnamon and fresh ginger." The most important figure in Kabbalah, Rabbi Isaac Luria, borrows his mother's recipe, which calls for three kinds of spices and seven kinds of mashed fruit. One contemporary rabbi describes the *charoset* savored by our ancients as more like Chinese duck sauce, made of apricots.

But while we are captivated by the scrumptious sweetness of *charoset,* we remember that it, too, is a symbol on our seder plates, a stark contrast to the pungent sharpness of *maror. Charoset* also represents the mortar that Israel was forced to produce for Pharaoh's pyramid cities. A Jewish soldier fighting in the American Civil War describes his efforts to make a seder in a West Virginia encampment with twenty of his coreligionists. "The necessaries for *charoset* we could not obtain, so we got a brick which, rather hard to digest, reminded us by looking at it, for what purpose it was intended."

While all members of Jewish families slaved in Egypt, turning straw into bricks and sand into mortar, the role of women is especially poignant. The Talmud brings together several aspects of the Exodus story, using *charoset* to cement the narrative together. Starting with words from Psalms, "Your wife shall be like a fruitful vine within your house" (Ps. 128:3), Sages next turn to the Song of Songs, referencing a legend that credits Jewish women with conceiving secretly in apple orchards: "Under the apple tree I roused you; / It was there your mother conceived you, / There she who bore you conceived you" (Song of Songs 8:5). Jewish women in Egypt also sought refuge under this same fruit tree to hide their newborn baby boys from Egyptian soldiers ordered to kill them.

Another *charoset* ingredient, red wine, brings more than its sweet flavor to this Pesach dish. At least twice in Torah, wine is referred to as *dam anavim,* "the blood of grapes" (Gen. 49:11; Deut. 32:14), a description filled with ominous portents. A midrash paints a painful portrait of Egyptian slavery, again calling attention to the role of Israelite women: "Rabbi Akiva said: Pharaoh's taskmasters ordered Israel to make straw for bricks for them. The Israelites collected dry stubble in the wilderness. Their donkeys, women, and children trampled it into straw. The stubble pierced their heels so that blood ran all over the mortar." Women played such a significant role in Egypt that the medieval French commentator Joseph Tov Elem intuited this response: "Why dip [*maror*] in *charoset*? In memory of the mortar that the woman and her husband trampled."

We are left with just one additional *charoset* dilemma, the *koreich* (sandwich) controversy. Should the "Hillel sandwich" we eat right before serving the seder meal contain both *maror* and *charoset,* or should *charoset* be left out? Pro-*charoset* proponents point out that *koreich* literally means "bind together," and the more we combine, the merrier we attend to seder observance. Since we eat *charoset* when we eat *maror,* inclusionists applaud the heartier result. But the more traditional view restricts *koreich* to matzah and *maror* only, because the *maror* originates in the Bible while *charoset* is a rabbinic gloss. As an example, *The Family Haggadah,* published by ArtScroll, an Orthodox press, gives the following Haggadah instructions: "The head of the household takes . . . *maror,* dips it into *charoses* [*sic*], [and then] shakes off the *charoses.* . . ."

What do we need to "shake off"? Are we "shakers off" or "adders on"? As we complete this portion of our passage through Pesach, we've added to our understanding of several key holiday observances that perhaps we hadn't thought much about. And we've shaken off notions that these seder plate objects are mere anachronisms, with no contemporary meaning. We've now seen the seder as symbol, as storyteller, and as teacher. The many seder rituals deliver fuller, richer worlds of spiritual growth, in which ancient observances ground our actions with contemporary flair.

## From Our Tradition

Yea, you shall leave in joy and be led home secure.
Before you, mount and hill shall shout aloud,
And all the trees of the field shall clap their hands.
Instead of the brier, a cypress shall rise;
Instead of the nettle, a myrtle shall rise.
These shall stand as a testimony to *Adonai,*
As an everlasting sign that shall not perish.
(Isa. 55:12–13)

Torah uses the rare term *befarech* to describe the Egyptian harsh labor. Rabbi Elazar explained, "Don't read *be-farech* 'with harshness' but *be-fe-rach* 'with soft speech,' a silvery tongue. . . . Pharaoh told Israel:

"Please do me a favor today and give me a hand." Pharaoh took a rake and a basket and began to make mud bricks. Israel did the same, enthusiastically working with him the whole day. When it grew dark, Pharaoh appointed taskmasters over them to count the bricks. "That will be your daily quota." (*Tanchuma Buber, B'haalot'cha*)

Rabbi Bunam said: We eat matzah first and *maror* next, though it would seem the reverse order is appropriate, since we first suffered and later were freed. However, as long as there was no prospect of being delivered, Israel didn't feel the bitterness of the experience keenly. But as soon as Moses spoke to them of freedom, they awoke to the bitterness of their slavery. (Michael Strassfeld)

# The Third Cup—*V'gaalti*:
# The Many Moods of Miracles

I will redeem you with an outstretched arm and through extraordinary acts: judgments, chastisements. (Exod. 6:6)

And *Adonai* brought us forth out of Egypt with a mighty hand and an outstretched arm, with great awe-inspiring acts and with signs and wondrous portents. (Deut. 26:8)

To our jaded, world-weary sensibilities, it takes a lot to make a miracle. Our senses are constantly assaulted by newer, bigger, and most definitely louder phenomena, cultural commercialism going forward full throttle in order to change "ho hum" to "wow." But each year, Jews look past artificially created feats of wonder as we once again marvel at our own redemption. How could we, a people who lived as slaves for hundreds of years in a land not our own, pushed to our physical limits and beyond by unfeeling, uncaring masters, have ever escaped this fate?

Nothing we ourselves could do could remedy our terrible situation in Egypt. We felt doomed, unable to find a way out, when suddenly strange, unnatural things began to happen. The Nile River, that bountiful body of water on which all of Egypt was dependent, turned blood red and foul. The incessant croaking of frogs drove Egyptians mad; hailstorms and cattle pestilence destroyed grain fields and killed off what little animal life remained. Other horrors continued to plague the land and its people. Blaming their Jewish slaves for these awful events, Egyptian taskmasters made our lives even more difficult, forcing us to work even harder under the unrelenting desert sun.

Our tradition tells us that we could have done nothing to escape— on our own. We were trapped in an unending cycle of misery in Egypt until

... their cries for help rose up to God. God heard their moaning, and God remembered God's covenant with Abraham and Isaac and Jacob. God looked down upon the Israelites, and God took notice of them. (Exod. 2:23–25)

Only God's direct action could affect this stunning series of reversals, genuine miracles that altered the very nature of things God created. Hearing our pleas for help, God at the same time hardened Pharaoh's will to free his Jewish slaves until an ascendancy of misfortunes killed the firstborn in every Egyptian household. Then, did Pharaoh finally believe in the incredible power of the Jewish God? In the short run, absolutely. Then, did the astounded Israelite slaves finally accept the majestic devotion of God? In the short run, they did.

But because of our incurably brief memory spans, we need to be reminded at each Pesach seder of the miracles God performed for us. These marvels instruct us that God exists in the world. We are commanded to keep an eternal remembrance of what our eyes have witnessed and proclaim this testament to our most wondrous miracles of all, our children. Eternal doubters that we are, our adult sensibilities also benefit from the annual spiritual tune-up the seder affords us, renewing what the modern Jewish philosopher Abraham Joshua Heschel refers to as our "radical amazement," our "legacy of wonder." By the end of the seder, our reacquaintance with what God did for our people so long ago reinvigorates our faith in divine portents. The merciful acts God showered on us urge on the good deeds we do today, each for the other, another modern miracle of this Third Cup of Pesach.

## With an Outstretched Arm, with Signs and Wonders

The Haggadah is clear. If we fail to grasp its message the first time, the Bible emphasizes *Adonai*'s passionate involvement over and over again.

> I will pass through the land of Egypt on that night [I and no angel];
> I will slay all the firstborn in the land of Egypt [I and no seraph];
> and upon all the gods of Egypt will I execute Judgments [I and no messenger]; I, Adonai [it is I and no other]. (Exod. 12:12)

The Torah teaches that all signs and wonders, might and mystery, are the work of the hand of God. The plagues are not accidental, nor are they coincidental aberrations of nature, no matter what some scientists or skeptics suggest. Our tradition makes certain we understand that all the credit for Israel's redemption from Egypt goes to the One God, to *Adonai* alone. This directly contrasts with the theological panoply of Egypt, saturated with gods "explaining" natural occurrences. The sun god had as his responsibility warming the earth, while the moon god's paler brilliance shone after her more powerful peer "retired" for the evening. The Nile River god controlled the water's currents and direction. Numerous fertility gods either withheld or bestowed their beneficence.

Language from the traditional Haggadah asserts that the Egyptians' belief in their deities, with their omnipresent allure, also influenced the religious beliefs of Israel: "Our ancestors were idol worshipers." Only the most powerful weapons from God's personal arsenal, unleashed by God's own "hand," could wrest a theologically challenged Israel from the grasp of wholly idolatrous Egypt.

The late-eighteenth-century Lithuanian sage the Vilna Gaon likens God's outstretched arm to the sword God used to kill the firstborn of Egypt. Its visibility is said to have led the Children of Israel out of Egypt. In some Yemenite and Iraqi Haggadot, God explicitly warns the angels not to interfere with what is "going down" in Egypt. These interpretations also implicitly downplay any human assistance, specifically help from Moses, the first Jewish prophet. Maybe to devalue his Egyptian upbringing, or maybe to emphasize that this was the work of the Divine and not of a human, the Haggadah does not mention Moses even once in its narrative. One commentator notes that the phrase "God's outstretched arm" is found in the Septuagint, the early Greek translation of the Bible from the fourth century B.C.E. The exclusion of Moses' name from the Haggadah is thus a very old tradition.

But several other commentators point to the word "signs," *otot*, as an appeasement to the pro-Moses contingent. They equate *otot* with the shepherd's staff Moses first used when working for his father-in-law Jethro, tending the flocks in Midian, and which he then took to Egypt. There God told Moses to employ the staff's magical powers to convince both Jewish doubters and Pharaoh's advisors of the seriousness of God's intentions. Moses threw down his staff, turning it into a serpent, and then reversed this "sign," changing the snake back to a staff. Moses continued to make use of his staff to perform miracles, parting the Red Sea with it and miraculously sending water gushing from a rock in the wilderness. Might Moses have overextended his powers, appropriating acts God had reserved for God's own use, thus losing the right to enter the Promised Land? It is possible the editors of the Haggadah might have thought so, expunging the mention of Moses from the authorized Haggadah text.

## "I Will Lay My Hand upon the Egyptians . . . with Extraordinary Judgments" (Exod. 7:4)

The Torah has no such subliminal agenda. In the Book of Exodus, God directly employs Moses and his brother Aaron to carry out many of the miracles described there, including most of the Ten Plagues, *Eser Makot*. The plagues unleashed God's relentless strength against Egypt so that the Children of Israel could gain their freedom. The Ten Plagues were actually "ten blows" to the most powerful nation on earth, threatening to transform the fundamental order of nature into demonic chaos. The Talmud explains two ways of understanding the plagues. Rabbi Eliezer teaches that they demonstrated God's kindness to Israel, thus serving as manifestations of the Hebrew letters *yod-hei-vav-hei* (יהוה), the four-letter Tetragrammaton, the most sacred, never-pronounced visualization of God's name, representing God's attribute of mercy. Others dispute this meaning. Rabbi Akiva interprets the plagues as retribution paid to Egypt, calling up God's five-letter name, *Elohim—alef-lamed-hei-yod-mem* (אלהים)—distinguishing God's attribute of justice.

Not willing to make due with a mere ten kindnesses to Israel or punishments to Egypt, three of our most beloved Sages saw fit to engage in a little rabbinic hyperbole in the Haggadah. Rabbis Yose the Galilean, Eliezer, and Akiva either multiplied the number of plagues Egypt suffered while the Jews were still in their midst or created additional plagues the Egyptian soldiers were forced to withstand at the shores of the Red Sea. The contemporary scholar Adin Steinsaltz states that these Rabbis wanted to prove the plagues were even more harsh and difficult than as described in Torah. In contrast, the Vilna Gaon believed that overall a finite number of plagues existed. Therefore, the greater the number of afflictions inflicted upon the Egyptians at the time of the

Exodus, the fewer number of diseases or misfortunes Israel would suffer at a future date.

Thus, some of our teachers expanded the number of plagues. Yet Rabbi Judah shrank them to compose a mnemonic made up of words using the first Hebrew letters of each plague, *D'TZACH, ADASH,* and *B'ACHAV,* to help people remember them. Since these "words" represent the names of the plagues in Hebrew, and no similar memory aids exist in other languages, including English, they are less user friendly to the last few generations of Jews than they probably were to Jews of earlier times. For those who can make sense of the mnemonic, the talmudic dictum "A person should teach students succinctly" has fine merit. The medieval Spanish scholar Abarbanel states that each group of letters refutes a particular Egyptian heretical doctrine, transforming them into solid Jewish theology: *D'TZACH* = God as the source of all existence; *ADASH* = God's sweeping involvement with humanity's life on earth; and *B'ACHAV* = God's power is limitless.

A more practical explanation of the mnemonic comes from the mid-twentieth-century academic Solomon Zeitlin. Zeitlin believes that the reason Rabbi Judah thought it necessary to give a mnemonic rendering of the Ten Plagues has nothing to do with their discussion in the Book of Exodus, but their mention in other Jewish sacred books, which could cause confusion. For example, Psalm 78 describes only seven plagues, not mentioning *kinim,* "vermin"; *dever,* "pestilence"; or *choshech,* "darkness." Psalm 105 discusses eight, leaving out *arov,* "wild beasts," and *choshech* as well. The Book of Jubilees, a second-century B.C.E. text, lists all ten, but in an order different from that of Exodus. Even Josephus, the first-century-C.E. Jewish historian, lists only nine in his book *Antiquities,* omitting *dever.* Rabbi Judah's mnemonic performed a service for seder observers two thousand years ago, setting them straight on the number of plagues to commemorate and the order in which to list them.

A rational, scientific approach to the plagues could logically explain them as chain reactions to ecological catastrophe. For example, the first Egyptian plague, which the Bible describes as turning the water of the Nile River into blood, could have looked similar to what today we call "red tide." During the time of Israelite enslavement, this proliferation of algae might have killed off most of the fish, which therefore were not around to eat their usual quota of tadpoles. So, many more than the usual number of frogs metamorphosed, creating the horrific croaking associated with frogs, the second plague. Natural misfortunes, say the rationalists, continued to multiply, with more widespread devastation directly attacking the accumulated grain storage. The end result: contamination of the stored food supply, causing anyone who ate from it to die. Since Egyptian custom dictated that the firstborn eat first, this population was decimated by the time the rest of the Egypt became aware of the problem.

Whatever happened more than three thousand years ago in Egypt, Jews today commemorate this part of our birth story at the seder by pouring out sixteen drops from our wine cups. They symbolize blood, fire, and columns of smoke as described by the prophet Joel (3:3–4), the Ten Plagues, and the three mnemonic plague-group abbreviations of Rabbi Judah.

Partaking in the solemn ritual of remembering the plagues brings up an interesting dilemma, noted and discussed by our Rabbis. Of course, we justify the devastation and horrors caused by the plagues because of their end result, Jewish liberation. And yet, they caused grim suffering to human beings, each of whom, we believe, was created in the image of God. As the maxim from the Book of Proverbs tells us, "If your enemy falls, do not exult; if he trips, let your heart not rejoice" (24:17). Our tradition also places God squarely in the middle of this same quandary. A midrash quotes God's innermost thoughts as determined by the stern face of justice: "Since My children and I are partners in trouble; it is right that I Myself smite in requital those that hate them." A second narrative reveals God's more compassionate nature. The angels wanted to sing victorious songs to celebrate the drowning of Pharaoh's army in the Red Sea. God angrily told them to keep quiet: "My children are dying, and you are about to sing."

We take note of this dilemma during the seder. We rejoice in our freedom even as we mourn the Egyptian dead. The drops of wine we spill diminish our joy, causing us to praise and bless God with less than full glasses, our acknowledgment of the pain and suffering of others. As we notice when we read this part of the Haggadah, our tradition does not overly dwell on the plagues. The Sages go to great lengths to be sensitive to the plight of Egypt. To highlight the principle that we should not celebrate the downfall of our enemies, the Torah speaks of Pesach as the season of our liberation, rather than the time when Egypt was destroyed. A more modern text from the nineteenth century was written by a rabbi who was part of the Musar movement, whose main teaching focused on ethics. He describes feeling empathy for others, even one's enemies: "Our teachers listed the ability to help bear the burdens of others as a desirable quality for study of Torah. Sympathy for another flows from our power to put ourselves in the place of the other."

The contemporary Israeli scholar Menachem Kasher cites the Rabbis' expansion of a biblical text to emphasize this point among the Israelite slaves in Egypt: "And God saw the Children of Israel, and God knew" (Exod. 2:25). "What did God see? God saw the Israelites showing mercy to one another. When one completed the required quota of bricks, he proceeded to help his fellow. God saw these actions, and knew Israel to be worthy of divine compassion." When we preserve the life and well-being of those who are persecuted, be they enemy or friend, we preserve the life of another—our own.

## "He Lifted Up His Rod and Struck the Water of the Nile" (Exod. 7:20)

Two of the Ten Plagues stand out whenever we think of Pesach: the first plague, *dam*, "blood," and the last plague, *makat b'chorot*, "the slaying of the firstborn." *Dam*, turning the Nile into a river of blood, connects the specific Haggadah experience of the plagues with two earlier Exodus narratives. The first reminds us that the Nile waters were a refuge for the infant Moses, hiding him from the Egyptians sent to murder all of Israel's male infants. Therefore a midrash identifies Aaron, not Moses, as the person who actually "lifted up his rod" to turn the Nile into blood, in deference to the river's previous sheltering of his younger brother, the baby Moses. The second recalls that blood is not something to be feared for Israel, but the ultimate protective substance, a signal to God to pass over Jewish houses as *Adonai* purposely kills the firstborn of the Egyptians.

For the first nine *makot*, or plagues, any actual deaths of human Egyptians were incidental to the primary, designated intent. With the last, *makat b'chorot*, killing of the firstborn, God unleashes a divine fury never before seen in Egypt. Because Egypt had the audacity to enslave the people of Israel, whom God calls *b'nei v'chori*, "my own firstborn" (Exod. 4:22), God punished the entire nation by slaying their eldest:

> . . . from the firstborn of Pharaoh who sits on his throne to the firstborn of the slave girl who is behind the millstones; and all the firstborn of the cattle." (Exod. 11:5)

Just as Egypt in fact inflicted a living death on the Children of God, so God slew Egypt's firstborn children, as well as those of their cattle, their most important food supply. A midrash from *P'sikta Rabbati* describes the anguish of Egyptian parents: "Rabbi Nathan taught: It was customary in Egypt that when a firstborn died, a statue was fashioned that resembled the dead child. When God smote the firstborn, this statue was smashed as well, broken up into fragments. Parents regarded this destruction as their child's second death."

A second midrashic anthology, *P'sikta D'Rav Kahana*, lauds God's unerring powers in discerning the Egyptian birth order: "Rabbi Nehemiah said: No other being in the world is able to distinguish between the seed of a first birth and the seed that is not. Only the Holy One can so distinguish. For my part, said Moses, making a distinction of this kind is utterly beyond me." In our time, Elie Wiesel has assumed the burden of proclaiming the world's inhumanities, calling them to our attention by raising his voice and his pen in protest. In his commentary to the Haggadah, he tries to uncover God's motives for performing this terrible deed: "Why does God boast of killing innocent children, be they Egyptian? Why does He mention it so often? Is He proud of it? . . . Is He teaching us an essential lesson? That He alone may kill? And that no one has the right to imitate Him?"

## How Much More Should We Be Grateful to God!

Our passage through the plagues that presaged the Exodus makes the next seder observance, our singing God's praises, even more meaningful. Numbering our gratitude to the Divine, we sing the "Dayeinu," one of the most beloved seder songs. Each year during Pesach we are reminded of the difference between "more" and "enough," not an easy concept to come by in this, the Age of Conspicuous Consumption. We say thank you to God for overdoing it, expressing gratefulness for every facet of God's miraculous deliverance. Understanding that liberation comes in small steps, saying "Dayeinu" teaches us not to despair when our ultimate end seems distant. The sage Avraham Pam compares this to the experience of entering a perfumery. Even if we don't buy anything, we still leave the shop in an aura of its sweet surrounding scents.

We praise God, who not only brought the Jewish people out of slavery, but has continued to bestow kindnesses upon us throughout history. The medieval Spanish commentator Abarbanel credits Rabbi Akiva with deciding what to include and what not to include in our "Dayeinu" praises. As we introduce it, the familiar melody begins to play in our minds. First we ask together in Hebrew, *kamah maalot tovot,* "with how many good 'stages' [or levels] has God seen fit to bless us," for any one of them would have been enough to earn our most heartfelt thanks.

"Dayeinu" is composed of fifteen separate thanksgiving utterances, suggesting several other groups of fifteen in the Jewish lexicon. At the Temple in Jerusalem, fifteen steps led to the main altar, where the Levites stood when they sang hymns and praises to God during the daily sacrifices. A section of Psalms, called *Shir HaMaalot,* "Songs of Ascent," number fifteen; we chant several of them in our two-part Haggadah *Hallel.* And let us not forget that our seder is itself composed of fifteen steps, from *kadeish,* the blessing over the first cup of wine, to *nirtzah,* the conclusion of the seder. Finally, if we add the numerical significance of the Hebrew letters *yod* and *hei,* we get fifteen. *Yod* and *hei* spell *Yah,* a name of God often used when referring to the Divine in worship.

For the ancient editors of the Haggadah, celebrating Pesach as merely the physical escape of the Jewish people from Egypt was not sufficient. The traditional "Dayeinu" might begin with praising God for taking us out of Egypt, but it ends by commemorating our receiving of the Sabbath, our coming to Mount Sinai, our acceptance of Torah, and our worship of God in the Temple in the Land of Israel. These concepts define the ideologies of Judaism every bit as much as the matzah we eat during Pesach and place our passage on a holy trajectory in our history, which in the litany of the traditional Haggadah ends more than two thousand years ago. Recently two New York rabbis updated the "Dayeinu":

## IT WOULD HAVE BEEN ENOUGH . . .

Had God upheld us throughout two thousand years of Dispersion
But not preserved our hope for return

*Dayeinu!*

Had God preserved our hope for return
But not sent us leaders to make the dream a reality

*Dayeinu!*

Had God returned us to the land of our ancestors
But not filled it with our children

*Dayeinu!*

Had God filled it with our children
But not caused the desert to bloom

*Dayeinu!*

Had God planted in our hearts a covenant of one people
But not sustained in our souls a vision of a perfected world

*Dayeinu!*

## "After Eating the Pesach Offering, They Do Not End with *Afikoman*"
### (*Mishnah P'sachim* 10:8)

Our children—be they our sons or daughters, our nephews, nieces, or cousins, our friends or our students—are our most thrilling miracles, each containing elements of all four of the children described in the Haggadah. A high point of the seder is watching them search for the *afikoman,* running around in an explosion of at-last unleashed energy.

Though the current understanding of *afikoman* is a time filled with joy and laughter, the Mishnah purposefully forbids concluding the evening with its positive excitement. The Sages were reacting to the then-widespread Greek banquet custom of eating at one place and, after dinner, strolling from house to house, drinking and carousing. By the end of the evening, a sedate dinner might be long forgotten in the mind-dazing party atmosphere that followed. Equating *afikoman* with the Greek *epikomios,* successive wine-soaked processions from house to house, was frowned upon. It didn't fit with the family gatherings that define the first Jewish meal of Pesach, concentrating as it does on a multigenerational get-together.

So, following the Mishnah's instructions, we do not end the evening's festivities with the children's pursuit but ask them to look for the *afikoman* right after the meal, before they get too sleepy. Searching for the *afikoman* is the world's oldest treasure hunt, one more seder activity designed with the children in mind. We listen very attentively to the children's questions asked early in the evening and attempt to keep priming their curiosity by eating unusual foods and dipping them into each other. We cannot do without the active, inventive participation of the children. Since the seder cannot continue until they find the *afikoman* and give it back to us, they can make all sorts of demands, holding it and us hostage until we give in. Children usually play this to the hilt, reveling in the power they don't normally have, making seder night quite different and quite magical.

Designating the *afikoman* as the "stay at home" seder symbol takes us back to the Pesach in Egypt, when no Israelite dared set foot outside for the entire night. We read in Exodus:

> None of you shall go outside the door of your house until morning. (Exod. 12:22)

While today we all eat a small portion of the found matzah in a festive atmosphere, that first night was spent in uncertainty and fear. The *afikoman* also reminds us of the *pesach* sacrifice at the time of the Temple, when the roasted paschal lamb was the very last food eaten, to make sure that the memory of the Exodus lingered after the celebrating had concluded. After the Temple's destruction, the *afikoman* continued to be the very last food of the night, in commemoration of the *pesach* sacrifice. Two Rabbis from the Talmud, Samuel and Yochanan, thus translate *afikoman* as dessert, the final item on the menu, combining the sweet memories of the Exodus with the more somber concerns that preceded it.

Were we to look for the word *afikoman* in the list of seder steps taking us through the Haggadah, we would not find it. In its place we would discover *tzafun*, "that which is hidden." Even though the *afiko-man* matzah is concealed from sight, the children are still sure it is there. They just have to look a little harder, perhaps imagining themselves in the mind of the person who hid it in order to figure out the most likely place to find it. In the vast Jewish experience of memory, in our sacred texts and our precious rituals and observances lovingly passed down from parent to child, we feel confident that we will locate God, who at times seems quite unapproachable and distant. But first, we must become as children, seeking God with fresh, imaginative eyes.

Even for the fortunate few of us whose personal faith is rock solid, lingering uncertainties still occasionally appear. Most of us accept doubt as a constant companion. Though we sincerely want to believe the prayers we say and the blessings we sing, we freely admit how hard it is sometimes for our mind to affirm the feelings of our heart. Perhaps it might be possible to shift our focus, at least for one or two nights a year, and, like the broken matzah of the *afikoman,* our faith can be found and made whole once again. Perhaps beginning first at Pesach, if we work very hard to suspend our skepticism and genuinely locate ourselves in the marvels of the Exodus, we might discover that, like the afikoman, God really isn't so hidden after all. Now that would be a miracle indeed!

## From Our Tradition

Rabbi Abun said in the name of Rabbi Judah ben Pazi: Bithiah the daughter of Pharaoh was a firstborn. By what merit did she escape death? Through the merit of Moses' prayer for her. Of her it is written: "She perceived that Moses, who was called a goodly child, was a shield, and that therefore her lamp—her soul—had not gone out by night" (Prov. 31:18). . . . Hence it is assumed that on this night Bithiah's lamp did not go out—that is, her life was spared. (*P'sikta D'Rav Kahana* 7:10)

Rabbi Levi bar Zechariah taught in the name of Rabbi Berechiah: God set upon Egypt with the tactics of warrior kings. First God shut off their water conduits by turning the waters of the Nile into blood. Then God brought up loud voices to confuse them—frogs. After that God shot arrows at them—gnats. . . . Then God shot stones at them from catapults—hail. God arrayed scalers of walls against them—locusts. . . . God put them in prisons—threw them into darkness. And then God led forth . . . the oldest among each and every one and slew [them]—the plague of the firstborn at midnight. (*P'sikta Rabbati* 17.7)

We do not mean to suggest, *chalilah,* we would have been content not to have received these blessings [the "Dayeinu"]. How could we imagine not having been given Torah, the Sabbath, Eretz Yisrael, the Temple, and everything else mentioned in this song of gratitude? Rather our meaning is, any one of these gifts would have been sufficient to require infinite expressions of gratitude on our part. How much more grateful must we be that God has given us all of these precious gifts? (Malbim)

# The Fourth Cup—*V'lakachti*: Songs of Blessing and Praise to God

And I will take you to be My people, and I will be your God. (Exod. 6:7)

Therefore we are obligated to give thanks, to praise, to crown, to exalt, to elevate the One who did for us all these miracles and took us out of slavery to freedom, and let us say before God, Hallelujah. (*Mishnah P'sachim* 10:5)

When I was quite small, I remember being fascinated with lyrics to a popular song I heard on the radio: "When I'm weary, and I can't sleep, I count my blessings instead of sheep, and I fall asleep, counting my blessings." Suffering from insomnia even then, I used to sing the words to myself over and over again until I grew drowsy. Now I realize that I repeated the words to the song instead of following its advice because I didn't understand the concept of a blessing. I never thought to ask my parents, figuring it was one of those many "grown-up things" that would become clear to me as I grew older.

Several decades later I am well aware and, in saner moments, unimaginably thankful for my veritable deluge of blessings. Yet it is not these that I recount during all those 3 A.M. mornings, but the ogres of looming deadlines and the demons of unanswered e-mails. What should be the detritus of my life, mere debris barely acknowledged, now tends to take over even my semiconsciousness. I confess to being sorely in need of a comprehensive, cosmic reality check. To quote from another song of my youth, "How long has this been going on?"

Of course there is a simple, Jewish remedy. For more than two thousand years, Jews have begun each day by focusing not on themselves, but on God. Through the morning blessings we say and the psalms we recite to *Adonai*, we become automatically in tune to a higher purpose, to make God's work our work, transcending personal problems and pettiness. But for most of us, reciting prayers daily, much less three times a day as our tradition teaches, is not part of our lifestyle. So let us begin gradually, with the words we say and sing each seder. By determinedly reaching out to our Redeemer at least during Pesach, when we celebrate the very real redemption of Israel, we become God-centered almost subconsciously. Thanking our Provider for performing this wondrous deed for our people in the past, we can expand the occasions we offer thanks for our present abundance of blessings. And who knows? We might very well start a pattern of recognizing all sorts of sacred opportunities, resolutely drawing closer to God and glorying in the relationship.

## "Let Us Sing a New Song, Sing God's Praises. Hallelujah!" (*Mishnah P'sachim* 10:5)

In the previous chapter we discussed the "Dayeinu," recalling how any one gift from God would have been enough. Then the Haggadah talks about Rabban Gamliel's three obligations for celebrating Pesach, reviewing the meaning of the paschal sacrifice, matzah, and *maror*. We are reminded of our quite real duty to view ourselves as having been redeemed from Egypt, commanded to tell our children the story each year during Pesach. Our goal: to participate in the Exodus experience with the fervor of a just-freed slave.

Now we have arrived at a seminal point in our seder, approaching a critical mitzvah, the commandment to praise God. *L'fichach*, "therefore," we raise our wine glasses and exult *Adonai* with the list of nine acclamations from the Mishnah ("give thanks, praise, crown, exalt . . .") that began this chapter. The late-eighteenth-century commentator the Vilna Gaon relates these to the first nine plagues God inflicted on Egypt.

The Vilna Gaon also says that the tenth and final plague, the killing of the firstborn, talks figuratively of a future redemption, a *shirah chadashah*, a "new song" Israel will sing to God. After all, singing hymns to honor *Adonai* is a time-honored Jewish tradition. When Israel crossed the Red Sea, the spontaneous response, "I will sing to *Adonai*, for God has triumphed gloriously" (Exod. 15:1), shows that singing and praising God in response to divine intercession and redemption come naturally to a God-fearing people.

At our seders, we begin our homage to God's marvelous acts on our behalf by singing *Hallel,* songs of praise from the Book of Psalms. In fact, the first word in the first song, Psalm 113, is *hal'luyah,* combining *hallel,* "praise," with *Yah,* one of the names of God. We start with an almost perfunctory thank-you, "O servants of *Adonai,* give praise" (Ps. 113:1), a relatively simple, straightforward statement, then move steadily upward until we realize that what God has done for us is beyond thanks. No words exist to convey God's wondrous deeds and our emotional response. Nevertheless, we pile up verb after verb, song after song to honor the Holy One, until hopefully our passage leads into the actual experience of the holy, overflowing with passion for *Adonai.*

A firm historic base grounds these songs that revere God. Almost three thousand years ago, already during the time of the First Temple, singers coordinated their sacrifices with songs. This practice continued in a more elaborate fashion as part of the Second Temple pageantry, as Levites sang psalms to accompany the many sacrifices the priests performed. According to the Talmud, such songs were also chanted in the Temple on the day before Pesach, while the paschal lambs were slaughtered. After the Temple was destroyed and prayer substituted for sacrifice, it became clear that the early Rabbis sanctioned sacred singing by individuals as an important adjunct to Judaism's survival.

Medieval commentators called tosafists determined that the Jewish people could recite psalms in any language. A parable by Rabbi Eliahu Lopian, a nineteenth-century *musar* sage, gives voice to this ruling: "A simple man stood before a king and began to sing. They tried to shush him up, but he persisted. 'The king is my king,' he said. 'If he finds it fit to be my king, it is fitting that he hear my song.'" So, too, if it is fitting for *Adonai* to be called our Ruler, it seems right for God to hear our songs of praise, *Hallel,* however we are able to express them. The singing of these psalms at Pesach was so critical to Sages living in Palestine that they incorporated the following ruling into the Jerusalem Talmud (*Y'rushalmi*), the Talmud written in the Land of Israel: "In those parts of Galilee where most people were functionally illiterate, they assembled in their synagogue to recite *Hallel* under the leadership of a knowledgeable man," and then returned home to continue the seder with their families.

While these psalms are said throughout the year as part of the Shabbat and festival liturgy, their recital during the seder has a distinguishing flavor all its own. Even the name given to these particular psalms connotes a Pesach theme. Psalms 113–118 are referred to in the Talmud as "Egyptian *Hallel*" because of the mention of the Exodus at the beginning of Psalm 114. Only during the Pesach seder do we say them in the evening. There is a practical understanding for this, for only during daylight hours can God's many works be seen and thus honored. However, because the night of Pesach is unique in the Jewish calendar, the time of Jewish redemption, when for God "night is as light as day" (Ps. 139:12), saying psalms of thanks to God at night is certainly desired as well as justified. Usually when we chant *Hallel* in synagogue we stand, to give full honor to God. Only during the seder do we remain seated during *Hallel*, signifying our freedom from Egyptian tyranny. And although we continue to sing psalms for the duration of Pesach week, only during the seder is the complete Egyptian *Hallel* sung. A midrash relates that because Egyptian soldiers who pursued the people of Israel were drowned in the Red Sea on the seventh day of Pesach, Jewish triumph should be muted in deference to the suffering of the Egyptian people.

## "Before God's Presence, Tremble, Earth" (Ps. 114:7)

*Hallel* is sung in two parts during the seder. Psalms 113 and 114 appear in the Haggadah right before the meal. After eating, we "discover" that the *afikoman* is missing. Since we can't proceed without it, children scurry about in their search, and adults stand and move about, the "seventh-inning stretch" of the evening. We then all eat from the retrieved *afikoman* matzah, traditionally the last food of the evening. The *Birkat HaMazon*, the Blessing after Meals, is recited, another occasion to offer numerous accolades of tribute to God. Following *Birkat HaMazon* the mood shifts from acknowledgment of past redemption, the Exodus, to the promise of future salvation. Will this be the year that the prophet Elijah, the harbinger of the Messiah, at last comes to signal the beginning of eternal peace and harmony? After the door to welcome Elijah is closed, we proceed to the second part of *Hallel*.

This brief review of several seder observances prepares us for the remainder of the evening. The Mishnah records a lively debate between those classic combatants, the House of Hillel and the House of Shammai, over which Psalms are said before the meal and which are said following dinner: "Up to what point does [a person] recite the *Hallel*? The House of Shammai said, Until 'He sets the childless woman among her household as a happy mother of children,' [the end of Psalm 113]. The House of Hillel said, Until 'Tremble . . . at the presence of the Lord . . . who turned the flinty rock into a fountain' [the end of Psalm 114]. The House of Shammai's reasoning: Psalm 114 begins, 'When Israel went out of Egypt. . . .' If it is said together with Psalm 113, some could imply that the Jewish people were freed and left during the night. But they did not leave during the night; they were confined in their houses (to avoid being caught in the killing of the firstborns). So reciting Psalm 114 at this time is inappropriate. The House of Hillel responds: Since the Exodus did not occur until the next day, Psalm 114 should not be recited at all at the seder. So we might as well sing it together with Psalm 113, before the meal." Though not one of the more profound discussions of our Sages, it does offer a glimpse into their humorous, playful style, nonetheless.

## "Let the Name of *Adonai* Be Blessed Now and Forever" (Ps. 113:2)*

As the singing of the *Hallel* begins, the atmosphere of the seder changes from instruction to joyful expectancy. From the very beginning of Psalm 113, we sense that our status has been transformed. In Egypt, Jews were forced to act as Pharaoh's slaves. Once free, Jews blissfully become "servants of *Adonai*" (113:1). Even before we thank *Adonai* for God's special intervention in Egypt, we offer our gratitude to God for the miracle of our altered existence:

> Who is like *Adonai* our God,
> who, enthroned on high,

---

*Because *Passage to Pesach* explores the major themes of the holiday, discussion of specific psalms will be limited, giving only a brief taste of all the blessings and praises sung during seder. Hopefully readers will enjoy the sampling enough to seek out the psalms and blessings in their entirety. This chapter's "From Our Tradition" section is devoted to more comprehensive examples of their beautiful poetry.

sees what is below . . . ?
God raises the poor from the dust,
lifts up the needy from the refuse heap. (Ps. 113:5–7)

Psalm 113 concludes with the blessed promise of fertility, the assurance that there will be generations who come after us:

God sets the childless woman among her household
as a happy mother of children.
Hallelujah. (Ps. 113:9)

Psalm 114 speaks directly of the Exodus experience and of the special attention God paid to Israel at the time of the Exodus. The psalm's parallel imagery, a hallmark of biblical poetry, is especially magnificent here:

When Israel went forth from Egypt,
the House of Jacob from a people of strange speech,
Judah became God's holy one,
Israel, God's dominion. (Ps. 114:1–2)

Biblical commentators cite the people of Israel as deserving of extraordinary credit for not succumbing to Egyptian civilization and assimilating into the culture of their rulers, "a people of strange speech." Instead, they held on to their own language and faith, against the allure of Egypt's impressive array of deities and, by implication, their general immorality.

## "When You Have Eaten Your Fill, Give Thanks to *Adonai*" (Deut. 8:10)

The seder meal, filled as it always is with an overabundance of delicious food, lends another opportunity to celebrate God's incredible generosity to the Jews. We insert the festival meal into the midst of the *Hallel,* signaling that on this night, even eating too much is a form of praise to God. The Haggadah devotes one of its distinct "steps," *bare-ich,* to our expression of astounding thankfulness, as we sing *Birkat*

*HaMazon,* the Blessing after Meals. As Adin Steinsaltz states, "The Grace after meals is essentially an act of remembering as it progresses from the simple immediate to the abstract future. Ultimately, in its essence, it is an expression of gratitude to the Provider." The twentieth-century Jewish philosopher Emmanuel Levinas draws a parallel between the single act of reciting the *Birkat HaMazon* and one of the most spectacular of the Exodus wonders: "Saying grace is an act of the greatest importance. To be able to eat and drink is a possibility as extraordinary, as miraculous, as the crossing of the Red Sea."

Commentators traditionally separate the *Birkat HaMazon* into four main parts. It can be seen as a rising series of blessings, similar to the classic description of Psalm 126, "A Song of Ascents," which functions as a sort of preamble to the entire *Birkat HaMazon.* Although Psalm 126 focuses on a later event, the Jews' return from the Babylonian exile after the destruction of the First Temple, it surely could be viewed as an account of Israel's benumbed delight when at last freed from Egyptian bondage:

> When *Adonai* restores the fortunes of Zion
> we will be like dreamers.
> Then our mouths will be filled with laughter,
> our tongues with songs of joy. (Ps. 126:1–2)

The first *Birkat HaMazon* blessing is the primary one relating to the meal: "God gives sustenance to all flesh, for God's loving-kindness is everlasting." In the second blessing, thanks is offered for the land and for providing us with food from the earth: "We extend thanks to You, *Adonai* our God, for having given to our ancestors a lovely, good, and spacious land." The third blessing asks for the reestablishment of the city of Jerusalem as the Jewish spiritual center, calling to mind the heartrending words of another psalm:

> By the rivers of Babylon,
> there we sat and wept. . . .
> Our captors asked us there for songs . . .
> "Sing us one of the songs of Zion."
> How can we sing a song of *Adonai*
>     on alien soil? (Ps. 137:1, 3–4)

At peak moments of spirituality we are transported to Jerusalem, the place where our ultimate purpose and dreams connect. Our fourth and final blessing invokes God as all-merciful. We thank *Adonai* for the countless good things with which we have been favored. "God was bountiful to us, is bountiful to us, and will forever be bountiful to us— with grace, loving-kindness, compassion and relief, rescue and success, blessing and salvation."

## "Not to Us, O *Adonai* . . . but to Your Name Bring Glory" (Ps. 115:1)

The message of the Haggadah shifts from the past redemption of the Exodus to our fervent wish for final salvation, not for our own sake, but to bestow all ultimate honors to God. Since "the dead cannot praise *Adonai*" (Ps. 115:17), it is up to us, as long as we are blessed with breath, to "bless *Adonai* now and forever" (115:18). In Psalm 116, collective speech becomes personal: "I love *Adonai* for God hears my voice, my pleas" (116:1). Each individual begs for God's assistance to find just the right way to love God: "How can I repay *Adonai* for all Your bounties to me?" (116:12). Building on the theme of blessed thankfulness for no longer being forced to live as slaves of Pharaoh, we pledge fealty to *Adonai*:

> O *Adonai,*
> "I am Your servant,
> Your servant, the child of your maidservant;
> You have undone the cords that bound me." (Ps. 116:16)

The Alter of Kelm, a prominent nineteenth-century rabbi in the *musar* tradition, asks us to try to imagine ourselves as slaves who have been freed: "How would we contemplate the greatness of [our] Liberator? How would [we] sacrifice all [we] possessed—and [ourselves]—for Him?"

Composed of just two verses, Psalm 117 again changes voice. The previous poem spoke from deep within the individual Jewish soul. Here, Psalm 117 speaks to the *goyim*, the rest of humanity who as yet do not worship God. "Praise *Adonai*, all you nations; extol God, all you peoples" (117:1). The final Egyptian *Hallel,* Psalm 118, returns to the literary device of the "I," the words of an individual penitent. First recalling personal misery, "Out of the straits I called to You," we are relieved to hear God's immediate response, the very next words in the same verse, "*Adonai* answered me and brought me relief" (118:5). Some medieval Haggadot illustrate this scene by placing King David, the traditional author of the Book of Psalms, wedged between steep rocks, strumming on his harp. In Hebrew, the word for "straits" or "narrow place" is spelled מ-צ-ר, the same root as "Egypt," *Mitzrayim,* an obvious reference to the tightest, most uncomfortable place for Jews in biblical history.

The last verse of Psalm 118,

> Praise *Adonai* for God is good,
> God's steadfast love is eternal (118:29)

forms a perfect segue to the last full psalm sung at the seder, Psalm 136, *Hallel HaGadol,* "The Great *Hallel.*" Its first verse, "Praise *Adonai* . . ." repeats the just-quoted line in Psalm 118. While the kindness of God is continually demonstrated in both Psalms 118 and 136, the Great *Hallel* stands by itself as a triumphant anthem to God's eternal devotion. It recalls, in chronological order, God's marvelous deeds to the Jews, from the creation of the world to all the challenges of the Exodus. Already in Temple times, priests would sing a verse from Psalm 136, and the assembled throngs would then echo each wondrous occurrence with the words *ki l'olam chasdo,* "for God's *chesed* [kindness] endures forever." Some commentators put a midrashic spin on the psalm, saying that its twenty-six verses match the twenty-six generations between the world's beginnings and God's giving of Torah to Israel. Others note that the number twenty-six equals the numerical value of *yod-hei-vav-hei* (יהוה), the Tetragrammaton, the never-pronounced, ineffable name of God.

On this note of almost delirious exaltation, we bless the name of God with "the souls of all the living," and drink the fourth and final glass of wine of the seder meal. At least in spirit, God has indeed transported us to our Holy Land! With *nirtzah,* the last "step" in the Haggadah, we "accept" all of God's gifts and conclude the seder with the words in all of our hearts, *L'shanah habaah birushalayim,* "Next year in Jerusalem!"

## "God Is Most Mighty"

The formal part of our Pesach seder has thus ended. Our spirits are as full as our stomachs; we are overwhelmed by once again relating the story of our passage from slavery to freedom. Now the true merriment of the evening is about to begin as we sing our favorite Pesach *z'mirot,* table songs, just for the fun of it. Not only is it permissible, it is absolutely encouraged to relax and engage in all sorts of frivolity. We find an additional energy rush and sing, not because all the stories of the ballads genuinely happened, but because it feels so good to play the rhyming games and share the general silliness of the increasingly late hour, safe with family and friends.

The six songs that form most of the traditional post-seder repertoire divide into two parts. The first four are all Hebrew alphabetical acrostics; the first verse begins with the letter *alef,* and the verses proceed through the alphabet to the last letter, *tav.* These songs were written between about 600 and 1600 C.E. by Jewish poets who filled their words with messages of divine praise and adulation. It is believed that the last two songs are adaptations of popular folk songs, containing moral messages, yet geared to the child in all of us.

Before we get to the songs themselves, a few words about the genre in general are in order. Over the centuries, traditional Jewish liturgy has been embellished with emotional, heartfelt yearnings. They are known as *piyutim,* from the same Greek root that gives us the English words "poet" and "poem." Perhaps many were created during periods of religious persecution, when secular rulers forbade the chanting of Jewish litany. Other *piyutim* might have been written in times of relative calm, as substitution for the liturgy, when some Jews rebelled against what they perceived as unnecessary standardization and rigidity of fixed prayer. Originally the term designated every type of sacred Jewish poetry. As their usage developed, *piyutim* came to include only poems containing praise and thanksgiving to God, exactly the kinds of blessings and praises we have spoken of throughout this chapter.

The song "Uv'chein Vaihi BaChatzei HaLailah" (It Came to Pass at Midnight) lists in alphabetical order miracles that occurred to the Jews. According to this interpretation, the wicked were punished in the middle of the night, a recognition of God's direct action against Egypt in the form of the deaths of their firstborn. Early medieval compilers of some midrash collections expand this notion, asserting that all miracles of salvation that ever happened to the Jewish people occurred on the fourteenth of Nisan, the Pesach "night of watching." This particular *piyut* is thought to be the work of the sixth-century Palestinian poet Yannai, who originally wrote it for Shabbat HaGadol worship, on the Saturday immediately preceding Pesach. It became so popular that it was later incorporated into most Ashkenazi Haggadot. Because all events telescope into the very beginning of Pesach, customarily "It Came to Pass at Midnight" is recited only on the first seder night.

The seventh and last stanza of the song begins, "May the day draw near when it is no longer day or night. . . ." The word *kareiv,* "draw/bring near," comes from the same root as *korban,* "sacrifice." In this case we relate it to *korban pesach,* the paschal offerings made at the Temple bringing the people close to God. Today we hope that our Pesach prayers, blessings, and praises have the same effect and bring God ever nearer to us.

Eleazer Kalir, the most famous writer of *piyutim* and a pupil of Yannai, is thought to have composed the second song, "V'amartem Tzevach Pesach" (And You Shall Say: This Is the Feast of Pesach). In this song, another alphabetical acrostic, each verse details various Jewish events, which all converge on the same day, the fifteenth of Nisan. Because these events allegedly occurred on the first day of Pesach, the poem belongs to the second seder night. A midrash transports Pesach to the time of Abraham as it attempts to explain the following line from the *piyut*: "Abraham fed the angels *ugot* [cakes] on Pesach." As the story goes, the angels actually visited Abraham at midday (Gen. 18:1) of *erev* Pesach, just hours before the holiday began. The Rabbis forbade eating matzah after mid-morning on this day. This is why Abraham prepared matzah cakes, *matzah ugot,* made with eggs and fruit juice, which could be eaten *erev* Pesach. In fact, this particular food, *matzah ugot,* cannot be eaten to satisfy the commandment to eat matzah on the night of Pesach. Since *matzah ugot* may be eaten only until early afternoon of the pre-Pesach day, it explains why Abraham was in such a hurry to prepare the food for the angels (Gen. 18:6). If he had delayed even a little bit, it would have been too late to serve the cakes, since the holiday would have already started!

Several hundred years separate the composition of the first two songs and the remaining alphabetical acrostics. The third song, "Ki Lo

Na-eh" (For to God, Praise Is Proper), does not appear until the thirteenth century. The distinguishing characteristic of the song is the constant repetition of *l'cha*, "to You," appearing in each chorus seven times:

> To You, to You only,
> To You, just to You,
> To You, surely to You,
> To You belongs all dominion.

While having no direct connection to Pesach, its popularity as a general religious song led to its inclusion in medieval Haggadot.

If "Ki Lo Na-eh" seems a bit abstract to many of us, that is not the case with the fourth and final Pesach alphabetical acrostic, "Adir Hu" (Mighty Is He). One modern commentator calls this the all-time seder favorite, with a lovely melody that lingers in our minds. Its main theme, "May God build the Temple soon, Your House soon," combines praises to *Adonai* with the redemptive wish of restoring the Temple in Jerusalem. We praise God with the letters of the alphabet and look forward to the time when all of God's creatures will echo our praises.

## "Who Knows One?"

Our post-seder songs proceed from letters to numbers. Both "Echad Mi Yodei-a" (Who Knows One?) and our last song, "Chad Gadya" (An Only Kid), came from France and Germany in the fifteenth or sixteenth centuries and were originally written as Christian songs. "Who Knows One?" begins with the foremost Jewish theme of divine oneness, affirming our faith in the one omnipresent God, vibrant on earth and in the heavens. We resolutely repeat this same principle in each verse, until thirteen stanzas later we unabashedly proclaim our final ode to God, remarking on God's many attributes.

While the Christian world views the number thirteen as automatically unlucky, we Jews are drawn to the number thirteen. In addition to the number of the attributes of God as discussed in the Book of Exodus, "God is compassionate and gracious, slow to anger, abounding in kindness and faithfulness . . ." (34:6–7), the numerical value of the Hebrew word for "one," *echad,* is thirteen. If one counts the off-spring of Joseph's sons Ephraim and Manasseh as forming family units of their own, Israel was composed of not twelve, but thirteen tribes. Young Jewish children reach the age of responsibility, bat or bar mitzvah, when they reach thirteen. The medieval Jewish philosopher Maimonides identified thirteen faith principles of the Jewish people.

At my family seder we go around the table, demanding that each person recite one English stanza of "Echad Mi Yodei-a" all in one breath. Since the first stanza is quite short and the last are very long, about five minutes of serious horse trading occurs (e.g, "Mom, if you swap with me I promise to keep my room clean for a whole week"). A terrific time is had by all, as we pay tribute to our tradition of "two tablets, three patriarchs, four matriarchs, five books of Torah. . . ."

## "An Only Kid"

The evening is getting late. Both adults and children are tired and squirmy. Our rapidly diminishing powers of concentration hone in on a long-ago market scene, watching a doting Jewish father purchase a baby goat for his child. What happens next, and next, and next to *chad gadya,* this solitary animal, has been variously interpreted by Jewish commentators through the centuries. In premodern times, people could better accept the main theme of "Chad Gadya"—that for each catastrophe Jews endured, heavenly retribution would surely follow.

But today, after witnessing the most terrible deeds people inflict on each other with no divine recompense, many would agree with Elie Wiesel's impassioned words: "I loved this naïve little song in which everything seemed so simple, so primitive. . . . But that evening the song upset me. I rebelled against the resignation it implied. Why does God always act too late? Why didn't God get rid of the Angel of Death before he even committed his first murder?"

For most of us, there is no satisfactory answer to these questions, and there probably never will be. And yet, this hasn't stopped us from constantly singing God's praises, from relentlessly believing in a Holy One who truly is there for us. To whom else could we turn? How else could we continue? So each year we resolutely end the Pesach seder by proclaiming, in the present tense, words of never-ending passage and process:

The Holy, praise to Him, is coming and slaughtering the Angel of Death, who slaughtered the ox that drank the water that put out the fire that burned the stick that hit the dog that bit the cat that ate the kid that my father bought for two *zuzim,* a kid, a kid.

## From Our Tradition

Hallelujah.
Praise, O ye servants of the LORD,
Praise the name of the LORD.
Blessed be the name of the LORD
From this time forth and for ever.
From the rising of the sun unto the going down thereof
The LORD's name is to be praised. (Ps. 113:1–3)

O Israel, trust thou in the LORD!
He is their help and their shield! . . .
The heavens are the heavens of the LORD;
But the earth hath He given to the children of men. . . .
But we will bless the LORD
From this time forth and for ever, Hallelujah.
(Ps. 115:9, 16, 18)

I will give thanks unto Thee, for Thou hast answered me,
And art become my salvation.
The stone which the builders rejected
Is become the chief corner-stone.
This is the LORD's doing;
It is marvelous in our eyes.
This is the day which the LORD hath made;
We will rejoice and be glad in it. (Ps. 118:21–24)

To Him that smote Egypt in their first-born,
For His mercy endureth for ever;
And brought out Israel from among them,
For His mercy endureth for ever; . . .
O give thanks unto the God of heaven,
For His mercy endureth for ever. (Ps. 136:10–11, 26)

# ⨳ 13 ⨳

## The Fifth Cup—*V'heiveiti*:
## Elijah, Messianic Herald

And I will bring you into the land that I swore to give to Abraham, Isaac, and Jacob, and I will give it to you for a possession, I *Adonai*. (Exod. 6:8)

Pour out Your wrath upon the nations that do not know You, upon realms that do not invoke Your name. (Ps. 79:6)

If the compilers of the Pesach seder had a favorite number, it must have been four—we ask four questions, we speak of four children, four verses from the Book of Deuteronomy (26:5–8) guide us through the Haggadah narration. Four other biblical verses recited when opening the door for Elijah begin with the words from the Book of Psalms quoted above.* These four verses beseech God to open celestial floodgates of destruction, to take revenge on those who have mercilessly persecuted the Jewish people. But more on that later. For now, the number four focuses on yet another Haggadah quartet, the number of cups of wine everyone is required to drink, spread over the length of the seder.

As explained in the introduction to this section of *Passage to Pesach,* each of the first four "Wine Cup" chapters is based on one of the four divine promises of redemption from the Book of Exodus (6:6–7). The first begins, "I will bring you out from the labors of the

---

*Pour out Your wrath upon the nations that do not know You, upon realms that do not invoke Your name. For they have devoured Jacob and laid waste his home. (Ps. 79:6–7)

Pour out Your wrath upon them and may Your fierce anger overtake them. (Ps. 69:25)

Pursue them in anger and destroy them from under the heavens of Adonai. (Lam. 3:66)

Egyptians"; the last starts with the words "I will take you to be My people." So far, so good. But even the number of cups of wine in the seder ritual is rarely as straightforward as it seems. This holds true especially in matters of religious interpretation, and more especially in the spirited discussions that are the hallmark of Rabbinic Judaism. For the Talmud explains that an early-second-century Sage, Rabbi Tarfon, discusses a *fifth* cup of seder wine. Not coincidentally, later commentators validate Rabbi Tarfon's teaching by citing the biblical verse that immediately follows the four pledges from the Book of Exodus. It states:

> And I will bring you into the land. . . . (Exod. 6:8)

Wanting to distinguish the first four cups of wine from this fifth add-on, a respected early medieval rabbi explains: "There are those who say that the [first] four cups indicate four periods of exile, and the fifth cup indicates salvation." The dispute was resolved through a rare ritual compromise. A fifth cup is indeed poured, yet no one at the seder drinks from it. As the Haggadah explains, we reserve it for the prophet Elijah, who will finally resolve this controversy and all other perplexing questions when he returns to earth to announce the arrival of the Messiah.

Already in the second century, Rabbi Tarfon's fifth cup may have been viewed as a reference to the ultimate future redemption, a fervent hope building on our release from Egypt, the central redemptive event for Jews. But the connection of a fifth cup to Elijah in the Pesach Haggadah was not spelled out until a fourteenth-century rabbi, Zelikman Bingo, reported it. Since we expect Elijah to appear during the seder, wrote Bingo, we might as well prepare a cup for him before the seder begins. Otherwise, the Pesach celebration would be unnecessarily interrupted.

Even today there are various opinions about when this wine cup should be prepared. Should it be poured at the beginning of the evening, before we say *Kiddush* over the first cup, or should we pour it when we pour the fourth cup of wine? Over the past few years, our family has adopted a custom from the Chasidic rabbi Naphtali Tzvei, the "Ropshitser." We go around the table, and each person pours a little from his or her third cup of wine,

thus filling up Elijah's cup. This way, we all do our bit to has-
ten the coming of the Messiah. We pray this miraculous event will
indeed take place during Pesach, as the Talmud states: "In Nisan
they have been redeemed; in Nisan, they will be redeemed too in
the future."

Who knows? Perhaps, at this year's seder, someone will indeed spot
Elijah when we open the door for him! But how will we recognize him?
Just what do we know about this mysterious prophet?

## "Go Tell [Ahab]: Elijah Is Here" (I Kings 18:14)

Though Elijah is such a familiar figure, he is not mentioned at all in the
Torah. Elijah does not appear until the end of the historical section of
the Bible known as N'vi-im, the Prophets, in the very last books of this
section, the Books of Kings. Here, the Scriptures actually provide a
physical description of him, something usually reserved for the
Patriarchs from Torah: "[Ahaziah] asked them, 'What sort of a man
was [Elijah] . . . who came toward you and said these things to you?'
They replied, 'A hairy man with a leather belt tied around his waist.'
'That is Elijah the Tishbite!' he said" (II Kings 1:7–8).

The Books of Kings juxtaposes Elijah, a prophet of the one God,
with the idolatrous deeds of the ninth-century B.C.E. king of Israel,
Ahab, and his infamous wife, Jezebel. "[Ahab] erected an altar to Baal
. . . Ahab did more to vex Adonai, the God of Israel, than all the kings
of Israel who preceded him" (I Kings 16:32–33). At this time, there
must have been more than one Elijah who was a public figure, well-
known to the people. For when "our" Elijah is introduced, biblical
editors are careful to make sure we know exactly who is being talked
about, "Elijah the Tishbite, an inhabitant of Gilead" (I Kings 17:1).
Elijah announces that only he can bring rain to the land, severely
stricken by drought: "There will be no dew or rain except at my bidding" (I Kings 17:1), until Ahab and Jezebel foreswear their false
deities and worship "Adonai, God of Abraham, Isaac, and Israel" (I
Kings 18:36).

In the context of Pesach, we see Elijah as the central messianic figure who will announce his presence by drinking wine from the cup
bearing his name. Throughout our history, Jews have had good reason

to long for him fervently, to put an end to the many periods of intolerance and persecution. Because Jews have desired this time so intensely, we have built in additional occasions in the Jewish calendar that also summon Elijah. Each week, as the Sabbath ends, his presence is requested during *Havdalah* worship through the song "Eliyahu HaNavi" (Elijah the Prophet). Legend has it that he also attends each *b'rit milah* (circumcision) and watches over male Jewish infants as they ritually take their place among the Jewish people. In past centuries, many synagogues provided a richly decorated "Elijah's chair" for precisely this occasion.

In the Bible, one of Elijah's miraculous feats was on behalf of a child, whom he brought back to life: "Then he stretched out over the child three times, and cried out to *Adonai,* saying, 'O *Adonai* my God, let this child's life return to his body!' *Adonai* heard Elijah's plea . . . and he revived" (I Kings 17:21–22). Most marvelously, the singular event that Elijah will achieve to presage the Messiah, as chronicled in the Book of Malachi, will also return the lives of children, metaphorically speaking. This is the basis of the Shabbat HaGadol haftarah reading, studied right before Pesach: "I will send the prophet Elijah to you before the coming of the awesome, fearful day of *Adonai.* He shall reconcile parents with children and children with their parents . . ." (Mal. 3:23–24). Jewish tradition has long portrayed Elijah as the ultimate protector of Jewish children. So we trust that at the seder, when we send our children, our most precious of God's gifts, to the opened door to search for him, Elijah will guarantee their safety.

Since Elijah figures so prominently in Jewish legend and folklore, it seems that he should merit significant reference in the traditional Haggadah text. But like Moses, mortal redeemer of the Jewish people from Egyptian persecutors, Elijah's name is never directly mentioned. He appears only as part of the usual *Birkat HaMazon* sung after completing the meal: "Compassionate One! May God send Elijah the prophet to us, and may he bear good tidings of salvation and comfort." Might Haggadah compilers of old have feared that, like Moses, Elijah's role as the final redeemer of the Jewish people had become too conspicuous, threatening to usurp God's role as the sole, ultimate Deity? Or maybe the editors of the Mishnah, the second-century Jewish law code that contributes the basic Haggadah format, found another potential problem. Perhaps they were worried that a comparison between Elijah, the Jewish prophet, and Jesus, the young Jew who became the Messiah for the newly established Christian church, would be too alluring. Perhaps, then, Jewish Sages took out even a hint of similarity, even if this pruning removed all references to the beloved Elijah.

## "Let Us See Whether Elijah Will Come to Save Him"
### (Matt. 27:49)

Adding to the possibility of an Elijah-Jesus connection are several discussions in early church writings linking the holiday of Pesach and the crucifixion of Jesus. The Christian redemption story hinges on the reason for Jesus' final trip to Jerusalem, where he met his death. It was to celebrate Pesach by sacrificing at the Temple. The authors of the New Testament Books of Matthew, Mark, and Luke refer to the final meal Jesus ate with his followers, which Christians call "the Last Supper," as a seder, "the Feast of Unleavened Bread." "The Teacher says, 'Where is my guest room, where I am to eat the passover [sic] with my disciples?'" (Mark 14:12). According to these same sources, Jesus was crucified on the fifteenth of Nisan, the first day of Pesach.

An interesting aside for tracking the development of the Elijah character is the telling allusion to the prophet's legendary miraculous powers in Christian Scriptures, which affirms how ingrained the idea of Elijah as savior had become. The Book of Mark relates that, as Jesus suffered his final agonies, "one of the bystanders said, 'Behold, he is calling Elijah . . .' [And another said], 'let us see whether Elijah will come to take him down'" (Mark 15:35–36).

Much of the language of the Christian Scriptures is neutral narrative, merely moving the story along. Unfortunately, other words are more menacing. When written, the ideas may have put forward a particular political agenda, but for hundreds of years they have meant terror and tragedy for Jews residing in Christian lands: "It was now two days before the Passover and the Feast of Unleavened Bread. And the [Jewish] chief priests and the scribes were seeking how to arrest him [Jesus] by stealth, and kill him" (Mark 14:1).

## "For They Have Devoured Jacob and Laid Waste His Home" (Ps. 79:7)

So it seems a little surprising that, given the language and tone of the most sacred of Christian literature, not until the twelfth century did widespread massacres of the Jews take place in Christian lands. The first incidents of massive Jewish killings occurred as Crusaders decimated Jewish populations in the Rhineland, modern-day Germany. Around the same time, the insidious notion of blood libel first took shape. In the spring of 1144, in Norwich, England, of all places, a dead Christian child was found in an area where Jews lived. Not long afterward, several Jewish men were accused of murdering the child in order to use his blood to prepare Passover matzah. This denunciation directed at Jews was endlessly repeated at Easter, the sacred Christian holiday coinciding with Pesach. The carnage continued at this same time of year through the centuries.

The idea that Jews somehow needed human blood to make matzah is absolutely preposterous. Blood, the foundation of human existence, is so precious to Jews that it is fit only for God. Even a trace of it in our meat makes otherwise acceptable, kosher food *treif*, unsuitable for Jews to eat.

Yet even in modern times, this accusation followed the Jews. In Czarist Russia in 1911, a Jew named Mendel Beilis was charged with blood libel, accused of killing a Christian boy. Fifty years later, the Jewish writer Bernard Malamud wrote a fictionalized account of this travesty in his highly acclaimed novel *The Fixer*.

## *Sh'foch Chamat'cha:* "Pour Out Your Wrath upon the Nations . . ." (Ps. 79:6)

Thus, for hundreds of years, Jews were persecuted before being expelled from most of the countries of Europe. It seems appropriate that, as we celebrate our first redemption in the privacy of an evening meal, we find the courage to decry the dreadful accusations that seemed to haunt us. The biblical verses beginning with the words *Sh'foch chamat'cha*, "Pour out your wrath upon the nations that do not know You" (Ps. 79:6), form a definitive part of the Haggadah, beginning in the troubled times of the Middle Ages. It is rare to find other examples of as explicit a plea for divine retribution as this one.

We Jews do not think of ourselves as a vengeful people, especially considering the scope of our own persecution. For us today, residing in blissful freedom, it remains difficult to say these words, particularly in the context of joy surrounding a seder. We must force ourselves to remember the dark times as well as the more happy occasions of our history, which is, after all, one of the main purposes for participating in the evening's observances.

Yet other examples exist of Jewish demands for vengeance, both in traditional Jewish and secular literature. A midrashic selection is quite forthright in its measure-for-measure message: "They that were to be slain, slew; they that were to be destroyed, destroyed; they that were to be hanged, hanged." Writing what he took to be a universal law of human nature, William Shakespeare put these words into the mouth of the Jewish character Shylock in his play *The Merchant of Venice*: "And if you wrong us, shall we not revenge? The villainy you teach me I will execute, and it shall go hard, but I will be better the instruction."

Do we really believe this today, that we can benefit from such acts? Perhaps the emotional satisfaction in knowing our enemies will be punished someday makes memories of incomprehensible suffering easier to handle. The nineteenth-century commentator known as the Sefat Emet finds a more socially acceptable way for Jews to get satisfaction from avenging the wrongs done to us by our enemies. His interpretation comes from this verse in Exodus: "No one should go out through the door of his house until morning" (12:22). While acknowledging that God did not allow Jews to witness the punishment that befell the Egyptians before the first Exodus, the Sefat Emet explains that Jews will be permitted to watch our enemies' defeat "in the morning," when the Messiah comes.

Scholars have identified a few Jewish manuscripts written in an apologetic tone, trying to downplay or smooth over the vengeful statements in the Haggadah. For instance, a sixteenth-century Haggadah from the German city of Worms substitutes the words "Pour out Your love" for the "Pour out Your wrath" invective of Psalms. The obvious motive was to promote a more healthy, stable atmosphere for Jewish life among a gentile population: "Pour out Your love on nations who have known you and on kingdoms who call upon Your name. For they have shown loving-kindness to the seed of Jacob, and they defend Your people Israel. . . ." A second example comes from the seventeenth-century commentator Moses Rivkes: "We stand on guard to pray continually for the welfare and success of the kingdoms and ministers in whose shade we Israelites are exiled among, and among whom we are dispersed. . . ." A third example, also from late medieval times, expressly excludes biblical curses from falling upon people of "monotheistic faiths"—any Christians or Moslems who ruled lands in which Jews were living—the dominant cultures in which virtually the world's entire Jewish population lived.

## "That Was for *Adonai* a Night of Watching [*Leil Shimurim*]" (Exod. 12:42)

Whether polemic or apologetic, the Haggadah does not lose sight of the mission of the Exodus, to keep close vigil on Jews so that, one day, Elijah will indeed herald the beginning of eternal peace and a return to the Promised Land for a much-reviled Jewish people. From a focus on the past redemption of the Egyptian Exodus, when Jews huddled behind closed doors, Jews lose their slave mentality and fling open the door as the seder concludes, unafraid to hope for better future times.

Opening the door while appealing to God to destroy one's enemies takes a fair amount of chutzpah. It shows that Jews are not afraid of what might be lurking just beyond their doorways. It helps Jews to stand resolute in defiance of external threats, while affirming the faith that God will indeed come to their rescue. Opening the door extends the isolated space most Jews lived in. Just knowing that Jews all over the world are performing the same ritual connects the people to each other, as it has for a thousand years. Rabbi Sue Levi Elwell echoes our sentiments as we perform this time-honored seder ritual:

Tonight, we walked through walls of words
And filled our mouths with wine and song.
As darkness deepens, we look to the future and begin to dream.

We wake the children who doze in our laps,
And gather those who have strayed.
It is time to open the door.

## "Pursue Them in Anger and Destroy Them . . ."
### (Lam. 3:66)

Commentators warn that, while we want to fight back against the injustices done to us, we ourselves must not take action on our own. At the time of the first Exodus, the instructions clearly name the sole Affecter of all punishment.

> For that night I will go through the land of Egypt . . . I will mete out punishments . . . I *Adonai*. (Exod. 12:12)

We are strictly forbidden to take matters into our own hands. Quite simply, *Adonai* told the people to leave revenge to God. And what better time is there to express our faith and trust in the God of justice than on Pesach, the commemoration of the first time Jews were guarded and shielded from all harm by *Adonai*. It also helps to remember explicit teachings of Torah denying Jews this very act on our own behalf: "Mine are vengeance and payback" (Deut. 32:35).

For many of us today, the ultimate demonstration of Jewish refusal to sanction vengeance came in Europe in the spring of 1945. Holocaust survivors have related countless stories of their last days as inmates of German concentration camps. The following is a tale from Theresienstadt, the Czech fortress that served as the "model ghetto" of the Nazis: "When the main body of the Germans had fled and the Russians had not yet arrived, one German officer remained. . . . [He] went from gate to gate, [on a bicycle and without a weapon,] closing each one and collecting the keys. . . . Silently the Jews watched. Not one of them moved. [Then Leo Baeck, the great German rabbi and the only leader of this stature to survive confinement in Theresienstadt, made this observation:] 'Look at it. This can only happen with Jews. Of all these Jewish people here, not one person lifted a stone to throw at him. They could have strangled him if they wanted.'"

Many Haggadot published in the last fifty years include readings from Holocaust-era diaries, poetry, and narratives, either as additions to the "Pour out Your wrath" verses or as substitutes for them. One of the most moving selections, *Ani Maamin*, attaches a haunting melody to the twelfth of Maimonides' Thirteen Principles of Faith: "I believe in perfect faith in the coming of the Messiah. . . ." It is said that some Jews chanted these words as they were led into the gas chambers. Their unyielding devotion to God even as they knew their lives were about to end, that God could not save them from their terrible fate, gives a heartbreaking edge to Pesach festivities.

## "Today, If You Will But Listen to the Voice of God"
### (Ps. 95:7)

At Pesach we are given a mandate we ignore at our own peril: It is up to us to bring Elijah and the Messiah to earth. We must work together to end the plagues of poverty and hopelessness, the lack of basic health care and education. Words from the Reform *A Passover Haggadah* echo this edict: "The injustice of this world still brings to mind Elijah who in defense of justice, challenged power. In many tales from Jewish lore, he reappears to help the weak. . . . For every undecided question, then, of pain and sorrow, of unrewarded worth and unrequited evil, Elijah would someday provide the answer. . . . Elijah opens up for us the realm of mystery and wonder."

> To unlock fetters of wickedness,
> And untie the cords of lawlessness,
> To let the oppressed go free;
> To break off every yoke.
> It is to share your bread with the hungry,
> And to take the wretched poor into your home;
> When you see the naked, to clothe them,
> And not to ignore your own kin. (Isa. 58:6–7)

"Let us now open the door for Elijah!"

## *From Our Tradition*

*Eliyahu haNavi, Eliyahu haTishbi,*
*Eliyahu, Eliyahu, Eliyahu haGiladi.*
*Bimheirah v'yameinu, yavo eileinu*
*Im Mashiach ben David, im Mashiach ben David.*

(Elijah the prophet, Elijah the Tishbite, Elijah from Gilead. Come quickly to us, bringing the Messiah, son of David.)

I believe with all my heart in the coming of the Messiah, and although He will be late, I will wait each and every day for His arrival. (*Ani Maamin*)

The fortune of the house has come; the fortune of the world has come; Elijah has come, who will overthrow the foundation of the heathen. (*B'reishit Rabbah* 71:9)

The smallest vengeance poisons the soul. (Yiddish proverb)

In the past, when someone performed a good deed, a prophet placed it on record; but nowadays, when someone performs a good deed, who records it? Elijah records it, and the Messiah and the Holy One subscribe their names to it. (*Ruth Rabbah* 5:6)

# 14

## The Sixth Cup: Miriam, Pesach Prophetess

Now Miriam the prophetess, Aaron's sister, took a timbrel
in her hand, and all the women went out after her with timbrels
and with dancing. Miriam chanted to them:

> Sing to *Adonai*, for God has triumphed, yes tri-
> umphed; The horse and its charioteer God flung into
> the sea! (Exod. 15:20–21)

Feisty, fearless Miriam! Your mother Yocheved, desperate with worry, sent you to guard your baby brother Moses as he drifted helplessly along the banks of the Nile River. You watched out of sight as Pharaoh's daughter found him in the bulrushes and drew him out of the water. Then you found your voice and approached the Egyptian princess, offering the services of your mother as wet nurse, reuniting the family for a few more precious years. You grew into a capable leader of women who eagerly followed your example, serving God through fiery rhetoric and exuberant spirit. When you left Egypt, you made sure the women packed their musical instruments among their few provisions. Standing together with your family at the shores of the Red Sea, you watched helplessly as Pharaoh's warriors pursued you, then were amazed as all Israel "crossed on dry ground . . ." but "*Adonai* hurled the Egyptians into the sea" (Exod. 14:29, 27). Miriam, your ecstasy was boundless—and contagious! All the women of Israel picked up their drums and joined you in impassioned song and dance, a frenzied thanksgiving to *Adonai*.

You are one of the few women described in the Bible as *han'viah*, "the prophetess," yet none of your words of wisdom are quoted there. The Rabbis stepped in to fill this void, fleshing out the bare biblical skeleton with meaty anecdotes that capture your vivacity and your wiliness. A midrash explains that, when you were a little girl, you courageously reprimanded the all-powerful Pharaoh for his cruel deeds against the Jewish slaves. Only your mother's tearful pleas prevented him from putting you to death on the spot.

Years later, once more unable to keep silent in the face of a misdeed by Moses, his marriage to "the Cushite woman" (Num. 12:1), you and Aaron spoke out against your own brother, yet only you were punished with leprosy and sent outside the camp. The people would not break camp and leave without you, so strong was their love for you (Num. 12:15). Years before, you waited at the Nile until you knew Moses was safe, so the people waited until you recovered before moving to their next desert destination. About your death, the Bible says tersely that you died on the first new moon (Num. 20:1); the Rabbis embellish this, explaining that you died during the month of Nisan, the anniversary month of the redemption from Egypt.

 

≈∿ We come to Miriam in our passage through Pesach, celebrated during our modern seders and elsewhere in the Jewish calendar as the unsung hero in our tradition. Tantalizing glimpses of Miriam reveal a woman who exercised religious leadership in the wilderness community, claiming authority as a spokesperson for the Divine. But there are very few ancient texts that adequately describe her status and importance in Jewish lore. Some scholars believe that her single verse of song, "Sing to *Adonai,* for God has triumphed gloriously . . . (Exod. 15:21)," originally preceded, rather than followed the much longer Song of the Sea (Exod. 15:1–19) that Moses is usually credited with authoring. Perhaps a whole "Book of Miriam" once existed, now irretrievably lost. While today we mourn these unknown passages, the words of Miriam we do have motivate us to compose our own lyrics and melodies, singing our songs alongside hers.

Translations of the name "Miriam" reflect her many facets. One meaning connects two Hebrew words, *mar,* "bitter," and *yam,* "sea," to describe the oppressions of Israelite slavery or the foulness of the water in the wilderness encountered by the people of Israel after they left Egypt. It was Miriam who magically and repeatedly found fresh sources of water for the wandering Jews. A second, contrasting translation of her name comes from Arabic; the word *ra'im,* "to love tenderly," fits both the special emotions Miriam held for the people and the reciprocal feelings of genuine love the people of Israel showed her. Yet another translation looks to the ancient Egyptian language for clues. Just as the name of Moses has an Egyptian root ("to draw out [of water]"), so Miriam was called "beloved," derived from the word *mer* in the same language.

## "Good Gifts Were Given at Their Hand . . . The Well, Because of the Merit of Miriam" (BT *Taanit* 9a)

Miriam was called "beloved" because of her wondrous ability to find fresh water in the wilderness, sustaining the Israelites throughout their forty years of wandering. Inspired by rabbinic midrash, scholar and storyteller Ellen Frankel has created this lovely "Legend of Miriam's Well":

> At twilight of the sixth day of Creation, Shekhinah, The Holy-One-Who-Dwells-in-This-World, created the miracles. . . .
> Of all the miracles, Miriam's Well was perhaps the most marvelous. Resembling a round white millstone, it gave forth water whenever a woman sang to it with the proper heartsong.

Other sources from Jewish tradition also describe the well's amazing origin and qualities. "Ten things were created on the eve of the Sabbath, at twilight: the mouth of the earth [which engulfed Korach]; the mouth of the well [which supplied the Israelites with water in the wilderness]. . . ." The well "resembled a rock in the form of a beehive, accompanying the tribes wherever they went. From it came all the good things Israel enjoyed: fruit, vegetables, trees, wine." Our folklorists have even addressed why Miriam, almost voiceless in the Bible, was given the honor of discovering this endlessly running source of life for the entire Jewish people. "It was believed that God gave the well in Miriam's name, since Moses could barely speak, let alone sing, while the voice of Aaron, the priest, was so loud that it frightened both children and animals."

There was another ancient Jewish ritual involving water that defined the Jewish people when the Temple still stood, an eagerly anticipated ceremony of pageantry and grandeur that Miriam would have loved, though she would not have been allowed to take part. At the fall holiday of Sukkot during the time of the Second Temple, a priestly procession worked its way to the spring of Shiloach, outside Jerusalem. There, a golden flask was filled with water and brought back to the Temple, where the water was transferred to a massive silver bowl. Beginning on the second night of Sukkot, some of this water was poured on the Temple altar as a libation, a liquid offering in the form of a religious ritual. Thus the *Simchat Beit HaSho-eivah,* the "Water Libation Rite," was a magnificent Sukkot attraction, drawing thousands to the Temple to revel in the holiday with singing, dancing, and acrobatics. The glow from three huge golden candlesticks was so bright, "there was not a courtyard in Jerusalem did not reflect the light" of the *Beit HaSho-eivah*; whoever had seen witnessed this ritual "had never witnessed real joy in his life." The festivities of the Water Libation Rite were said to have taken place in the women's court, a huge area within the Temple precincts. Yet it is unlikely that women were permitted to participate. They had to be satisfied to observe the goings-on from a balcony that skirted the court, well distanced from the actual merriment.

## "Israel Was Redeemed from Egypt on Account of Righteous Women" (BT *Sotah* 11b)

Inspired by Miriam, new rituals have been created by Jewish women, the half of our population who for so long were relegated to balconies, rendered silent by ancient law and custom. One such observance is Rosh Chodesh, a monthly gathering of Jewish women of all ages who seek to explore much of Jewish tradition in decidedly untraditional ways. Rosh Chodesh celebrates the new lunar month in an atmosphere of female Jewish conviviality.

In 1989, a group of Boston women spent one Rosh Chodesh meditating on the meanings and teachings of Miriam's well. The next week, a member of this group reflected on her experience as she prepared for the Sabbath. She set a crystal goblet in the middle of the Sabbath table and filled it with spring water. That evening, each member of her family drank from the glass she referred to as *kos Miryam.*

Three years later, other women linked the cup of Miriam concept to Pesach, creating an additional observance and another ritual object to grace the seder table.

LEADER: This is the cup of Miriam, the cup of living waters, which we drink to remember the Exodus from Egypt.

ALL: These are the living waters, God's gift to Miriam, which gave new life to Israel as we struggled with ourselves in the wilderness. . . .

As word of this ceremony spread, its meaning was enhanced by additional flourishes. At some seders, everyone is invited to add water from her or his glass to Miriam's cup. By involving all seder participants, the interaction increases the magic of the entire evening, building shared memories of Pesach. Here are words from another *kos Miryam* ceremony that accompany the cup as it passes from person to person.

Let us each fill the cup with water from our own glasses, so that our daughters may continue to draw from the strength and wisdom of our heritage.

RAISE GOBLET: We place Miriam's cup on our seder table to honor the important role of Jewish women in our tradition and history, whose stories have been too sparingly told.

Another, subtler message may be found in the *kos Miryam* rituals. When we raise our glasses to honor Miriam, we also tacitly toast and thank the seder providers, for the most part women. Their supreme efforts in "making Pesach" have long been unacknowledged. And we also rectify an unbelievable omission: women are not mentioned at all in the traditional Haggadah, except in some seder directions that were added long after the Haggadah became finalized. Worse yet, when formative seder rules were first established almost two thousand years ago, women were not even invited to attend the Pesach meal. The whole institution of the seder was created for fathers to relate to their sons and for teachers to instruct their students.

Early on, Rabbis engaged in lively discussion to determine if the honored Jewish law exempting women from doing positive commandments within a specific time frame extended to Pesach rituals. For example, the Mishnah explains in detail a man's Pesach obligations, which in Temple times referred to eating the paschal lamb sandwiched between matzah and bitter herbs, precursor of the "Hillel sandwich."

Since there was no reference to the need of women to do this, the Mishnah excused them from participating in these rituals. So during Pesach, women were not obligated to eat matzah. However, the Talmud, written several hundred years after the Mishnah, quotes a third-century Rabbi for the express purpose of reversing this ruling. Rabbi Elazar declared that anyone who is obligated to abide by the restrictions of Pesach is also obligated to engage in the positive rituals of the holiday. Thus, since women are prohibited from eating leavened food on Pesach, they are therefore required to eat matzah.

Another talmudic ruling adds further requirements for women during Pesach, giving a moral rather than a legal justification. "Rabbi Yehoshua ben Levi said: Women are obligated to drink these four cups, since they were also saved by the same miracle." By the time of the Rashbam, an eleventh-century French sage, women were instructed to observe all the commandments of the seder night as their privilege and duty.

## "When God Appeared at the Red Sea, Women Recognized God First" (BT *Sotah* 11b)

Thus for hundreds of years, women have been very much involved in the family seder, both preparing for and participating in the festivities. Yet, beginning in the 1970s that was no longer enough. With rising female consciousness, women started to feel the need not only for involvement, but also for ownership. The first women's seders, led by women and mostly for women, were held at this time. They were created by small groups, most of whom were independent from one another. Each of these women's seders tried to define for themselves specific aspects of Pesach that spoke to Jewish females. They created ceremonies like those for *kos Miryam,* calling attention to roles played by females, from securing freedom from Egypt to overcoming a host of contemporary social, economic, and political grievances.

A book by author Esther Broner describes twenty years of her own experiences organizing and running women's seders with a high-profile group of Jewish feminists, including the activist-writer Gloria Steinem and the late activist-politician Bella Abzug. Broner's first alternative seder took place in Israel and featured a then-heretical role reversal.

Men were invited only to prepare the meal, serve it, and clean up afterward, allowing women time to contemplate the essential issues of the holiday, which included writing new, relevant prayers to update the traditional Haggadah.

Rivka, the mother of Naomi Nimrod, Broner's co-author of *The Women's Haggadah,* was an observant elderly woman, the widow of a well-known cantor. She could not understand the necessity of revising a book that had been perfectly acceptable for hundreds of years. And she would not believe that there were almost no women mentioned in the Exodus from Egypt. She lived in Haifa, the beautiful northern port of Israel, with an excellent maritime museum. "'Surely,' Rivka thought, 'with all the ancient artifacts, all those representations of the sea with people crossing, women will be represented. How is it not possible?' Rivka asked to see the museum's extensive collection . . . no women were depicted leaving Egypt. 'How could there be a Jewish people if there were no women?' Rivka asked the curator in exasperation."

About the same time, the San Diego Woman's Institute for Continuing Jewish Education scheduled its first seder. Finding the right hall and scheduling the event was easy. Finding a Haggadah to use that fit the spirit of the evening proved much more difficult. Finally, like Broner and Nimrod, the women from San Diego stopped searching and wrote their own. They surrounded Pesach's traditional tale of liberation from bondage with personal stories of freedom, describing the roles of foremothers as well as forefathers. For women, talking about their lives, giving an account of it, is essential to leading that life rather than being led through it.

## "All the Women Went out after [Miriam] with Dancing"
### (Exod. 15:20)

For some, the focal point of their women's seder is the special readings of the evening. Hearing the stories makes them important and real. For me, however, all prayers and rituals are mere preludes to what really defines it—the dancing! When men are around, many decidedly middle-aged women like myself still hear the voices of our mothers whispering in our ears, "Remember who you are. Remember what you are. Remember where you are. Always act like a lady." But when it's just us, we don't have to remember. All we need to do is look at the faces to our right and to our left to realize we are safe and among friends, even if we've never seen each other before. The music starts. Just try to keep us in our chairs!

Somehow, dancing seems a part of the language of religion. Physical movement—more than getting up from our seats, standing in place, and sitting down again—becomes an outward expression of our intense emotions of faith. When Jewish men (and they all were men) of the nineteenth century, each one a paragon of rationalist integrity, sought to "reform" Judaism, they deleted more than words. They also removed many rituals that allowed our souls to move to the dance of our long history. They tried to make us forget those aspects of Judaism not based on a highly decorous notion of morality.

Yet long ago, outward appearances of correctness mattered less than basic belief. When Jewish sacred books were being debated for biblical canonization, there was no question about the propriety of, say, Psalms, which brims with prayerful movement. "Let them praise God's name in dance" (Ps. 149:3) and "Praise God with timbrel and dance" (Ps. 150:4) speak of wholehearted physicality, in which God seems to delight. The Bible contains eleven Hebrew words to describe dance, suggesting that several thousand years ago ritual choreography was extensive and highly sophisticated. In a defining moment for ancient Israel, women celebrated their victory against Pharaoh by dancing, led by a spirited female. After crossing the Red Sea, the prophetess Miriam was well within her right to behave as she and the other women did. And more than three thousand years later, so are we.

## "Miriam Died from a Kiss from God" (BT *Bava Batra* 17a)

As long as Miriam was alive, the well of nurturing waters that bore her name kept thirst far away from the people. "Whenever the people journeyed, the well traveled with them, and when they camped, it settled opposite the Tabernacle. Twelve crones, chosen by the women from each of the twelve tribes, would then bring their spindles to the well and declare, 'Spring up, O Well!' And the water would shoot up from the white stone, as high as the tallest date palms, then cascade into great rivers." Miriam's well provided the water that the people of Israel used for drinking and for bathing, supplying all the water they needed to keep themselves and their animals alive and functioning.

But that changed once Miriam died. In its usual terse way, the Bible gives us little information surrounding her death besides the place and time of year.

> The Israelites arrived in a body in the wilderness of Zin on the first new moon, and the people stayed at Kadesh. Miriam died there and was buried there. (Num. 20:1)

However, the very next biblical verse reveals important details in the lives of the people, without directly linking them to what had just happened to Miriam.

> The community was without water, and they joined against Moses and Aaron. (Num. 20:2)

Suddenly the life-giving waters that had been so abundant, whose appearance wherever the Jews rested in the wilderness had become so routine that it was taken for granted, disappeared. Yet perhaps the biblical authors were trying to tell us something else. In her declining years, Miriam might well have lost much of her spunk. From her youthful role as a leader, she undoubtedly began to slow down, becoming withdrawn and quiet. Where once she lit up a place by her presence, now no one took note of her coming or going.

That is, until the day she died. Only then did the people remember all that Miriam had done for them and realize how much they would miss her. In their grief, they tried to cry out for Miriam, to tell her how much they loved her. But Miriam was not there to hear the people's love for her. Words lost their meaning; thoughts shriveled; the people turned against each other.

The writer Tamara Cohen imagines what might have taken place so long ago: "As soon as Miriam died, the well dried up and a great thirst grew among the people. Women who had learned from Miriam how to raise their voices in song suddenly felt their throats grow parched and dry. The children could not dance. . . ." Without a compassionate appreciation of the present, an understanding that each moment is precious, never to be relived, the glorious dance of life fades from view.

Taking up Miriam's timbrel, life rebounds—if we could only remember where we put it down the last time we danced with it . . .

### "I Hope You Dance"

I hope you never lose your sense of wonder,
You get your fill to eat but always keep that hunger,
May you never take one single breath for granted,
God forbid love ever leave you empty-handed.
I hope you still feel small when you stand beside the ocean,
Whenever one door closes I hope one more opens,
Promise me that you'll give faith a fighting chance,
And when you get the choice to sit it out or dance,
I HOPE YOU DANCE! I HOPE YOU DANCE.

And so, Miriam, a new generation of Jewish women now follows your lead, singing and dancing your praises. E. M. Broner describes you as "caretaker rather than searcher, predictor rather than actor . . . the angry one who cries out for . . . justice." Your deeds still inspire women who seek to honor God with strong words and emotion. "Mine is the voice of joy, of victory, of power. I prophesy the redemption of all our people. My vision is clear and limitless . . . I am the Singer, the Dancer, the Drummer of Israel. I celebrate the myriad contributions of Jewish women through the ages."

## From Our "Tradition"

*Since the Miriam's cup phenomenon is so recent, the poetry that follows reflects a tradition in the making, written expressly for the new seder ritual.*

### Miriam Hanevi'ah

Miriam the Prophet,
strength and song are in her hand.
Miriam will dance with us
to swell earth's song.
Miriam will dance with us

to redeem the world.
Soon, in our day,
she will bring us
to the waters of redemption. (Ellen Frankel)

### God

. . . I remember the moment
when the Great One
split the Red Sea for us,

and all the people tread on the precious shore
and Miriam sang,
and in the distance
the beauty of the songs sounded,
and the air responded with reverberations
the prophetic lips quivered:

You allowed me to take part in these songs
in this prophetic exile
and gave me uncertain knowledge
and the ardor of the righteous heart.
So now with earthly sounds and my mortal music
let me glorify Your regal Name
beyond the seas of the sun. (Feiga Izrailevna Kogan)

### I Shall Sing to the Lord a New Song

I, Miriam, stand at the sea
and turn
to face the desert
stretching endless and
still.
My eyes are dazzled
the sky brilliant blue
Sunburnt sands unyielding white.
My hands turn to dove wings.
My arms
reach

for the sky
and I want to sing
the song rising inside me.
My mouth open
I stop.
Where are the words?
Where is the melody?
In a moment of panic
my eyes go blind.
Can I take a step
without knowing a
Destination?
Will I falter
Will I fall
Will the ground sink away from under me?
The song still unformed—
How can I sing?

To take the first step—
to sing a new song—
Is to close one's eyes and dive
into unknown waters.
For a moment knowing nothing risking all—
but then to discover

The waters are friendly
the ground is firm.
And the song—
the song rises again.
Out of my mouth
come words lifting the wind.
And I hear
for the first
the song
that has been in my heart
silent
unknown
even to me. (Ruth Sohn)

# Epilogue: Passage from Pesach to Shavuot

When you enter the land I am giving to you and you reap its harvest, you shall bring the first sheaf of your harvest to the priest . . . (Lev. 23:10)

And from that day . . . you shall count off seven weeks. They must be complete. (Lev. 23:15)

The Pesach seder has ended. The seder plate and matzah cover, all the symbols that make Pesach so special, have been returned to china cabinets and drawers until they are needed again next year. Our thoughts turn "post-Pesach" to all of the things that make up our day-to-day existences the other fifty-one weeks of the year.

While we absorb the themes and ideas of this holiday, there is still one observance begun during the seder that continues through the days and weeks ahead. Those who customarily attend a seder on only the first night probably do not associate Pesach with these additional rituals, since they don't begin until the second night. Even many who do attend an additional seder might not be aware of the observance that takes place on this second night, late in the evening, when the seder is almost over.

During Pesach's second seder, we proclaim again "Next year in Jerusalem" and sing several Pesach songs, including one sung on this night only, "And You Shall Say: This Is the Feast of Pesach." As we complete the recounting of the Exodus story, we also begin a special counting that continues for the next forty-nine nights, ending with the holiday of Shavuot.

This ritual, called the counting of the *Omer*, commemorates an ancient Temple tradition. Each year, after Jews ate the *pesach* sacrifice in Jerusalem and returned to their homes, they harvested the first spring crops, including barley. Then they brought some of the barley harvest to the Temple to be blessed by the priests. This measured grain taken to Jerusalem for priestly blessing was called an *Omer*. Today we are not sure how this translates into modern units of measurement. Nonetheless, the Rabbis have given us ways to update this ancient rite. A blessing is said each night at home or in the synagogue, thanking God for giving Jews the commandment to count the *Omer*. And then we mark that day by noting the length of time since Pesach has ended and the *Omer* counting has begun.

This is what is said on the second night of Pesach:

> Praised are You, *Adonai* our God, Sovereign of the universe, who sanctified us through Your commandments and commanded us about the counting of the *Omer*.

> Today is day one of the *Omer*. [On the eighth day of counting we say, for example: "Today is day one of the second week of the *Omer*."]

Once the Temple was destroyed and Jews no longer could bring sacrifices to Jerusalem, the Rabbis transformed what was essentially an agricultural festival into the anniversary of the giving of the Torah at Mount Sinai, *z'man matan Torateinu*. According to Scriptures, this occurred some three months after the Jews left Egypt (Exod. 19:1). Thus Pesach, the celebration of physical redemption, is directly connected to Shavuot, the time that God entered into a covenant with the Jewish people, signaling a spiritual redemption as well.

Perhaps because we tend to concentrate our Jewish focus so single-mindedly on Pesach, the most celebrated holiday in the Jewish calendar, Shavuot is undercelebrated. No biblical or rabbinic rituals make Shavuot special, calling it to our attention. The Reform Movement has made an effort to celebrate confirmation at Shavuot, sharing the day of a teenager's commitment to Judaism with the historic covenant of the entire Jewish people at Sinai. Still, Shavuot remains the best-kept secret among Jewish holidays. A midrash written hundreds of years ago relates that this was probably always the case. "Rabbi Yannai said: The way it is with mankind, when a man buys a pound of meat in the marketplace, how much trouble he goes to, how much time and money he gives to the effort. . . . Yet while mortals sleep, the Holy One causes winds to blow, clouds to rise, rains to come down, fruits to grow plump—and you are asked to give God in return no more than the *Omer* of barley!"

Pesach and Shavuot are in fact quite closely connected to each other. They are both *chagim*, Jewish pilgrimage festivals, and are celebrated in the spring, the beginning of the agricultural year. The Hebrew meaning of *s'firat HaOmer*, "counting the *Omer*," and *sipeir*, the *telling* of the story of the Exodus, share the same three-letter root, ס-פ-ר. An additional link between the two holidays is only slightly more abstract. History-defining and glorious as the Exodus event was, it was exactly that, a one-time, long-ago occurrence. Shavuot represents the remarkable spiritual fulfillment of the Exodus, the giving of the Torah, an eternal ideal instructing us in the ways that God wants us to live. Today when we celebrate Shavuot, we build on the understanding of freedom as bound to timeless ethical obligations. Without the focus of caring and compassion found in Torah, the redemption of the Jews would seem hollow, lacking in overall purpose.

Thus the spiritual revelation at Sinai, celebrated by Shavuot, completes the physical redemption of the Jews from Egypt, a sacred climax to the Pesach story of liberation. Rabbi Shlomo Riskin, spiritual leader of the city of Efrat, Israel, has explained that Pesach is the first promise of salvation, close to the birth of the Jewish people. Shavuot marks the culmination of redemption, the acceptance of the Torah by a mature people.

## "You Must Count until the Day after the Seventh Week—Fifty Days" (Lev. 23:16)

As noted, the traditional way to count the *Omer* is spelled out quite precisely. It must be preceded by a special blessing. It must mention both the number of days and, after day seven, the number of weeks, describing the specific length of time that has elapsed since the end of the first full day of Pesach. We stand when we say the blessing and recite the counting. It should be done immediately following the evening service in the synagogue, just after twilight, the time when one day ends and the next one begins.

To keep track of the days, it was fairly common practice to consult an "*Omer* calendar" with either movable numbers or a changeable marker circling the proper day. In recent years, Jewish craftspersons have created innovative *Omer* calendars that can be displayed as works of art all year long. To bring *Omer* counting into the twenty-first century, Web sites e-mail daily *Omer* reminders to anyone requesting this service.

With so many rules and regulations regarding the counting of the *Omer,* it is not surprising that a fair amount of institutional solemnity accompanies this time. Observant Jews assume some of the traditions associated with Jewish mourning. They do not cut their hair for the seven-week period; men don't shave or trim their beards. Weddings are not scheduled, nor is festive music played for entertainment purposes. The medieval philosopher Maimonides gives one rationale for marking this time with gravity in his aptly named text, *The Guide of the Perplexed*: "In order to increase the importance of this day [Shavuot] . . . we count the days that pass since the preceding festival. [In the same way,] one who expects his most intimate friend on a certain day, counts the days and even the hours. That is . . . why we count the *Omer* from the day of the Exodus until the day of the giving of the Law . . . [it is] the aim and object of the Exodus from Egypt."

The period of *Omer* counting is therefore a minor Jewish time of sorrow, yet one with obscure origins. One explanation states that Jews remember a plague that occurred at this time of year in the beginning of the second century, killing many students of Rabbi Akiva. Scholars note that other faiths experience a similarly muted period in the early spring, such as the Christian Lent that precedes Easter. Going back to times when Jews were mainly farmers, the season producing the first harvest was always a time of apprehension and worry. It was believed that God executed judgment on the people by withholding or sending too much rain, thereby controlling the vital grains, their sustaining food.

There is one respite during the *Omer* sobriety, which is celebrated on the thirty-third day of counting—Lag BaOmer. Jewish tradition says the plague that had afflicted Rabbi Akiva's students ended on this day. In modern-day Israel, the people celebrate Lag BaOmer by going to the beaches and mountains for evening cookouts lit by giant bonfires.

Taken together, these fifty days between Pesach and Shavuot present opportunities for quiet reflection. A cerebral activity celebrated throughout the Jewish world is the study of *Pirkei Avot*, the "Words of

Our Fathers," on the six Shabbat afternoons between Pesach and Shavuot. We move from the dependence of Egyptian slavery to communal self-reliance under the divine constitution of Torah, from subservience under Egyptian taskmasters to taking responsibility for our own actions, following God's direction. Thus the themes of Passover and Shavuot fuse. In order to receive the Torah, the Jewish people first had to become a free people. The deliverance they experienced at Pesach freed them to receive the Law at Sinai during Shavuot.

For Jews, freedom on its own does not work. Merely being released from slavery is incomplete. In the Jewish tradition, freedom means so much more. It is always yoked to additional moral and social responsibilities. It is not "freedom from," a self-absorbed posture that ignores the needs of others, but "freedom to," assuming the duty to help those in need, defined by the covenant between *Adonai* and the Jewish people and commemorated on Shavuot.

Several holidays in the Jewish calendar are associated with biblical books, or *m'gillot,* scrolls read in the synagogue as part of holiday festivities. As noted earlier, the love song of courtship between God and the Jewish people, *Shir HaShirim,* the Song of Songs, traditionally is read during both Pesach seders and Pesach synagogue worship. At Shavuot we read the very moving personal narrative in the Book of Ruth, the story of a Moabite woman who converts to Judaism to honor the faith of her Jewish mother-in-law, Naomi. The words Ruth utters as Naomi tries to convince her to return to her own people following the deaths of both of their husbands have become watchwords of individual devotion and Jewish inclusivity: " . . . Wherever you go, I will go . . . your people shall be my people, and your God my God" (Ruth 1:16).

This verse and those surrounding it have added meaning at Shavuot. Ruth and Naomi return to the Land of Israel, to the city of Bethlehem, "the house of bread," after a terrible famine has recently ended. They enter Bethlehem "at the beginning of the barley harvest" (Ruth 1:22), the same set of circumstances that brought Jewish farmers to the Temple to offer sacrifices of appreciation, which in turn became the counting of the *Omer.* Ruth's loyalty to Naomi broadens to symbolize Israel's loyalty to Torah, whose giving is commemorated on Shavuot. And the last verses of the Book of Ruth inform us that she is the ancestor of King David (4:18–22), from whose line, our Sages have assured us, will come the Messiah, the longed-for Messenger of peace.

# "You Shall Not Gather the Gleanings of Your Harvest"
## (Lev. 23:22)

A final seminal Torah theme connects Ruth and the holiday of Shavuot to Pesach. Immediately following the explanation in Leviticus of the laws regarding the counting of the *Omer,* a single biblical verse describes an act of social responsibility that serves as classic Jewish canon:

> And when you reap the harvest of your land, you shall not reap all the way to the edges of your field, or gather the gleanings of your harvest; you shall leave them for the poor and the stranger; I am *Adonai* your God. (Lev. 23:22)

In ancient Israel, the poor of the land received sustenance by becoming gleaners. They walked behind the harvesters and picked up the few stalks of grain left in the fields, which saved them from starvation. When Ruth and Naomi arrived in Bethlehem, they were destitute. So Ruth offered to glean in the fields owned by her late husband's relative, to feed herself and her aging mother-in-law.

> Ruth the Moabite said to Naomi, "I would like to go to the fields and glean among the ears of grain, behind someone who may show me kindness." (Ruth 2:2)

While gleaning, Ruth caught the eye of the prosperous owner of the field, Naomi's cousin Boaz, who fell in love with Ruth and married her (Ruth 4:13).

We recall how, on countless occasions, the Bible tells us to attend to the needs of the stranger, "because you were strangers in the land of Egypt." From the time of the Exodus, Jewish concerns for the poor have become paramount because we remember our many struggles on alien soil and those who aided us in our many times of need. Especially in our passage from Pesach to Shavuot, we remember these words of Torah and heed them, just as our ancestors replied to Moses at Mount Sinai:

> Then [Moses] took the record of the covenant and read it aloud to the people. And they said, "All that *Adonai* has spoken we will do and obey [*naaseh v'nishma*]. (Exod. 24:7)

◅ Thus our passage to Pesach ends. A journey that began six weeks prior to Pesach with Shabbat Sh'kalim, the first of the special Shabbatot, concludes with Shavuot, seven weeks after the Passover holiday. Through Jewish texts we have experienced the sights and sounds, the tastes and smells, the rituals and prayers that give the Pesach season its glorious meaning. We have proceeded through the seder meal, expanding our understanding of the major themes that have traditionally defined Pesach. We have increased our awareness of how we Jews have commemorated Pesach over our long history. And we've seen how the holiday has been transformed in modern times by the empowerment of Jewish women.

Each spring Jews all over the world renew the first experience of freedom granted to us by God and pass this timeless heritage to those who follow. For us, for our children, we say, *Amen.* We wait until next year, when our passage begins anew.

# Abbreviations

| | | | |
|---|---|---|---|
| b. | ben | Judg. | Judges |
| B.C.E. | before the Common Era | Lam. | Lamentations |
| BT | Babylonian Talmud | Lev. | Leviticus |
| C.E. | Common Era | Mal. | Malachi |
| Deut. | Deuteronomy | Matt. | Matthew |
| Eccles. | Ecclesiastes | Neh. | Nehemiah |
| Exod. | Exodus | Num. | Numbers |
| Ezek. | Ezekiel | Ps. | Psalms |
| Gen. | Genesis | R. | Rabbi, Rabban, Rav |
| Hos. | Hosea | RSV | Revised Standard |
| Isa. | Isaiah | | Version (of Christian |
| Josh. | Joshua | | Bible) |
| JT | Jerusalem Talmud | Sam. | Samuel |

# Notes

### Chapter 1: Preparing for Passage

3  close to 90 percent of American Jewry . . . : Council of Jewish Federations, 1990 National Jewish Population Survey (New York, 1991), in *Encyclopaedia Judaica*, CD-ROM ed.

3  hundreds of young trekkers . . . : Joel A. Zack, "The Legendary Seder in Katmandu," in Zion and Dishon, *Leader's Guide*, 52.

3  "I Go Die-O": *Jewish Community Store Passover Newsletter* (March 14, 2001).

4  "When we were leaving . . . ": Wouk, *Will to Live On*, 13.

4  With Egypt portrayed as archetypal enemy and Jerusalem symbolizing ultimate synthesis . . . : Fredman, *Passover Seder*, 35.

4  "starting in disgrace and ending in praise": *Mishnah P'sachim* 10:4.

5  past humiliations . . . present joys . . . : Chaim Bermant, "A Living Religion Lovingly Preserved," in *Encyclopedia of Judaism*, 1547.

5  if we take the bones of our ancestors with us . . . : Lawrence A. Hoffman, "Sabbath Week," *Jewish Week*, February 9, 2001.

6  "On this day every dwelling . . . ": Philo, *Special Laws* 2:145–146, in Bokser, *Origins of the Seder*, 9.

6  "The meal is not just for a special class . . . ": *Mishnah P'sachim* 10:1.

6  "atmosphere of *communitas*": Bokser, *Origins of the Seder*, 81.

6  The embracing atmosphere of the seder . . . : Fredman, *Passover Seder*, 10.

9  And we receive our wedding present . . . the Land of Israel: Wylen, *Settings of Silver*, 136.

### Chapter 2: Ancient Pesach: How Many Passages?

10  Thus Pesach was first celebrated by farmers . . . : Ernst Kutsch, "Critical View, Passover," in *Encyclopedia Judaica*, CD-ROM ed.

11  The animal blood . . . protected them . . . : Raphael, *Feast of History*, 39.

12  Not even Moses himself knew many of the details . . . : Ibid., 38.

15 The military outpost was first established in the early years of the sixth century B.C.E. . . . : Ibid., 127.

15 A papyrus written by the Persian ruler Darius . . . : Bokser, *Origins of the Seder,* 20.

16 *Chavurot,* table-fellowship groups . . . : Hoffman, "Liturgy of Judaism: History and Form," in *Encyclopedia of Judaism,* 823.

16 in the city of Alexandria, Egypt . . . : Raphael, *Feast of History,* 133.

16 "So joyful were they that in their vast enthusiasm . . . ": Philo, *Special Laws* 11:27, in Bokser, "Unleavened Bread," in *Anchor Bible Dictionary,* 762.

17 the redaction of the Mishnah . . . reflected several centuries of religious and cultural activity: Raphael, *Feast of History,* 69.

17 Blessings and benedictions on wine and food . . . : Ibid., 72.

18 Sometime in the second century C.E., before the Mishnah's final editing . . . : Hoffman, "Passover Meal in Jewish Tradition," 13–14.

18 *Pesach Sheini* . . . is actually significantly older than *Pesach Rishon* . . . : Arnost Zvi Ehrman, "Pesahim," in *Encyclopaedia Judaica,* CD-ROM ed.

18 The ultimate sign of rabbinic worthiness . . . : Bokser, *Origins of the Seder,* 95.

18 "When the Israelites saw that the uncircumcised . . . ": *Sh'mot Rabbah, Bo,* 19:5.

## Part II: Our Tradition's Measured Passage to Pesach: Five Special Shabbatot

23 The Talmud states, "One should raise issues and give expositions . . . ": BT *P'sachim* 6a.

### Chapter 3: Shabbat Sh'kalim: Touching the Mundane, Striving for the Sacred

28 As *Mishnah Sh'kalim* relates . . . : *Mishnah Sh'kalim* 1:1.

28 those who count give life . . . : *Pentateuch and Rashi's Commentary,* vol. 2, 171.

29 "Just as wheat is measured and stored away . . . ": *B'midbar Rabbah* 1:4.

29 "On the first of Adar . . . ": JT *Sh'kalim* 1:1–2.

30 Rabbi Joseph Hertz . . . connected . . . : Hertz, ed., *Pentateuch and Haftorahs,* 352.

30 A *piyut* . . . : Marmorstein and Marmorstein, trans., *Piyyutim,* 69.

30 God tallied the people three times: *P'sikta Rabbati* 10:4.

31 An ancient Jewish processing method . . . : *Mishnah Sh'kalim* 8:3.

31  everyone . . . also has possessions that may be numbered . . . : *Mishnah B'rachot* 9:7.

32  Jewish historian Josephus . . . : Josephus, *Jewish Antiquities* 16:3, in *New Complete Works of Josephus*, ed. Maier, 527.

32  "When God lifted Moses' head . . . ": *P'sikta Rabbati* 10:6, 181.

32  It contrasts the one Jewish fee to the many taxes . . . : *P'sikta D'Rav Kahana* 2:3.

33  Even if someone was ritually unclean . . . : JT *Sh'kalim* 6:4.

34  The angels were about to celebrate . . . : BT *M'gillah* 10b; *Sanhedrin* 39b.

35  "When You make Israel aware . . . ": *Exodus Rabbah*, trans. Lehrman, 458 n. 3.

35  "God said to Moses, 'Take special care of this nation . . . '": *P'sikta Rabbati* 10:11.

35  "A King had many purple cloaks . . . ": *P'sikta Rabbati* 10:11.

35  "Rabbi Judah bar Simon said . . . ": *P'sikta D'Rav Kahana* 2:10.

36  God as dwelling *among* the people . . . : Sarna, *Exploring Exodus*, 203.

36  "Rabbi Levi said: Why did God keep counting . . . ": *P'sikta Rabbati* 10:5.

36  "Each year I face the same question . . . ": Siegel, "Who Will Lead," 220.

36  "As for myself, how precious to me . . . ": Marmorstein and Marmorstein, trans., *Piyyutim*, 67.

### Chapter 4: Shabbat Zachor:
### Seeing Our Memories as They Define Us Today

38  "Jews have six senses . . . ": Foer, *Everything Is Illuminated*, 198–199.

40  "Amalek got into Egyptian archives . . . ": *P'sikta D'Rav Kahana* 3:10.

40  "Rabbi Yose ben Chalafta says . . . ": *M'chilta D'Rabbi Yishmael*, 136.

40  Haman is the only Amalekite who attempts to exterminate . . . : Jacob, *Second Book of the Bible*, 492.

40  if we fail to read this passage . . . : *P'sikta Rabbati* 12:2.

41  of the entire list . . . indication of his lowly birth: Sarna, *Exploring Exodus*, 124.

42  "As R. Banai . . . ": *P'sikta D'Rav Kahana* 3:4.

42  "If you use false weights and measures . . . ": *Rashi's Commentary: Deuteronomy* (New York: Hebrew Publishing, 1934), 123.

42  The late chief rabbi of Great Britain, J. H. Hertz, explains . . . : Hertz, *Pentateuch and Haftorahs*, 258.

42  Pharaoh's oppression of Israel . . . : Jacob, *Second Book of the Bible*, 490.

43  And finally, there is the moral argument . . . : *P'sikta Rabbati* 12:3.

43  "Memory! An impossible subject . . . ": Rosenblatt, "Monster Memory."

44  "remember with utterances of your mouth": *Sifre*, Piska 296, Hammer, trans., 286.

44  Deut. 25:17 . . . requires continuous public reading: Drazin, trans., *Targum Onkelos*, 227 n. 24.

44  "God will remember you again and again . . . ": *P'sikta D'Rav Kahana* 11:25.

44  "Rabbi Berechiah Berabbi said: A king had an orchard . . . ": *P'sikta Rabbati* 12:12.

45  it was the memory of this first battle . . . : Plaut, ed., *The Torah*, 1507.

45  "the place was named Massah and Meribah . . . ": Davis, trans., *Metsudah Chumash, Rashi*, 219.

45  "think of a mighty man . . . ": Ibid., 220.

45  God's call to remember . . . Israel doubted God's presence: *P'sikta Rabbati* 12:12.

45  the name Rephidim can be broken down into two Hebrew roots . . . : *P'sikta D'Rav Kahana* 3a.

45  the first mention of writing something down in the Bible . . . : Sarna, *Exploring Exodus*, 123; Jacob, *Second Book of the Bible*, 483.

46  an actual memorial book . . . : Nachmanides, *Commentary on Torah*, trans. Chavel, 245.

47  In one such place . . . as inappropriately "abstract art.": Kimmelman, "Behind Sealed Doors," E1.

48  One scenario punishes Saul . . . : Friedlander, trans., *Pirke de Rabbi Eliezer*, 349.

49  A close reading of the Hebrew in this passage . . . : Plaut, ed., *Haftarah Commentary*, 549.

50  such outright condemnation of an entire people . . . : Leibowitz, *Studies in Devarim*, 251.


*Chapter 5: Shabbat Parah: Following the Scent of a Red Heifer*

52  Legend has it that only nine such cows . . . : Maimonides, *Mishneh Torah, Hilchot Parah Adumah* 3:4.

53  "God told Moses . . . ": Marmorstein and Marmorstein, trans., *Piyyutim*, 145.

53  "Rabbi Aibu said . . . ": *B'midbar Rabbah*, 19:8.

54  Just two non-red hairs sprouting . . . : *Mishnah Parah* 2:5.

54  She could never have been worked in the field . . . : *Mishnah Parah* 2:3.

54  When Abraham . . . : *P'sikta Rabbati* 14:3.

55  Even King Solomon . . . : *Yalkut Shimoni* 759.

55  "We shall never know . . . ": Hertz, *Pentateuch and Haftorahs*, 652.

55  Rabban Yochanan ben Zakkai's faith . . . : *B'midbar Rabbah* 19:8.

56  "Because other nations taunted Israel . . . ": Rosenbaum and Silberman, trans., *Pentateuch and Rashi's Commentary*, 92.

56  "You have no right to investigate it . . . ": "MiGinzeinu Ha-Atik," in *Torah Gems*, "Hukkat," ed. Greenberg, 97.

58  Because blood was thought to be synonymous with life . . . : Milgrom, *JPS Torah Commentary*, 159.

59  King Herod, had to force people . . . : Josephus, *Jewish Antiquities* 18:2.3, in *New Complete Works of Josephus*, ed. Maier, 588.

60  some commentators have said that the reason impurity caused by corpse contamination . . . : Hizkuni, in *Torah Gems*, ed. Greenberg, 102.

60  Perhaps . . . priests threw hyssop . . . : *Encyclopaedia Judaica*, Jehuda Feliks, "Hyssop," in CD-ROM ed.

60  researchers have associated our sense of smell . . . : Good, "Emotional Malady," F7.

62  Plaut notes that the Hebrew root ח-ל-ל . . . : Plaut, ed., *Haftarah Commentary*, 558.

62  God had to purify Israel . . . : Eichrodt, *Ezekiel*, 497.

62  In the words of Rabbi Akiva: "Happy are you, O Israel! . . . ": BT *Yoma* 85b.

63  "The cedar alludes to haughtiness . . . ": Greenberg, ed., *Torah Gems*, 99.

63  "The mixture of water and ashes . . . ": Gray, *Critical and Exegetical Commentary on Numbers*, 247, cited in Plaut, ed., *The Torah*, 1149.

### Chapter 6: Shabbat HaChodesh: Tasting Pesach in Public Places, in Private Spaces

64  The early twentieth-century French Jew Marcel Proust . . . : Proust, *Remembrance of Things Past*, 62.

64  in freedom, people can choose what they eat: Greenberg, *Jewish Way*, 55.

65  our additional Torah reading . . . . contains the very first biblically given mitzvot found in Torah: Leibowitz, *Studies in Shemot*, pt. 1, 78.

65  It specifies a foreign country . . . : Sarna, *JPS Torah Commentary*, 53.

65–66  Jewish commentator Solomon ibn Verga describes . . . . : "Shabet Yechudah," in Goodman, *Passover Anthology*, 27–28.

66  "King Agrippa once wished to count the hosts of Israel. . . . ": BT *P'sachim* 64b.

67 Tradition from Mishnaic times tell us . . . : *Mishnah P'sachim* 7:1, 7:3, 10:3.

67 Since the pagan peoples . . . often ate their sacrificial meat raw . . . : Hertz, *Pentateuch and Haftorahs*, 255.

67 they celebrated the thirty-day interval that includes Pesach . . . : Nachmanides, *Commentary on Torah*, 118–19.

67 Just imagine the audacity of slaves . . . : Leibowitz, *Studies in Shemot*, 198–201.

68 Its biblical Hebrew name is Chodesh HaAviv . . . : "Nisan," *Encyclopaedia Judaica*, CD-ROM ed.

68 talmudic Sages called the first day of Nisan "the new year for kings and festivals": *Mishnah Rosh HaShanah* 1:1; JT *Rosh HaShanah* 1:2.

68 "During each of the 2,448 years before the Children of Israel went out . . . ": *P'sikta D'Rav Kahana* 5:2.

68 A *piyut* links the lamb sacrificed . . . : Marmorstein and Marmorstein, trans., *Piyyutim*, 163.

68 Because of Nisan's special status, fasting is not permitted . . . : Goodman, *Passover Anthology*, 430.

68 Because, he says, we begin counting all months with this one . . . : Nachmanides, *Commentary on Torah*, 116.

70 "The primary hallmark of freedom . . . ": Greenberg, *Jewish Way*, 40.

70 a family exiting Egypt included . . . : *Pentateuch and Rashi's Commentary*, vol. 2, 53a.

71 The Old French meaning . . . : Ibid., 55.

71 Another definition also highlights the skipping act itself . . . : Raphael, *Feast of History*, 40.

71 we have a description of a dapper, lighthearted . . . : *P'sikta Rabbati* 15:8.

71 is the same length of time it takes a circumcision wound to heal: Leibowitz, *Studies in Shemot*, pt. 1, 195–96.

71–72 "The time has come for the foreskin to be cut . . . ": *P'sikta D'Rav Kahana* 5:9.

72 a hurried, harried departure for the glory of God . . . : Shmuel Himelstein, "Rabbi Tzadok Ha-Kohen," in *Torah Gems*, ed. Greenberg, 87.

72 "One who is taking a journey . . . ": BT *Tannit.* 10b.

72 Rabbi Samuel bar Nachman said . . . ": *P'sikta Rabbati* 15:25.

73 Redactors also rather inelegantly combine two ancient holidays . . . : Fox, ed., *Five Books of Moses*, 312.

73 "It is My will that in this month you shall be redeemed": *P'sikta D'Rav Kahana* 5:7.

73  Our tradition gives the term *Pesach Dorot* . . . : Sarna, *JPS Torah Commentary,* 57.

73  now a display of matzah . . . : Hoffman, "A Symbol of Salvation," in *Passover and Easter,* ed. Bradshaw and Hoffman, 116.

73  Jews asked each other Three Questions . . . : Tabory, "Towards a History of the Paschal Meal," 69.

73  The large room is elegantly but sparsely furnished . . . : Leyerle, "Meal Customs," 30–31.

74  We're told that the typical meal . . . : Ibid., 34.

74  The first Jewish philosopher, the Egyptian-born Philo . . . : Kolatch, *Great Jewish Quotations,* 356.

74  God's place of residence thus extended . . . : Jacob Neusner, "Religious Meaning of Halakhah," in *Encyclopedia of Judaism,* vol. 1, 358–59.

74  "If three persons have eaten together and did not discuss Torah . . . ": Silverman, ed., *Passover Haggadah,* x.

74  believers view the Exodus as both a past and future event: Bradshaw and Hoffman, "Passover and Easter," 5.

74  *Exodus '47'* does not go unnoticed: Greenberg, *Jewish Way,* 53.

75  "It can be compared to a king who betrothed a woman . . . ": *Sh'mot Rabbah* 15:31.

75  "Rabbi Joshua says . . . ": BT *Rosh HaShanah* 11b.

75  "When they arrived at the mountains which surround Jerusalem . . . ": Solomon ibn Verga, in Goodman, *Passover Anthology,* 26.

75  *"This month shall be to you. . . . "*: Sforno, *Commentary on the Torah,* 297.

## Chapter 7: Shabbat HaGadol:
### Hearing One Another to Listen for God's Voice

77  "One should raise questions . . . ": BT *P'sachim* 6a.

77  "If the first day of the month Adar . . . ": *Mishnah M'gillah* 3:4.

77–78  Because talmudic Sages are silent as well about the existence of Shabbat HaGadol . . . : Zeitlin, "Liturgy of the First Night of Pesach," 457.

78  *Machzor Vitry,* an early prayer book . . . : Yuval, "Passover in the Middle Ages," 133.

78  Other scholars maintain . . . : Hoffman, "The Great Sabbath and Lent," 18.

78  making the day seem especially "long," *gadol*: Washofsky, *Jewish Living: A Guide to Contemporary Reform Practice,* 389.

78  since a long-standing custom in traditional synagogues requires . . . : Hoffman, "The Great Sabbath and Lent," 20.

78 This reasoning assumes a balancing Jewish need . . . : Yuval, "Passover in the Middle Ages," 138–40.

78 Since the Israelites were able to offer the paschal sacrifices . . . : BT *Shabbat* 87b.

79 Elijah became the symbol of healing and support . . . : Hertz, *Pentateuch and Haftorahs,* 1008.

80 others say he is Mordecai, cousin of Esther . . . : BT *M'gillah* 15.

80 Yet if either man authored this work . . . : Lipinski, "Malachi," in *Encyclopaedia Judaica,* CD-ROM ed.

80 dating the work between 500 and 450 B.C.E.: Plaut, *Haftarah Commentary,* 576.

81 "A Message for an Age of Discouragement": "Malachi," in *The Interpreter's Bible,* vol. 6, 118.

81 but had become a wilderness: Guttmacher, *The Jewish Encyclopedia,* vol. 8, 275.

82 This document is similar to . . . : Hill, "Malachi," *The Anchor Bible Dictionary,* vol. 4, 484.

82 "Haggai, Zechariah, and Malachi are the last prophets . . . ": BT *Yoma* 9b.

83 R. Levi bar Zechariah taught . . . ": *P'sikta D'Rav Kahana* 7:11.

83 "Moses said to Pharaoh . . . ": Ginzberg, *The Legends of the Jews,* vol. 2, 369–70.

83 "There were corpses as if they had been strangled in every house . . . ": Marmorstein and Marmorstein, trans., *Piyyutim,* 191.

84 "When Jews took the firstborn lambs . . . ": *Tosafot, Shabbat* 87b; *P'sikta Rabbati* 17:5.

85 "A woman was about to bring charges against her son . . . ": *P'sikta D'Rav Kahana* 9:5.

85 "Once parents used to teach their children to talk . . . ": Swarner, *Yiddish Wisdom,* 49.

85 a primal purpose of Pesach . . . : Jonathan Sacks, in Jeffrey M. Cohen, *1,001 Questions and Answers on Pesach,* ix.

85 The Talmud commends a person who teaches Torah to his friend's offspring . . . : BT *Sanhedrin* 19b.

85–86 "Rabbi Tanchuma discussed an unmarried man . . . ": *P'sikta D'Rav Kahana* 9:2.

86 "the month of ear-forming . . . ": *The New Brown-Driver-Briggs-Gensenius Hebrew and English Lexicon* (Peabody, Mass.: Hendrickson Publishers, 1979), 1.

87 "One who looks at his father is like one who sees God . . . ": Stephen Zweig, in Jeffrey Salkin, *Putting God on the Guest List* (Woodstock, Vt.: Jewish Lights, 1992), 20.

87   "When [Israel] the bride received news of her coming exaltation . . . ": Benjamin ben Zerach, *Piyyutim*, trans. Marmorstein and Marmorstein, 185.

87   "Pharaoh rose in the night of smiting": Ginzberg, *Legends of the Jews*, vol. 2, 368.

88   "Jews who long have drifted from the faith . . . ": Heinrich Heine, "Rabbi von Bacharach," in Kolatch, *Great Jewish Quotations*, 190.

## Part III: Pesach as Passage: Cups of Wine, Biblical Promises

91   Custom has it . . . : Steinsaltz, *Passover Haggadah*.

91   "Even the poorest in Israel . . . ": *Mishnah P'sachim* 10:1.

92   Various answers have been given to the question of why four . . . : Kasher, *Passover Haggadah*, 17; Silverman, *Passover Haggadah*, 64; Chaim Stern, *Gates of Freedom* (Bedford, N.Y.: New Star Press, 1981), 6; Goldschmidt, *Passover Haggadah*, 9.

92   or the four world empires that conquered . . . : JT *P'sachim* 10:1.

92   "To life! To freedom! . . . ": Raphael, *Feast of History*, 17.

92   "We remember not out of curiosity . . . ": Leonard Fein, "A Toast to Freedom," in Zion and Dishon, *Different Night*, 117.

93   viewing the promises made by God to Israel in an ascending order: My reading of Nehama Leibowitz's *New Studies* series, particularly her selections from German scholar Benno Jacob's work, greatly clarified my thinking in this matter. Leibowitz, *New Studies in Shemot, Exodus*, pt. 1, 123–29.

94   So, if a little wine is spilled . . . : Eugene B. Borowitz, "Introduction," in Stern, *Gates of Freedom*, vii.

### Chapter 8: History of the Haggadah: Telling the Pesach Story through the Ages

Since most of this chapter contains information found in a variety of sources, texts are cited by author rather than by the order in which they appear in the chapter.

Balin, "Modern Transformation of the Ancient Passover Haggadah."

Bokser, *Origins of the Seder*.

Finkelstein, "The Oldest Midrash."

Finkelstein, "Pre-Maccabean Documents in the Passover Haggadah."

Fredman, *Passover Seder*.

Friedland, "David Einhorn and *Olath Tamid*," and "Messianism in the Progressive Passover Haggadah."

Goldschmidt, *Passover Haggadah.*

Ernst D. Goldschmidt, Joseph Guttmann, Bezalel Narkiss, Cecil Roth, Robert Weltsch, "Haggadah, Passover," in *Encyclopaedia Judaica,* CD-ROM ed.

Goodman, *Passover Anthology.*

Guttman, "Haggadah Art."

Kaplan, Kohn, and Eisenstein, eds., *New Haggadah for the Pesach Seder.*

Steingroot, *Keeping Passover.*

Touster, ed., *Survivors' Haggadah.*

Wiesel, *Passover Haggadah.*

Wolfson, ed., *First Cincinnati Haggadah CD.*

### Chapter 9: The First Cup—V'hotzeiti: Matzah, Soul Food of Freedom

105   To paraphrase the sixteenth-century Italian sage Obadiah . . . : Zion and Dishon, *A Different Night,* 37.

105   what one modern scholar has deemed a "dialectical relationship": Fredman, *The Passover Seder,* 84.

106   Because this matzah-like substance was difficult to digest . . . : Scherman, *Haggadah Treasury,* 34.

106   "already/not yet" Jewish syndrome . . . : Richard Hirsh, in Levitt and Strassfeld, *Night of Questions,* 32.

106   matzah can also symbolize a situation we may not feel prepared for . . . : Roekard, *Santa Cruz Haggadah,* 35.

106   no one knew what to do until Nachshon . . . : BT *Sotah* 36.

107   "One by one, [people] would enter a room in the community house . . . ": Wiesel, *Passover Haggadah,* 24.

107   a good deed performed by the third-century Sage Rav Huna: BT *Taanit* 20b.

107   Helping to relieve deprivation wherever it appears . . . : My thanks to Rabbi Melanie Aron, Congregation Shir Hadash, Los Gatos, Calif., for sharing these thoughts with me from her April 1997 sermon. She recounts her "religious witnessing" on behalf of migrant strawberry pickers in Watsonville, Calif.

107   Some commentators ascribe . . . : JT *P'sachim* 10:5.

108   Others more matter-of-factly . . . : BT *P'sachim* 116a.

108   changing . . . *lechem oni,* "poor person's bread" . . . : Mallin, *Maharal Haggadah,* 58.

108   In the days of the Talmud . . . some Jewish bakers . . . : Goodman, *Passover Anthology,* 86–88.

108 Jews living in Germany in the fourteenth century . . . : Yuval, "Passover in the Middle Ages," 143.

108 In the mid-nineteenth century, an enterprising Austrian Jew . . . : Guggenheimer, *Scholar's Haggadah*, 201.

108 handmade matzah called *sh'murah* . . . : Birnbaum, *Birnbaum Haggadah*, 18.

108 the length of time it takes to walk a (Roman) mile: BT *P'sachim* 46a.

109 during Pesach, a third "loaf of bread" was added to the standard double portion . . . : Silverman, *Passover Haggadah*, 6.

109 Early practice in Palestine mandated only two pieces of matzah . . . : Hoffman, "Symbol of Salvation in Pesach Haggadah," *Worship* 53, no. 6 (1979), 530.

109 At the end of the eighteenth century in Lithuania, the scholar known as Vilna Gaon . . . : Herczeg, *Vilna Gaon Haggadah*, 7.

109 these matzot represent the three mitzvot of the seder . . . : Moline, *More than You Ever Need.*

109 Rabbi Sherira Gaon . . . : Guggenheimer, *Scholar's Haggadah*, 201.

110 Egyptian masters sought to deplete . . . : Scherman, *Haggadah Treasury*, 29.109

110 The sixteenth-century Bohemian rabbi known as the Maharal . . . : Mallin, *Maharal Haggadah*, 62.

110 *s'or* refers to the old leavening enabler, while *chameitz* . . . : Louis Isaac Rabinowitz, "Hamez," in *Encyclopaedia Judaica*, CD-ROM ed.

111 Rabbi Alexandri ended his daily silent devotions . . . : BT *B'rachot* 17a.

111 Moses and the angels were involved in a dispute . . . : BT *Shabbat* 88b.

112 This taste of reality we call matzah . . . : Yosef Konowitz, in Moline, *More than You Ever Need.*

112 The scholar Moshe Greenberg believes . . . : Bokser, "Unleavened Bread and Passover," 757.

112 "The bread is unleavened . . . ": Philo, *Special Laws*, bk. 2, 158–61, in Goodman, *Passover Anthology*, 135–36.

113 "It was only a few days before Passover . . . ": Mordechai Kamenetzky, March 29, 2001, Drasha@torah.org.

*Chapter 10: The Second Cup—V'hitzalti:*
*Seder Plate Objects, Sacred Symbols*

114 As Elie Wiesel has noted, the entire story of the Haggadah . . . : Wiesel, *Passover Haggadah*, 10.

115 He lined up the symbols in two vertical columns . . . : Mallin, *Maharal Haggadah,* 374.

115 "One does not bypass an obligation": BT *Yoma* 33a.

115 [The Vilna Gaon] placed *charoset* and the egg . . . : Herczeg, *Vilna Gaon Haggadah,* 7.

115 seder plate arrangement created by the sixteenth-century mystic Isaac Luria . . . : Steingroot, *Keeping Passover,* 30.

116 The two-triangle Star of David design . . . : Guggenheimer, *Scholar's Haggadah,* 202.

116 "They brought before him . . . ": *Mishnah P'sachim* 10:3.

116 *Karpas* was a late rabbinic addition . . . : Wolfson, *Art of Jewish Living,* 99.

116 Greek *karpos,* "fruit of the soil": Zion and Dishon, *A Different Night,* 31.

116 the Persian and Aramaic *karafas,* "celery": Michael Strassfeld, in Levitt and Strassfeld, *A Night of Questions,* 36.

116 Solomon Ganzfried suggests yet another food . . . : Goodman, *Passover Anthology,* 179.

117 All upper-class Greek and Roman banquets began . . . : Silverman, *Passover Haggadah,* 5.

117 Rabbi Menoah of Narbonne . . . : quoted by Riskin, *The Jewish Sentinel,* April 25, 1997.

118 As the classical commentator Yismach Yisrael relates . . . : *Haggadah Treasury,* 28.

118 A midrash uses the egg as a symbol of both mortal beginnings and endings . . . : BT *Rosh HaShanah* 11a.

118 The hotter life is made for us . . . : Steingroot, *Keeping Passover,* 39.

119 Since the destruction of the Temple . . . : Silverman, *Passover Haggadah,* 35.

119 Because of its prominence in the Pesach narrative, *z'roa* is located . . . : Fredman, *Passover Seder,* 133.

120 "Whoever has not explained the following three things on Passover . . . ": *Mishnah P'sachim* 10:5.

120 In traditional Haggadot, the leader does not even point to . . . : Wolfson, *Art of Jewish Living,* 310.

121 the preferred *chazeret* is called *chasah* . . . : Guggenheimer, *Scholar's Haggadah,* 332.

121 The Mishnah describes . . . : *Mishnah P'sachim* 2:6.

121 in antiquity, lettuce was used for medicinal purposes . . . : Guggenheimer, *Scholar's Haggadah,* 333.

121 When it first sprouts, *chazeret* . . . : Jehuda Feliks, "Lettuce," in *Encyclopaedia Judaica*, CD-ROM ed.

121 "Rabbi Shmuel ben Nachman said: How is Egypt similar to *chazeret*? . . .": BT *P'sachim* 39.

121 *maror*, called *chrein* in Yiddish: Zion and Dishon, *Leader's Guide to a Different Night*, 12.

121 *chazeret* is missing from some modern seder plates . . . : Steingroot, *Keeping Passover*, 38.

121 This legal code, known for its brevity, nonetheless mentions two Pesach actions . . . : *Mishnah P'sachim* 10:3.

121 Reuven Bulka defines *maror* . . . : Bulka, *Haggadah for Pesah*, 15.

122 *Maror* reawakens the pain and bitterness . . . : Roekard, *Santa Cruz Haggadah*, 36.

122 That is why, says Israeli scholar Menachem Kasher . . . : Kasher, *Passover Haggadah*, 151.

122 "[Bitter herbs] are manifestations of a psychic migration . . . ": Philo, *Special Laws*, bk. 1, 15, in Goodman, *Passover Anthology*, 137–38.

123 *Chazeret* may also be related to the Hebrew word *lachzor*, "to return" . . .: Wolfson, *Art of Jewish Living*, 190.

123 in the Aramaic vernacular of ancient Jewish life . . . : Kasher, *Passover Haggadah*, 145.

123 Several ingredients of *charoset* are compared to themes of love . . . : Solomon Ganzfreid, in Goodman, *Passover Anthology*, 179.

123 "Take dates, dried figs, or raisins . . . ": Steingroot, *Keeping Passover*, 239.

124 The most important figure in Kabbalah, Rabbi Isaac Luria . . . : Guggenheimer, *Scholar's Haggadah*, 334.

124 One contemporary rabbi describes the *charoset* . . . : Wylen, HUCalum 536, April 13th, 2000.

124 A Jewish soldier fighting in the American Civil War . . . : "Passover in a Union Camp," in Goodman, *Passover Anthology*, 53.

124 The Talmud brings together several aspects of the Exodus story . . . : BT *Sotah* 13b.

124 At least twice in Torah, wine is referred to . . . : Zeitlin, "Liturgy of the First Night of Passover," 437.

124 A midrash paints a painful portrait of Egyptian slavery . . . : *Pirkei D'Rabbi Eliezer* 48.

124 Joseph Tov Elem intuited this response . . . : Yuval, "Passover in the Middle Ages," 154.

125 *koreich* literally means "bind together" . . . : Wolfson, *Art of Jewish Living*, 190.

125 *The Family Haggadah* . . . : Scherman, *The Family Haggadah*, 51.

125 "Torah uses the rare term *befarech* . . . ": *Tanchuma Buber, B'haalot'cha*, in Zion and Dishon, *A Different Night*, 87.

126 "Rabbi Bunam said, We eat matzah first . . . ": Strassfeld, in Levitt and Strassfeld, *A Night of Questions*, 83.

### Chapter 11: The Third Cup—V'gaalti: The Many Moods of Miracles

128 We are commanded to keep an eternal remembrance of what our eyes have witnessed . . . : Kasher, *Passover Haggadah*, sect. 48.

128 Abraham Joshua Heschel refers to as our "radical amazement," our "legacy of wonder": Heschel, *God in Search of Man*, 43, 45.

128 all signs and wonders, might and mystery . . . : Bulka, *Haggadah for Pesah*, 64.

129 Vilna Gaon likens God's outstretched arm to the sword . . . : Herczeg, *Vilna Gaon Haggadah*, 58.

129 In some Yemenite and Iraqi Haggadot . . . : Guggenheimer, *Scholar's Haggadah*, 299.

129 the phrase "God's outstretched arm" is found in the Septuagint: Ibid., 259.

129 the word "signs," *otot*, as an appeasement . . . : Bulka, *Haggadah for Pesah*, 65; Guggenheimer, *Scholar's Haggadah*, 300.

130 The Ten Plagues were actually "ten blows" . . . : Fredman, *Passover Seder*, 106.

130 The Talmud explains two ways of understanding the plagues . . . : Scherman, *Haggadah Treasury*, 100–101.

130 Adin Steinsaltz states that these Rabbis wanted to prove . . . : Steinsaltz, *Passover Haggadah*.

130 the Vilna Gaon believed that overall . . . : Herczeg, *Vilna Gaon Haggadah*, 64.

131 "A person should teach students succinctly": BT *P'sachim* 3b.

131 Abarbanel states that each group of letters . . . : Fox, ed., *Passover Haggadah*, 83.

131 Zeitlin believes that . . . : Zeitlin, "Liturgy of the First Night," 455.

131 A rational, scientific approach to the plagues . . . : Mair and Malloy, *Ten Plagues in Egypt*.

132 "Since My children and I are partners in trouble . . . ": *P'sikta Rabbati* 49:6.

132 "My children are dying, and you are about to sing": BT *M'gillah* 10b.

132 our tradition does not overly dwell on plagues: Wolfson, *Art of Jewish Living*, 155.

133 "Our teachers listed the ability to help bear the burdens . . . ": The Alter of Kelm, in Wallach, *Pesach Haggadah*, 27.

133 Menachem Kasher cites the Rabbis' expansion of a biblical text . . . : Kasher, *Passover Haggadah*, 145.

133 Therefore a midrash identifies Aaron, not Moses . . . : Ibid., sect. 36.

133 but the ultimate protective substance . . . : Bokser, *Origins of the Seder*, 15.

133–134 Because Egypt had the audacity to enslave the people of Israel . . . : Scherman, *Haggadah Treasury*, 96.

134 "Rabbi Nathan taught . . . ": *P'sikta Rabbati* 17:5.

134 "Rabbi Nehemiah said . . . ": *P'sikta D'Rav Kahana* 7:2.

134 "Why does God boast of killing innocent children . . . ": Wiesel, *Passover Haggadah*, 51.

134 we are reminded of the difference between "more" and "enough" . . . : Roekard, *Santa Cruz Haggadah*, 30.

134–135 We say thank you to God for overdoing it . . . : Zion and Dishon, *A Different Night*, 104.

135 liberation comes in small steps . . . : Toba Spitzer, in Levitt and Strassfeld, *Night of Questions*, 70.

135 The sage Avraham Pam compares this . . . : Scherman, *Haggadah Treasury*, 105.

135 Abarbanel credits Rabbi Akiva . . . : Fox, ed., *Passover Haggadah*, 90.

135 At the Temple in Jerusalem, fifteen steps . . . : Steinsaltz, *Passover Haggadah*.

135 A section of Psalms . . . : Guggenheimer, *Scholar's Haggadah*, 308.

135 if we add the numerical significance . . . : Steingroot, *Keeping Passover*, 139.

136 "IT WOULD HAVE BEEN ENOUGH . . . ": Steven Greenberg and David Nelson for CLAL, the National Jewish Center for Learning and Leadership, in Greenberg, *Jewish Way*, 424–25.

137 Equating *afikoman* with the Greek *epikomios* . . . : BT *P'sachim* 119b.

137 Searching for the *afikoman* is the world's oldest treasure hunt . . . : Goodman, *Passover Anthology*, 378.

137 The *afikoman* also reminds us of the *pesach* sacrifice . . . : Steinsaltz, *Passover Haggadah*.

137 Two Rabbis from the Talmud, Samuel and Yochanan, thus translate *afikoman* as dessert . . . : BT *P'sachim* 10:8.

137–138 we would discover *tzafun*, "that which is hidden": Yuval, "Passover in the Middle Ages," 146.

138 like the broken matzah of the *afikoman*, our faith . . . : Olitzky, *Preparing Your Heart*, 24.

139 "We do not mean to suggest, *chalilah,* we would have been content . . . ": Malbim, in Scherman, *Haggadah Treasury,* 102–3.

### Chapter 12: The Fourth Cup—V'lakachti: Songs of Blessing and Praise to God

141 commanded to tell our children . . . : This commandment appears four times in the Torah: Exod. 12:26–27, 13:8, 13:14; Deut. 6:20–21.

141 The late-eighteenth-century commentator the Vilna Gaon relates these . . . : Herczeg, *Vilna Gaon Haggadah,* 76, 79.

141 When Israel crossed the Red Sea, the spontaneous response . . . : Bokser, *Origins of the Seder,* 19.

142 We start with an almost perfunctory thank-you . . . : Bulka, *Haggadah for Pesah,* 85.

142 already during the time of the First Temple . . . : Bokser, *Origins of the Seder,* 124 n. 21.

142 According to the Talmud, such songs were also chanted . . . : BT *P'sachim* 5:7.

142 A parable by Rabbi Eliahu Lopian . . . : Wallach, *Pesach Haggadah,* 178.

142 "In those parts of Galilee . . . ": JT *Sukkah* 10:1.

143 Even the name given to these particular psalms . . . : Cohen, *The Psalms,* 378.

143 Only during the Pesach seder do we say them in the evening: Scherman, *Haggadah Treasury,* 112.

143 Usually when we chant *Hallel* in synagogue we stand . . . : Wolfson, *Art of Jewish Living,* 174.

143 And although we continue to sing psalms . . . : Moses Aberbach, "Pharaoh," in *Encyclopaedia Judaica,* CD-ROM ed.

144 "Up to what point does [a person] recite the *Hallel?* . . . ": *Mishnah P'sachim* 10:6.

144 In Egypt, Jews were forced to act as Pharaoh's slaves . . . : Wolfson, *Art of Jewish Living,* 173.

145 Biblical commentators cite the people of Israel as deserving . . . : *Midrash T'hillim* 114:4.

146 "The Grace after meals is essentially an act of remembering . . . ": Steinsaltz, *Passover Haggadah.*

146 "Saying grace is an act of the greatest importance . . . ": Emmanuel Levinas, adapted from *Nine Talmudic Readings,* trans. Annette Aronowicz (Bloomington: Indiana University Press, 1994), 133, in Elwell, ed., *The Open Door,* 79.

147  At peak moments of spirituality . . . : Roekard, *Santa Cruz Haggadah*, 46.

147  The Alter of Kelm, a prominent nineteenth-century rabbi in the *musar* tradition . . . : Wallach, *Pesach Haggadah*, 103.

148  Some medieval Haggadot illustrate this scene . . . : Steingroot, *Keeping Passover*, 148.

148  Some commentators put a midrashic spin . . . : Scherman, *Haggadah Treasury*, 156.

148  Others note that the number . . . : Goodman, *Passover Anthology*, 443.

149  They are known as *piyutim* . . . : Heinemann and Petuchowski, *Literature of the Synagogue*, 205.

149  Other *piyutim* might have been written in times of relative calm . . . : Ibid., 208.

149  Originally the term designated every type of sacred Jewish poetry . . . : Elbogen, *Jewish Liturgy*, 167.

149–150  Early medieval compilers of some midrash collections . . . : see, for example, *Pirkei de Rabbi Eliezer* and *Sh'mot Rabbah* in Guggenheimer, *Scholar's Haggadah*, 380.

150  This particular *piyut* is thought to be the work . . . : Heinemann and Petuchowski, *Literature of the Synagogue*, 223.

150  The word *kareiv*, "draw/bring near," comes from the same root . . . : Steingroot, *Keeping Passover*, 154.

150  Eleazer Kalir, the most famous writer of *piyutim* . . . : Elbogen, *Jewish Liturgy*, 241.

150  A midrash transports Pesach to the time of Abraham . . . : Scherman, *Haggadah Treasury*, 176–77.

150–151  The third song, "Ki Lo Na-eh" . . . : Zion and Dishon, *A Different Night*, 153.

151  One modern commentator calls this the all-time seder favorite: Wolfson, *Art of Jewish Living*, 222.

151  Both "Echad Mi Yodei-a" . . . : Steingroot, *Keeping Passover*, 155.

152  "I loved this naïve little song in which everything seemed so simple . . . ": Elie Wiesel, in Levitt and Strassfeld, *Night of Questions*, 106.

153  From Our Tradition: All the translations in this section come from *The Holy Scriptures* (Philadelphia: The Jewish Publication Society of America, 1917).

*Chapter 13: The Fifth Cup—V'heiveiti: Elijah, Messianic Herald*

155  For the Talmud explains that . . . : BT *P'sachim* 118a.

155  "There are those who say . . . ": Rabbenu Sherira Gaon, in Kasher, *Passover Haggadah*, 333.

155 The dispute was resolved through a rare ritual compromise . . . : Wolfson, *Art of Jewish Living*, 212.

155 Already in the second century, Rabbi Tarfon's fifth cup . . . : Hoffman, "A Symbol of Salvation in the Passover Haggadah," *Worship* 53, no. 6 (1979), 527 n. 32.

155 But the connection of a fifth cup to Elijah in the Pesach Haggadah . . . : Guggenheimer, *Scholar's Haggadah*, 365–66.

156 a custom from the Chasidic rabbi Naphtali Tzvei . . . : Steingroot, *Keeping Passover*, 43.

156 "In Nisan they have been redeemed . . . ": BT *Rosh HaShanah* 11a.

157 In past centuries, many synagogues provided a richly decorated "Elijah's chair" . . . : *Encyclopaedia Judaica*, CD-ROM ed.

157 Might Haggadah compilers of old . . . : Friedlander, "Shefoch Chamatcha," 76.

158 The authors of the New Testament Books of Matthew, Mark, and Luke refer . . . : Matt. 26:17, Mark 14:1, Luke 22:1.

159 In the spring of 1144 in Norwich, England . . . : Stuart Schoffman, "Tales of the Red Matzah," in Zion and Dishon, *Leader's Guide to a Different Night*, 67.

159 In Czarist Russia in 1911 . . . : Raphael, *Feast of History*, 141.

160 We Jews do not think of ourselves as a vengeful people . . . : Wolfson, *Art of Jewish Living*, 210.

160 "They that were to be slain, slew . . . ": *P'sikta Rabbati* 19.

160 "And if you wrong us, shall we not revenge? . . . ": Shakespeare, "The Merchant of Venice," act 3, scene 1.

160 The nineteenth-century commentator known as the Sefat Emet . . . : Grossbard, *Sefas Emes Haggadah*, 159.

160 "Pour out Your love . . . ": Zion and Dishon, *A Different Night*, 143.

161 "We stand on guard to pray continually for the welfare . . . ": Moses Rivkes, in Raphael, *A Feast of History*, 143.

161 expressly excludes biblical curses . . . : in the Haggadah commentary of Eliezer Ashkenazi (Venice, 1583), in Goldschmidt, *Passover Haggadah*, 66.

161 Opening the door extends the isolated space . . . : Fredman, *Passover Seder*, 126.

161 "Tonight, we walked through walls of words . . . ": Elwell, in Elwell, ed., *The Open Door*, 85.

162 "When the main body of the Germans had fled and the Russians had not yet arrived . . . ": Baker, *Days of Sorrow and Pain*, 318.

163 "The injustice of this world still brings . . . ": Bronstein, ed., *Passover Haggadah*, 68–70.

163 "Let us now open the door for Elijah!": Ibid., 70.

164 "The smallest vengeance poisons the soul": Kumove, *More Words, More Arrows,* 64.

### Chapter 14: The Sixth Cup: Miriam, Pesach Prophetess

165 You are one of the few women described in the Bible as *han'viah*: Others are Deborah (Judg. 4:4), Huldah (II Kings 22:14), and Noadiah (Neh. 6:14). Plaut, *The Torah,* 490.

165 A midrash explains that . . . : *Sh'mot Rabbah* 1:13.

166 Years before, you waited at the Nile . . . : BT *Sotah* 11a.

166 the Rabbis embellish this . . . : Louis Ginzberg, *The Legends of the Jews* vol. 3, 317.

166 Tantalizing glimpses of Miriam reveal . . . : Burns, "Miriam," 870.

166 One meaning connects two Hebrew words . . . : Frankel, *Five Books of Miriam,* 113.

166 the word *ra'im* . . . : Guggenheimer, *Scholar's Haggadah,* 284.

167 the name of Moses has an Egyptian root . . . : Zion and Dishon, *Leader's Guide to A Different Night,* 81.

167 Miriam was called "beloved" . . . : *Five Books of Miriam,* 113.

167 "At twilight of the sixth day . . . ": Ibid., xv, from *B'midbar Rabbah* 1:2.

167 "Ten things were created . . . ": *Pirkei Avot* 5:8.

167 The well "resembled a rock . . . ": BT *Taanit* 9a.

167 "It was believed that God gave the well in Miriam's name . . . ": *Legends of the Jews,* vol. 3, 53–54.

167–168 At the fall holiday of Sukkot . . . : *Mishnah Sukkah* 5:1–4, in Abram Kanof, "Sukkot," *Encyclopaedia Judaica,* CD-Rom ed.

168 "there was not a courtyard in Jerusalem . . . ": Ibid.

168 "had never witnessed . . . ": Ibid.

168 They had to be satisfied . . . : Klagsbrun, *Jewish Days,* 43.

168 In 1989, a group of Boston women . . . : Cohen, "Filling Miriam's Cup," 18.

169 "LEADER: This is the cup of Miriam . . . ": Ritari, Angelou, and Berkenfield, *iworship* 95.

169 "Let us each fill the cup . . . ": Lerner, "Let Each of Us Fill a Cup." www.miriamscup.com/RitualFirst.htm.

169 women were not even invited . . . : Goodman, *Passover Anthology,* 308.

169 For example, the Mishnah explains in detail . . . : *Mishnah P'sachim* 2:5–6.

170 Rabbi Elazar declared that anyone who is obligated . . . : BT *P'sachim* 91.

170 "Rabbi Yehoshua ben Levy said: Women are obligated . . . ": BT *P'sachim* 108a.

171 "'Surely,' Rivka thought . . . ": E. M. Broner, *The Telling*, 11.

171 Finding a Haggadah to use that fit the spirit . . . : *San Diego Women's Haggadah*, vii.

171 For women, talking about their lives . . . : Friedlander, "Shefoch Chamatcha," 90.

172 The Bible contains eleven Hebrew words to describe dance . . . : Plaut, ed., *The Torah*, 492.

172 women celebrated their victory against Pharaoh by dancing . . . : Selma Jeanne Cohen, "Dance," in *Encyclopaedia Judaica*, CD-ROM ed.

172 "Whenever the people journeyed, the well traveled with them . . . ": Frankel, *Five Books of Miriam*, xvii–xviii.

173 "As soon as Miriam died . . . ": Cohen, "Filling Miriam's Cup," 17.

174 "I Hope You Dance,": Lee Ann Womack, in Womack, *I Hope You Dance*.

174 "caretaker rather than searcher . . . ": Broner, *The Telling*, 139.

174 "Mine is the voice of joy . . . ": Frankel, *Five Books of Miriam*, xxii.

174 "*Miriam Hanevi'ah*": Ibid., 304.

175 "God": Feiga Izrailevna Kogan, translated by Balin in *To Reveal Our Hearts: Jewish Women Writers in Tsarist Russia*, 148–49.

175 "I Shall Sing to the Lord a New Song": Sohn, in Levitt and Strassfeld, *Night of Questions*, 67.

### Epilogue: Passage from Pesach to Shavuot

178 "Rabbi Yannai said: The way it is with mankind . . . : *P'sikta D'Rav Kahana* 8:1.

179 Pesach is the first promise of salvation . . . : Riskin, "Nazir's Promise."

180 Web sites e-mail daily *Omer* reminders . . . : www.sefira@torah.org.

180 "In order to increase the importance of this day . . . ": Maimonides, *Guide of the Perplexed* 3:43.

180 The period of *Omer* counting is therefore . . . : Green, *These Are the Words*, 253.

180 the season producing the first harvest . . . : Theodor Gaster, *Festivals of the Jewish Year*, in Zarren-Zohar, "From Pesach to Shavuot," 80.

181 In order to receive the Torah . . . : Person, "Shavuot," May 2001, www.clickonjudaism.com.

# Glossary

**Adar:** Hebrew lunar month in which the special Shabbatot Sh'kalim, Zachor, and Parah occur.

**"Adir Hu":** "Mighty Is He," one of the concluding seder songs.

*Adonai-nisi:* "God is my miracle/banner." Soon after leaving Egypt, the Jews defeated the Amalekites in the first battle they fought as a free people. In gratitude, Moses built an altar to God and named it *Adonai-nisi.*

*afikoman:* The larger part of the middle of the three seder matzot on the seder table, which is hidden at the beginning of the seder and is searched for and found immediately following the meal so that the seder can proceed.

*aggadah:* Narrative or homiletic writings of rabbinic literature, as opposed to *halachah,* legal texts.

**Amalek:** As the Israelites left the Red Sea, Amalek and his followers attacked the weak and the sick, the most vulnerable. Thus he and his descendants symbolize the worst enemies of the Jews. Amalek is remembered in the Torah portion for Shabbat Zachor.

*Ani Maamim:* "I believe [in perfect faith in the coming of the Messiah]." Taken from Maimonides' Thirteen Principles of Faith, these words were turned into a song that was sung in the death camps of the Holocaust.

**Antiochus:** Syrian-Greek ruler of Judea whose repression of Judaism led to the Maccabean revolt in the second century B.C.E.

*Arba Parashiyot:* The first four special Shabbatot before Pesach: Sh'kalim, Zachor, Parah, and HaChodesh.

*arbeh:* Locusts; the eighth plague.

**Ari:** Name for Rabbi Isaac Luria, a sixteenth-century mystic and creator of Lurianic Kabbalah in Safed, Israel.

*arov:* Wild beasts; the fourth plague.

*Aseret HaDibrot:* "The ten things"; the Ten Commandments.

*atzmiyut:* "Essence"; in this context, used as a Hebrew wordplay with *atzumot,* "bones." When the Israelites left Egypt, they carried the bones of the patriarch Joseph with them in their wandering through the wilderness. They also took the moral essence of all of their ancestors, what they needed to guide them successfully on their journey to the Promised Land.

*atzumot:* "Bones"; "And Moses took with him the bones of Joseph, who had exacted an oath from the Children of Israel, saying, 'God will be sure to take notice of you: then you shall carry up my bones from here with you'" (Exod. 13:19).

*aviv:* "Ear-forming"; spring.

*barad:* Hail; the seventh plague.

*Bareich:* Blessing after the meal *(Birkat HaMazon)*; the twelfth seder step.

*beitzah:* hard-boiled or roasted egg; a seder plate symbol; the stand-in for the *pesach* sacrifice.

*B'farech:* "With harshness." "The Egyptians ruthlessly imposed [with harshness] upon the Israelites the various labors that they made them perform" (Exod. 1:13).

*Birds' Head Haggadah:* Fourteenth-century Haggadah manuscript portraying Jews with heads of birds.

*Birkat HaMazon:* Blessings said after eating.

*b'midbar:* The wilderness in which Jews wandered for forty years after leaving Egypt; the fourth book of Torah.

*b'nei vichori:* "My own firstborn."

*Book of Wars of the Eternal:* Ancient memorial book referred to in the Bible, now lost.

*B'rit milah:* Circumcision.

"*Chad Gadya*": "An Only Kid," one of the concluding seder songs.

*Chag HaAviv:* "The Holiday of Springtime"; another name for Pesach.

*chagigah:* Special festival sacrifice during Temple times.

*chagim:* The three Pilgrimage Festivals—Pesach, Shavuot, Sukkot; more generally, a Jewish holiday.

*chalilah:* "Heaven forbid!" Hebrew/Yiddish expression that was probably taken from the root ח-ל-ל, "to profane."

*chameitz:* Food containing leavening, forbidden at Pesach.

*charoset:* Mixture of fruit, nuts, and wine depicting the mortar the Israelite slaves made in Egypt; seder plate symbol.

*chasah:* Type of lettuce mentioned in the Talmud and used as *chazeret*; seder plate symbol.

*chavurot:* Two thousand years ago, table-fellowship groups emphasizing worship around food; in modern times, informal worship communities.

*chazeret:* Lettuce; additional seder plate symbol for bitter herbs.

**Chimielnitzki:** Seventeenth-century Cossack who led pogroms, killing tens of thousands of Russian Jews.

*chodesh:* "Month."

*Chodesh HaAviv:* "Month of Spring."

*choshech:* Darkness; the ninth plague.

*chrein:* Yiddish term for horseradish root used as *maror.*

*chuppah:* Wedding canopy.

*dam:* Blood; the first plague.

*dam anavim:* "Blood of the grapes"; biblical reference to wine.

**"Dayeinu":** "It would have been enough"—even one of the many miracles that God performed for us as we were leaving Egypt would have been sufficient. A well-known song that is part of the seder ritual.

*dever:* Pestilence; the fifth plague.

*D'TZACH, ADASH, B'ACHAV:* Three-word Hebrew mnemonic for the Ten Plagues found in the Haggadah.

**"Echad Mi Yodei-a?":** "Who Knows One?"—one of the concluding seder songs.

Egyptian *Hallel:* Psalms 113–118, which are included in the Haggadah.

*eirusin:* Traditional engagement period prior to marriage.

**Elephantine:** Site of Egyptian military outpost in the sixth century B.C.E., which was staffed primarily by Jewish soldiers.

**Elijah:** Prophet whose visit to the Pesach seder will signal the coming of the Messiah.

**"Eliyahu HaNavi":** "Elijah the Prophet," popular song from the *Havdalah* service also sung during seder when the door is opened for Elijah.

*Eser Makot:* The Ten Plagues.

**Feast of Unleavened Bread:** A name for Pesach from the Bible.

*First Cincinnati Haggadah:* Fifteenth-century Ashkenazi Haggadah manuscript now residing at the Cincinnati campus of Hebrew Union College–Jewish Institute of Religion.

*gerim:* "Strangers"; " . . . for you [Israel] were strangers in their [Egypt's] land" (Exod. 23:9 and throughout the Bible), an oft-cited proof text defining the rationale for proper Jewish moral behavior.

*g'nut:* "Disgrace," spoken during the beginning of the seder as part of the statement: "We start with disgrace and end with praise" (BT *Mishnah P'sachim* 10:4).

**haftarah:** A reading from the Prophets that follows the Torah reading on Shabbat and the Festivals.

**Haggadah:** Book used as service for Pesach seders.

*ha lachma anya:* "This is the bread of affliction," from the beginning of the *Magid* section of the Haggadah.

*Hallel:* "Praises"; psalms praising God; the fourteenth seder step.

*Hallel HaGadol:* "The Great Hallel," Psalm 136, which is part of the seder service.

**Hallelujah:** "Praises to God."

**Herod:** Roman-appointed king of the Jews at the turn of the Common Era who began massive renovation of the Jerusalem Temple.

*Hilchot Chameitz Umatzah:* Part of the *Mishneh Torah* by Maimonides that comments on the laws of Pesach.

**Hillel sandwich:** Bitter herbs between two pieces of matzah (some add *charoset*), eaten immediately before the seder meal.

**Hyssop:** Wild shrub common in ancient Israel used to apply blood on the Jews' doorposts during their last night in Egypt, which signaled to the Angel of Death to pass over their homes.

**Josephus:** Jewish general of the first century C.E. who defected to the Romans at the time of the destruction of the Temple; he wrote books of Jewish history still existing today.

*Kaddish:* A prayer recited by mourners praising God; also used to separate major sections of the worship service.

*kadeish:* Reciting the *Kiddush* at the beginning of the seder; the first seder step.

**Kalir:** Most famous writer of *piyutim*, liturgical poetry, who lived in Palestine in the sixth to seventh century.

*kamah maalot tovot:* "With how many good 'levels' [or stages] [has God blessed us]"; said immediately before the "Dayeinu" during the seder.

*k'arah:* Seder plate.

*kareiv:* "[To] draw near," the phrase taken from the last stanza of the Pesach song "It Came to Pass at Midnight"—"May the day draw near when it is no longer day or night," a reference to the coming of the Messiah.

*karpas:* [Usually] green vegetable symbolizing spring and dipped into salt water; the third seder step.

*kesef hakipurim:* Expiation money.

*ketubah:* Official marriage contract document.

*Kiddush:* Blessing over wine on the Sabbath and Pesach, Shavuot, and Sukkot.

*ki l'olam chasdo:* "For God's kindness endures forever," repeated phrase in Psalm 118.

**"Ki Lo Na-eh":** "For to God, Praise Is Proper," one of the concluding seder songs.

*kinim:* Vermin; the third plague.

*kohein:* Descendant of a Temple priest; name sometimes given to first of three ritual seder matzot.

*koreich:* "Bind together"; sandwich composed of bitter herbs and usually *charoset* between matzah; the tenth seder step.

*kos Miryam:* "Miriam's cup"; in recent years, cup of water dedicated to Miriam that is placed on the seder table.

**Last Supper:** Meal Jesus ate with his disciples in Jerusalem shortly before his arrest and crucifixion; some think it was a Pesach seder.

*l'chayim:* "To life."

*lechem chameitz:* Leavened bread, forbidden during Pesach week.

*lechem oneh:* "Bread of reciting"; a midrashic interpretation of what matzah represents in the seder meal.

*lechem oni:* "Poor person's bread"; the traditional understanding of matzah as a seder symbol.

*leil shimurim:* "Night of watching" (Exod. 12:42); the first night of the first, Egyptian Pesach.

**Levite:** Descendant of an assistant to the Temple priests; one from the biblical tribe of Levi; name sometimes given to second of three ritual seder matzot.

*L'shanah habaah birushalayim:* "Next year in Jerusalem," said at the end of seder.

*Machzor Vitry:* Twelfth-century prayer book.

*Magid:* Narrative section of the Haggadah; the fifth seder step.

**Maimonides:** The great medieval philosopher/physician also known as the Rambam who lived in Spain, Palestine, and Egypt toward the end of the twelfth century. He is best known for his systemic work on Jewish rationalism, *Guide to the Perplexed,* and his comprehensive legal code, *Mishneh Torah.*

*makat b'chorot:* "Death of the firstborn"; the tenth plague.

*makot:* "Plagues."

**manna:** Food sent by God to feed the people during their forty years of wandering in the wilderness.

*mar:* "Bitter."

*maror:* "Bitter herbs"; the ninth seder step and seder plate symbol.

**Massah:** "Trial"; ancient biblical site.

**matzah:** Unleavened bread made from wheat, barley, spelt, rye, or oats and water and eaten instead of leavened bread during Pesach; the eighth seder step.

*mei-nidah:* "Water for sprinkling" (i.e., purification, found in Numbers 19).

*mer:* Egyptian, "beloved"; possible root of Miriam's name.

**Meribah:** "Quarrel"; ancient biblical site.

*m'gillot:* "Scrolls."

**Mi chamochah ba-eilim Adonai?:** "Who is like You, Eternal One?", part of the Song of the Sea (Exodus 15).

*mikveh:* Ritual bath.

*minhag:* Jewish custom or practice often having the force of law.

**Miriam:** Older sister of Moses; prophetess who led the women in song and dance at the Red Sea.

**Miryam han'viah:** "Miriam the Prophetess."

**Mishnah:** Law code compiled in Palestine in 200 C.E.; basis of the Talmud.

*Mitzrayim:* Egypt.

**mitzvah (mitzvot):** A commandment; figuratively, a good deed.

*m'ot chitim:* "Wheat money"; charity collected pre-Pesach to provide Jewish poor with special holiday foods.

*Motzi:* "Who brings forth bread from the earth"; blessing over bread or matzah said prior to eating seder meal; the seventh seder step.

**Musar movement:** Nineteenth-century Jewish philosophy emphasizing a rigorous, ethical pietism in study and observance.

*naaseh v'nishma:* "We will do and obey" (Exod. 24:7).

**Nachmanides:** Also known as the Ramban, he lived in thirteenth-century Spain and was the leading talmudic scholar of his time.

*nidah:* Traditional idea of female impurity.

**Night of watching:** The first Pesach in Egypt.

*nirtzah:* "Acceptance" or "conclusion"; the fifteenth and last seder step.

**Nisan:** Akkadian, "To start"; "the first of months" in the Book of Exodus; month of Pesach.

*Omer:* A sheaf of first spring grain sacrificed at the Temple; later, a unit counted every day for the forty-nine-day period between Pesach and Shavuot.

*otot:* "Signs"; physical examples of the miracles God performed on behalf of the Jews in order to convince Pharaoh to free Israel from Egyptian bondage.

*parah:* "Heifer."

*parah adumah:* Completely red heifer used in purification ceremony described in the Book of Numbers.

*parashiyot:* Specific Torah or haftarah portions read on the Sabbath or Festivals.

*pesach:* the sacrifice.

**Pesach:** "To pass over"; spring festival celebrating the Hebrew slaves' Exodus from Egyptian bondage.

**Pesach Dorot:** "Pesach of the Generations"; all Pesachs after the first, Egyptian holiday.

**Pesach Mitzrayim:** "Egyptian Pesach"; the first Pesach, when God spared the lives of the Hebrew firstborns.

**Pesach Rishon:** The first section of *Mishnah P'sachim.*

**Pesach Sheini:** The second section of *Mishnah P'sachim.*

**Philo:** The first Jewish philosopher, who lived in the first century C.E. in Alexandria, Egypt.

*piyutim:* Medieval liturgical poetry.

**Prague Haggadah:** Sixteenth-century Haggadah printed in Yiddish.

**P'sachim:** Mishnaic book dealing with laws of the holiday.

**P'sikta D'Rav Kahana:** A midrashic anthology compiled during medieval times.

**P'sikta Rabbati:** A large midrashic anthology compiled about two hundred years after *P'sikta D'Rav Kahana.*

**Puah:** Midwife in Egypt, along with Shiphrah, who disobeyed Pharaoh and saved the lives of newborn Jewish male infants.

*rachtzah:* Washing hands prior to seder meal accompanied by a blessing; the sixth seder step.

*ra-im:* Arabic, "to love tenderly"; possible root of Miriam's name.

**Rashi:** Seminal eleventh-century Jewish thinker noted for his clear biblical and talmudic commentaries.

**Rephidim:** Site of first biblical battle after Israelites were freed from Egypt.

**Rosh Chodesh:** "The head of the month"; monthly holiday celebrated by women marking Jewish feminist themes.

**Samuel ben Salomon of Falaise:** Thirteenth-century French scholar who developed the fifteen steps of the Pesach seder.

*Sarajevo Haggadah:* Fourteenth-century Spanish Haggadah manuscript.

**seder:** "Order"; ritual Pesach meal.

*s'firat HaOmer:* "Counting of the *Omer*"; the ceremonial counting for the forty-nine-day period between Pesach and Shavuot.

**Shabbat HaChodesh:** "Sabbath of the Month"; the fourth special Shabbat before Pesach celebrating the first Sabbath of the month of Nisan.

**Shabbat HaGadol:** "The Great Sabbath"; the fifth special Shabbat before Pesach immediately before the holiday begins.

**Shabbat Parah:** "The Sabbath of the Heifer"; the third special Shabbat before Pesach especially dedicated to Jewish laws of purity.

**Shabbat Sh'kalim:** "The Sabbath of Counting"; the first special Shabbat before Pesach when Jews in Temple times paid their annual tax to Jerusalem.

**Shabbat Zachor:** "The Sabbath of Remembrance"; the second special Shabbat before Pesach closest to Purim when the wicked deeds of Amalek are remembered.

*sh'chin:* Boils; the sixth plague.

**shekel tax:** Annual payment to Jerusalem by Jews for upkeep and maintenance of the Temple.

*Sh'foch chamat'cha:* "Pour out Your wrath"; the first of four biblical verses traditionally recited during seder before the door is opened for Elijah.

**Shiphrah:** Midwife in Egypt, along with Puah, who disobeyed Pharaoh and saved the lives of newborn Jewish male infants.

*shirah chadashah:* "A new song" that is sung at the beginning of the blessing after the meal.

*Sh'ma:* "Hear/Listen!"; first word of the most important prayer in Jewish liturgy.

*Sh'moneh Esreih:* "The Eighteen Benedictions"; one of several names for the group of petition-blessings that is the center of each Jewish service.

*Sh'murah:* "Guarded or watched"; refers to closely watched production of matzah grain from harvest through baking.

*Shulchan Aruch:* "Prepared Table"; name of the definitive code of Jewish law compiled by Joseph Caro in sixteenth-century Safed that is still followed by observant Jews today.

*simchah:* Joyous celebration.

**Simchat Beit HaSho-eivah:** "Water Libation Rite" performed during Sukkot at the Jerusalem Temple.

*s'or:* "Sour dough"; ancient leavening agent.

**Special Shabbatot:** The Sabbaths before Pesach during which holiday themes are studied through special Torah and haftarah portions.

**Sukkot:** The festival of Tabernacles celebrating the fall harvest.

**Tabernacle:** The portable sanctuary the freed Israelites took with them in their forty years of wandering.

*tallit:* Jewish prayer shawl.

**Temple Mount:** The elevated area of Jerusalem where both Temples were built; thus, the holiest Jewish place.

**Ten Plagues:** The ten punishments inflicted by God against Egypt that culminated in Pharaoh's freeing of the Hebrew slaves.

**Tetragrammaton:** Four never-pronounced Hebrew letters that spell God's most sacred name.

*T'fillin:* "Phylacteries"; square leather boxes tied to the hand and head for the morning service containing biblical passages Exod. 13:1–10; 13:11–16; Deut. 6:4–9; 11:13–21.

**Tishrei:** The month in the Jewish calendar in which Rosh HaShanah and Yom Kippur occur.

**Titus:** Roman general who destroyed Jerusalem and the Temple in 70 C.E.

*torat lishmah:* Jewish study for its own sake.

**Torquemada:** The head of the Spanish Inquisition at the end of the fifteenth century.

*Tosefta:* Teachings of the rabbinic period not included in the Mishnah but accepted as secondarily authoritative.

*t'shuvah:* "Repentance."

*tzafun:* "Hidden"; eating the afikoman after the seder meal; the twelfth seder step.

*Tz'fardei-a:* "frogs"; the second plague.

*tzimtzum:* "Contraction"; in kabbalistic mysticism, God's withdrawal before creating the world to make room for earthly things.

*ugot:* "Cakes."

*Union Haggadah:* First official Reform Haggadah published by the Central Conference of American Rabbis in 1908.

*ur'chatz:* Ceremonial washing of hands without saying a blessing; the second seder step.

**"Uv'chein Va'hi BaChatzei Halailah":** "It Came to Pass at Midnight"; one of the concluding seder songs, it is sung only on the first night of Pesach.

**"V'amartem Tzevach Pesach":** "And you shall say: this is the Feast of Pesach"; one of the concluding seder songs, it is sung only on the second night of Pesach.

*v'gaalti:* "And I will redeem you [with an outstretched arm]" (Exod. 6:6).

*v'heiveiti:* "And I will bring you [into the Land]" (Exod. 6:8).

*v'hitzalti:* "And I will deliver you [from their bondage]" (Exod. 6:6).

*v'hotzeiti:* "And I will bring you out [from the Egyptians]" (Exod. 6:6).

*v'lakachti:* "And I will take you [to be My people]" (Exod. 6:7).

*yachatz:* "Dividing"; the fourth seder step.

*YaKenNeHaz:* Hebrew phrase in Haggadah that begins Saturday night seder, mistakenly translated into German as *Jagen-has,* "hare hunt."

*yam:* "Sea."

**Yannai:** Sixth-century poet living in Palestine who wrote *piyutim,* liturgical poetry.

*yetzer hara:* "The inclination to do evil."

*yetzer hatov:* "The inclination to do good."

**Yizkor:** Memorial service held at the conclusion of Pesach, Shavuot, Yom Kippur, and Sukkot.

**Yochanan ben Zakkai:** First-century rabbi credited with helping transform Judaism from a religion of sacrifice into a religion of prayer after the destruction of the Temple in 70 C.E.

**Yom HaShoah:** Annual commemoration of the Holocaust.

*Y'rushalmi:* The Talmud written in Israel around 450 C.E.

*zachor:* "Remember."

*Zevach Pesach:* Early sixteenth-century Haggadah written by the Sephardic commentator Don Isaac Abarbanel.

*z'man cheiruteinu:* "The time of our freedom"; a name for Pesach.

*z'man matan Torateinu:* "The time of the giving of the Torah"; a name for Shavuot.

*z'mirot:* Table songs sung at Shabbat and the Festivals.

*z'roa:* "Shank bone"; seder plate symbol; also referred to in the Haggadah as the *pesach.*

*z'roa n'tuyah:* "Outstretched arm" of God.

*zuz(im):* Unit(s) of money during Roman times.

# Bibliography

Adelman, Penina V. *Miriam's Well*. New York: Biblio Press, 1986.

Baker, Leonard. *Days of Sorrow and Pain: Leo Baeck and the Berlin Jews*. New York: Macmillan Publishing, 1978.

Balin, Carole B. "The Modern Transformation of the Ancient Passover Haggadah." In *Passover and Easter: Origin and History to Modern Times*, edited by Paul F. Bradshaw and Lawrence A. Hoffman. Vol. 5 of *Two Liturgical Traditions*. Notre Dame, Ind.: University of Notre Dame Press, 1999.

———. *To Reveal Our Hearts: Jewish Women Writers in Tsarist Russia*. Cincinnati: Hebrew Union College Press, 2000.

Birnbaum, Philip. *The Birnbaum Haggadah*. New York: Hebrew Publishing, 1953, 1976.

Blackman, Philip, ed. *Tractate Shekalim*. New York: The Judaica Press, 1963.

Bokser, Baruch M. *The Origins of the Seder: The Passover Rite and Early Rabbinic Judaism*. Berkeley: University of California Press, 1984.

———. "Unleavened Bread and Passover, Feasts of." In *The Anchor Bible Dictionary*. Vol. 6. New York: Doubleday, 1992.

Bradshaw, Paul F., and Lawrence A. Hoffman. "Passover and Easter: The Symbolic Shaping of Time and Meaning." In *Passover and Easter: The Symbolic Structuring of Sacred Seasons*, edited by Paul F. Bradshaw and Lawrence A. Hoffman. Vol. 6 of *Two Liturgical Traditions*. Notre Dame, Ind.: University of Notre Dame Press, 1999.

Braude, William G., and Israel J. Kapstein, trans. *Pesikta de-Rab Kahana*. Philadelphia: Jewish Publication Society of America, 1975.

Braude, William G., trans. *Pesikta Rabbati*. New Haven: Yale University Press, 1968.

Broner, E. M. *The Telling*. San Francisco: HarperCollins, 1992.

Bronstein, Herbert, ed. *A Passover Haggadah*. Rev. ed. New York: Central Conference of American Rabbis, 1994.

Brueggeman, Walter. *First and Second Samuel: Interpretation*. Louisville: John Knox Press, 1990.

Bulka, Reuven P. *The Haggadah for Pesah*. Jerusalem: Machon Pri Ha'aretz, 1985.

Burns, Rita J. "Miriam." In *The Anchor Bible Dictionary*. Vol. 4. New York: Doubleday, 1992.

Cardin, Nina Beth. *The Tapestry of Jewish Time*. Springfield, N.J.: Behrman House, 2000.

Cassuto, Umberto. *Commentary on the Book of Exodus*. Jerusalem: Magnes Press, 1967.

Cohen, Andrew, ed. *The Psalms*. London: Soncino Press, 1945.

Cohen, Jeffrey M. *1,001 Questions and Answers on Pesach*. Northvale, NJ: Jason Aronson, 1996.

Cohen, Tamara R. "Filling Miriam's Cup." In Miriam's Cups Exhibit Catalogue, *Drawing From the Source: Miriam, Women's Creativity, and New Ritual*. New York: Ma'yan: The Jewish Women's Project, 1997.

Cohn, Robert. *Two Kings*. Collegeville, Minn.: Liturgical Press, 2000.

Davis, Avrohom, trans. *Metsudah Chumash, Rashi*. Vol. 2. Hoboken, N.J.: KTAV, 1993.

Drazin, Israel, trans. *Targum Onkelos to Deuteronomy*. Hoboken, N.J.: KTAV, 1982.

Eichrodt, Walter. *Ezekiel: A Commentary*. Philadelphia: Westminster Press, 1970.

Eisemann, Moshe. *Yechezkel, The Book of Ezekiel*. Vol. 2. Brooklyn: Mesorah Publications, 1980.

Elbogen, Ismar. *Jewish Liturgy: A Comprehensive History*. Philadelphia: Jewish Publication Society, 1993.

Elman, Yaakov. *The Living Nach*. New York: Moznaim Publishing, 1984.

Elwell, Sue Levi, ed. *The Open Door: A Passover Haggadah*. New York: Central Conference of American Rabbis, 2002.

*Encyclopaedia Judaica*. CD-ROM edition. Jerusalem: Judaica Multimedia, 1997.

*Encyclopedia of Judaism*. New York: Continuum, 1999.

Finkelstein, Louis. "The Oldest Midrash: Pre-Rabbinic Ideals and Teachings in the Passover Haggadah." *Harvard Theological Review* 31, no. 4 (1938): 291–317.

———. "Pre-Maccabean Documents in the Passover Haggadah." *Harvard Theological Review* 35, no. 4 (1942): 291–332.

Foer, Jonathan Safran. *Everything Is Illuminated*. New York: Houghton Mifflin, 2002.

Fox, Everett, ed. *The Five Books of Moses*. New York: Schocken Books, 1995.

Fox, Shlomo, ed. *The Passover Haggadah with Commentary of Don Isaac Abarbanel*. Brooklyn: Mesorah Publications, 1990.

Frankel, Ellen. *The Five Books of Miriam*. New York: G. P. Putnam's Sons, 1996.

Fredman, Ruth Gruber. *The Passover Seder: Afikoman in Exile*. Philadelphia: University of Pennsylvania Press, 1981.

Freedman, H., and M. Simon, eds. *Midrash Rabbah*. 10 vols. London: Soncino Press, 1948.

Friedland, Eric L. "David Einhorn and *Olath Tamid*," and "Messianism in the Progressive Passover Haggadah." In *Were Our Mouths Filled with Song*. Cincinnati: Hebrew Union College Press, 1997.

Friedlander, Ariel J. "Shefoch Chamatcha: An Examination of Polemic and Apologetic Motifs in the Passover Haggadah." Rabbinic thesis, Hebrew Union College–Jewish Institute of Religion, 1996.

Friedlander, Gerald, trans. *Pirke de Rabbi Eliezer*. 4th ed. New York: Sepher-Hermon Press, 1981.

Ginzberg, Louis. *The Legends of the Jews*. Baltimore: Johns Hopkins University Press, 1998.

Goldschmidt, Ernst Daniel. *The Passover Haggadah*. Edited by Nahum N. Glatzer. New York: Schocken Books, 1953, 1969.

Good, Erica. "Emotional Malady Is Linked to Smell." *New York Times*, May 16, 2000.

Goodman, Philip. *The Passover Anthology*. Philadelphia: The Jewish Publication Society, 1993.

Gray, George. *A Critical and Exegetical Commentary on Numbers*. New York: Scribner's, 1903.

Gray, John. *I And II Kings: A Commentary*, Philadelphia: Westminster Press, 1970.

Green, Arthur. *These Are the Words: A Vocabulary of Jewish Spiritual Life*. Woodstock, Vt.: Jewish Lights Publishing, 1999.

Greenberg, Aharon, ed. *Torah Gems*. Tel Aviv: Y. Orenstein, Yavneh Publishing, Chemed Books, 1992.

Greenberg, Irving. *The Jewish Way: Living the Holidays*. New York: Simon & Schuster, 1988.

Grossbard, Simcha Leib. *The Sefas Emes Haggadah*. Smithfield, Mich.: Targum Press, 1995.

Guggenheimer, Heinrich. *The Scholar's Haggadah*. Northvale, N.J.: Jason Aronson, 1995.

Guttman, Joseph. "Haggadah Art." In *Passover and Easter: The Symbolic Structuring of Sacred Seasons*, edited by Paul F. Bradshaw and Lawrence A. Hoffman. Vol. 6 of *Two Liturgical Traditions*. Notre Dame, Ind.: University of Notre Dame Press, 1999.

Hammer, Reuven, trans. *Sifre: Tannaitic Commentary on Book of Deuteronomy*. New Haven: Yale University Press, 1986.

Hauptman, Judith. "Pesah: A Liberating Experience for Women." *Masoret*, winter 1991.

Heinemann, Joseph, and Jakob J. Petuchowski. *Literature of the Synagogue*. New York: Behrman House, 1985.

Herczeg, Yisrael Isser Zvi. *Vilna Gaon Haggadah*. Brooklyn: Mesorah Publications, 1993.

Hertz, J. H., ed. *The Pentateuch and Haftorahs*. London: Soncino Press, 1979.

Heschel, Abraham Joshua. *God in Search of Man: A Philosophy of Judaism*. New York: Farrar, Straus and Giroux, 1975.

Hoffman, Lawrence A. "The Great Sabbath and Lent: Jewish Origins?" In *Passover and Easter: The Symbolic Structuring of Sacred Seasons*, edited by Paul F. Bradshaw and Lawrence A. Hoffman. Vol. 6 of *Two Liturgical Traditions*. Notre Dame, Ind.: University of Notre Dame Press, 1999.

———. "Liturgy of Judaism: History and Form." In *Encyclopedia of Judaism*. New York: Continuum, 1999.

———. "The Passover Meal in Jewish Tradition." In *Passover and Easter: Origin and History to Modern Times*, edited by Paul F. Bradshaw and Lawrence A. Hoffman. Vol. 5 of *Two Liturgical Traditions*. Notre Dame, Ind.: University of Notre Dame Press, 1999.

———. "Sabbath Week," *Jewish Week*, February 9, 2001.

———. "A Symbol of Salvation in the Passover Haggadah." *Worship* 53, no. 6 (1979).

———. "A Symbol of Salvation in the Passover Seder." In *Passover and Easter: The Symbolic Structuring of Sacred Seasons*, edited by Paul F. Bradshaw and Lawrence A. Hoffman. Vol. 6 of *Two Liturgical Traditions*. Notre Dame, Ind.: University of Notre Dame Press, 1999.

*The Holy Bible, Revised Standard Version.* Cleveland: World Publishing, 1962.

*The Holy Scriptures.* Philadelphia: The Jewish Publication Society of America, 1917.

Hyatt, J. Philip. *Commentary on Exodus.* London: Marshall, Morgan and Scott Ltd., 1971.

Jacob, Benno. *The Second Book of the Bible, Exodus.* Hoboken, N.J.: KTAV, 1992.

Kamenestzky, Mordechai. March 29, 2001, **Drasha@torah.org.**

Kaplan, Mordecai, Eugene Kohn, and Ira Eisenstein, eds. *New Haggadah for the Pesach Seder.* New York: Behrman's Jewish Book House, 1941.

Kasher, Menachem M. *The Passover Haggadah.* New York: Shengold Publishing, 1975.

Kimmelman, Michael K. "Behind Sealed Doors, Opening the Past: After a Long Delay, A Stark Memorial in Vienna Confronts a Dark Legacy." *New York Times,* October 30, 2000.

Klagsbrun, Francine. *Jewish Days.* New York: Farrar, Straus, and Giroux, 1996.

Kolatch, Alfred J. *Great Jewish Quotations.* Middle Village, N.Y.: Jonathan David Publishers, 1996.

Kumove, Shirley. *More Words, More Arrows.* Detroit: Wayne State University Press, 1999.

Kutsch, Ernst. "Critical View, Passover." In *Encyclopedia Judaica.* CD-ROM edition. Jerusalem: Judaica Multimedia, 1997.

Lauterbach, Jacob Z., trans. *Mekhilta de Rabbi Ishmael.* Philadelphia: Jewish Publication Society of America, 1933.

Lehrman, S. M., trans. *Exodus Rabbah.* London: Sonsino Press, 1977.

Leibowitz, Nehama. *New Studies in Bereshit* (Genesis); *New Studies in Shemot* (Exodus); *New Studies in Vayikra* (Leviticus); *Studies in Bamidbar* (Numbers); *Studies in Devarim* (Deuteronomy). Jerusalem: Eliner Library, Department for Torah Education & Culture in the Diaspora, 1980–1993.

Lerner, Barry Dov. "Let Each of Us Fill a Cup." **www.miriamscup.com/RitualFirst.htm.** Wyncote, Pa.: Foundation for Family Education, 2001.

Levitt, Joy, and Michael Strassfeld. *A Night of Questions: A Passover Haggadah.* Elkins Park, Pa.: Reconstructionist Press, 2000.

Leyerle, Blake. "Meal Customs in the Greco-Roman World." In *Passover and Easter: Origin and History to Modern Times,* edited by Paul F. Bradshaw and Lawrence A. Hoffman. Vol. 5 of *Two Liturgical Traditions.* Notre Dame, Ind.: University of Notre Dame Press, 1999.

Maier, Paul, ed. *The New Complete Works of Josephus.* Grand Rapids, Mich.: Kregel, 1999.

Maimonides. *Mishneh Torah, Hilchot Parah Adumah.* In Nachmanides, *Commentary on the Torah: Numbers,* translated by Charles B. Chavel. New York: Shilo Publishing, 1975.

Mair, John S., and Curtis Malloy. *The Ten Plagues in Egypt.* TV documentary. The Discovery Channel, 1997.

Mallin, Shlomo. *The Maharal Haggadah.* Jerusalem: "Horev" Publishers, 1993.

Marmorstein, Emile, and Jennie Marmorstein, trans. *Piyyutim: Liturgical Poems for the Year's Special Sabbaths.* New York: Feldheim Publishing, 1983.

Milgrom, Jacob. *The JPS Torah Commentary: Numbers*. Philadelphia: Jewish Publication Society, 1990.

Moline, Jack. *More Than You Ever Need to Have a GREAT Seder*. Alexandria, Va.

Nachmanides. *Commentary on the Torah: Exodus*. Translated by Charles B. Chavel. New York: Shilo Publishing, 1973.

Neusner, Jacob, trans. *The Talmud of the Land of Israel*. Vol. 15, *Sheqalim*. Chicago: University of Chicago Press, 1991.

Noth, Martin. *Exodus: A Commentary*. Philadelphia: Westminister Press, 1962.

Olitzky, Kerry M. *Preparing Your Heart for Passover*. Philadelphia: Jewish Publication Society, 2002.

*The Pentateuch and Rashi's Commentary*. Vol. 2, *Exodus*. New York: S. S. & R. Publishing Co., 1977.

Person, Hara. "Shavuot." May 2001, **www.clickonjudaism.com.**

Piercy, Marge. "Maggid." In *Available Light*, 125. New York: Alfred A. Knopf, 1992.

Plaut, W. Gunther, ed. *The Torah: A Modern Commentary*. New York: UAHC Press, 1981.

———, ed. *The Haftarah Commentary*. New York: UAHC Press, 1990.

Proust, Marcel. *Remembrances of Things Past: Swann's Way*. New York: Modern Library, 1956.

Raphael, Chaim. *A Feast of History: The Drama of Passover through the Ages*. Jerusalem: Weidenfield & Nicholson; Steimatzky's Agency Ltd., 1972.

Riskin, Shlomo. "A Nazir's Promise." *The Jewish Week*, June 16, 2000.

———. Quoting Rabbi Menoah of Narbonne. *The Jewish Sentinel*, April 25, 1997.

Ritari, Stephanie Loo, Matia Angelou, and Janet Berkenfield. *iworship 95*, April 14, 2000, quoting *Lilith*, spring 1992.

Roekard, Karen G. R. *The Santa Cruz Haggadah*. Capitola, Calif.: Hineni Consciousness Press, 1992.

Rosenbaum, M., and Silberman, A. M., trans. *Pentateuch and Rashi's Commentary: Numbers*. New York: Hebrew Publishing Co., n.d.

Rosenberg, A. J. *II Kings: A New English Translation*. New York: Judaica Press, 1980.

Rosenblatt, Roger. "Monster Memory." *Newshour with Jim Lehrer*, October 2, 2000.

*San Diego Women's Haggadah*. 2d ed. San Diego: Women's Institute for Continuing Education, 1986.

Sarna, Nahum. *Exploring Exodus*. New York: Schocken Books, 1986.

———. *The JPS Torah Commentary: Exodus*. Philadelphia: Jewish Publication Society, 1991.

Scherman, Nosson. *The Haggadah Treasury*. Brooklyn: Mesorah Publications, 1989.

———. *The Family Haggadah*. Brooklyn: Mesorah Publications, 1994

Schorsch, Ismar. Sermon. Passover 5756, **www.learn.jtsa.edu.**

Sforno, Obadiah. *Commentary on the Torah*. Brooklyn: Mesorah Publications, 1999.

Shakespeare, William. *The Merchant of Venice*, act 3, scene 1. Ed. William Aldis Wright. Garden City: Doubleday & Co., 1936.

Siegel, Rachel Josefowitz. "Who Will Lead the Seder, Now That I Am Alone?" In *A Heart of Wisdom: Making the Jewish Journey from Midlife through the Elder Years,* edited by Susan Berrin. Woodstock, Vt.: Jewish Lights Publishing, 1997.

Silverman, Morris, ed. *The Passover Haggadah.* Bridgeport, Conn.: Prayer Book Press, 1975.

Sohn, Ruth. "I Shall Sing to the Lord a New Song." In Joy Levitt and Michael Strassfeld, *A Night of Questions: A Passover Haggadah.* Elkins Park, Pa.: Reconstructionist Press, 2000.

Steingroot, Ira. *Keeping Passover.* San Francisco: HarperCollins, 1995.

Steinsaltz, Adin. *The Passover Haggadah.* Jerusalem: Carta, 1983.

Stern, Chaim. *Gates of Freedom.* Bedford, N.Y.: New Star Press, 1981.

Swarner, Kristina. *Yiddish Wisdom.* San Francisco: Chronicle Books, 1996.

Tabory, Joseph. "Towards a History of the Paschal Meal." In *Passover and Easter: Origin and History to Modern Times,* edited by Paul F. Bradshaw and Lawrence A. Hoffman. Vol. 5 of *Two Liturgical Traditions.* Notre Dame, Ind.: University of Notre Dame Press, 1999.

Touster, Saul, ed. *A Survivors' Haggadah.* Philadelphia: The Jewish Publication Society, 2000.

Wallach, Shalom Meir. *The Pesach Haggadah Culled from Classic Musar.* Brooklyn: Mesorah Publications, 1997.

Washofsky, Mark. *Jewish Living: A Guide to Contemporary Reform Practice.* New York: UAHC Press, 2001.

Wiesel, Elie. *A Passover Haggadah.* Illustrated by Mark Podwal. New York: Touchstone, 1993.

Wolfson, Laurel S., ed. *The First Cincinnati Haggadah CD, Interactive Facsimile Edition.* Cincinnati: HUC-JIR, 2000.

Wolfson, Ron. *The Art of Jewish Living: The Passover Seder.* Woodstock, Vt.: Jewish Lights Publishing, 1988.

Womack, Lee Ann. *I Hope You Dance.* MCA Nashville audio CD, 2000.

Wouk, Herman. *The Will to Live On.* San Francisco: HarperCollins, 2000.

Wylen, Stephen M. *Settings of Silver.* Mahwah, N.J.: Paulist Press, 1989.

———. HUCalum 536, April 13th, 2000.

Yuval, Israel J. "Passover in the Middle Ages." In *Passover and Easter: Origin and History to Modern Times,* edited by Paul F. Bradshaw and Lawrence A. Hoffman. Vol. 5 of *Two Liturgical Traditions.* Notre Dame, Ind.: University of Notre Dame Press, 1999.

Zarren-Zohar, Efrat. "From Pesach to Shavuot." In *Passover and Easter: The Symbolic Structuring of Sacred Seasons,* edited by Paul F. Bradshaw and Lawrence A. Hoffman. Vol. 6 of *Two Liturgical Traditions.* Notre Dame, Ind.: University of Notre Dame Press, 1999.

Zeitlin, Solomon. "The Liturgy of the First Night of Passover." *Jewish Quarterly Review* 38 no. 4 (April 1948).

Zion, Noam, and David Dishon. *A Different Night: The Family Participation Haggadah.* Jerusalem: Shalom Hartman Institute, 1997.

———. *The Leader's Guide to a Different Night.* Jerusalem: Shalom Hartman Institute, 1997.

# Index